A Gil Vicente Bibliography

A GIL VICENTE BIBLIOGRAPHY (1975–1995)

With a Supplement for
1940–1975

C. C. Stathatos

Lehigh
University
Press

Bethlehem: Lehigh University Press
London: Associated University Presses

Associated University Presses
440 Forsgate Drive
Cranbury, New Jersey 08512

Associated University Presses
16 Barter Street
London WC1A 2AH, England

Associated University Presses
P.O. Box 338, Port Credit
Mississauga, Ontario
Canada L5G 4L8

The paper used in this publication meets the requirements
of the American National Standards for Permanence of Paper
for Printed Library Materials Z39.48-1984.

Library of Congress Cataloging-in-Publication Data

Stathatos, Constantine C. (Constantine Christopher)
  A Gil Vicente bibliography, 1975-1995 : with a supplement for 1940-1975 / C.C. Stathatos.
      p.   cm.
  Includes bibliographical references and index.
  ISBN 0-934223-48-3   (alk. paper)
    1. Vicente, Gil, ca. 1470-ca. 1536—Bibliography.   I. Title.
Z8941.7.S82 1997
016.8692'2—dc21   97-33332
                                                                        CIP

PRINTED IN THE UNITED STATES OF AMERICA

For Thomas R. Hart

CONTENTS

PREFACE

This bibliography covers the period 1975–1995 and, at the same time, supplements my *A Gil Vicente Bibliography (1940–1975)*—see entry no. B11. Book reviews are included regardless of their publication date.

The two decades covered witnessed a good deal of activity in Vicentine studies. Numerous interesting contributions appeared both in book and article form, some making original critical statements of decidedly lasting value, others reevaluating accepted critical opinions. Generally, Gil Vicente has been served well in this period, in spite of the occasional occurrence of esoteric and faddist criticism.

As in the past, my task as bibliographer was not an easy one. Anyone dealing with this area is surely aware of the difficulties involved: the unavailability of several Portuguese and Brazilian publications in this country as well as in Portugal and Brazil themselves, the inordinate length of time it takes to receive a publication from Portugal or Brazil, the increasingly prohibitive cost of borrowing books or getting copies of articles from major U.S. libraries, etc. The frustration generated by such obstructions, however, is counterbalanced by the realization that international interest in Gil Vicente is both alive and growing. The long list of celebrated *vicentistas* is constantly enriched by new names of scholars, some of whom introduce fresh ways of looking at Gil Vicente's works (consider Stanislav Zimic, João Nuno Alçada, J. A. Osório Mateus, Manuel Calderón Calderón, to name but a few). One can only hope that the present pace of Vicentine scholarship will continue unabated.

In terms of organization, I have followed here the same general format as in no. B11. In other words, I have divided the body of this bibliography into three principal parts: Editions and Adaptations, Translations, and Critical Studies. Entries in Part I and Section Cb of Part III are ordered chronologically: in Sections A, B, D of Part I, by date of publication; in Sections C of Part I and Cb of Part III, by date of composition or performance of each play, as the case may be, in accordance with the dates established by the late I.S. Révah in his discussion of Gil Vicente in *Dicionário de literatura portuguesa, brasileira, galega. Estilística literária*, ed. Jacinto do Prado Coelho, 3d ed. (Porto: Figueirinhas, 1973), vol. IV, pp. 1164–69. Entries in Part II are arranged alphabetically (by language); so are those in sections A, B, Cc, D of Part III, whereas in Section Ca they

9

are categorized thematically. Asterisks denote items which I have not been able to see.

A few of the entries included here have appeared before in "Supplement to *A Gil Vicente Bibliography (1940–1975)*" (see no. B14), "Gil Vicente Studies" (see no. B12), and "Gil Vicente Studies (1985–1990)" (see no. B13).

I would like to take this opportunity to express my appreciation to my colleagues Orpheus Johnson and Siegfried Christoph for their prompt answers to my calls for help. Thanks go also to Professors João Nuno Alçada, formerly of Rijksuniversiteit te Groningen, Stanislav Zimic, of the University of Texas at Austin, Osório Mateus, of the Universidade de Lisboa, and María Luisa Tobar, of the Università di Messina, for their several kindnesses; to the Committee on Research and Creative Activity, of the University of Wisconsin–Parkside, for having partially funded a research trip of mine to Portugal, and, finally, to B. J. Nielsen and Chris Anders, of the University of Wisconsin–Parkside Interlibrary Loan Service, for having been prompt and patient in handling my numerous requests.

C. C. S.
University of Wisconsin–Parkside

ABBREVIATIONS

ACCP	*Arquivos do Centro Cultural Português* (Paris)
ActaN	*Acta Neophilologica* (Ljubljana)
AHLM–I	*Actas do IV congresso da Associação Hispânica de Literatura Medieval* I: *Sessões Plenárias.* Colecção Medievalia, [I]. Lisboa: Cosmos, 1991.
AHLM–II	*Actas do IV congresso da Associação Hispânica de Literatura Medieval (Lisboa, 1–5 outubro 1991).* II: *Literatura medieval.* Organização de Aires A. Nascimento e Cristina Almeida Ribeiro. Colecção Medievalia, VII. Lisboa: Cosmos, 1993.
AHLM–III	*Actas do IV congresso da Associação Hispânica de Literatura Medieval (Lisboa, 1–5 outubro 1991).* III: *Literatura medieval.* Organização de Aires A. Nascimento e Cristina Almeida Ribeiro. Colecção Medievalia, VIII. Lisboa: Cosmos, 1993
Bcom	*Bulletin of the Comediantes* (Los Angeles)
BEP	*Bulletin des Études Portugaises et de l'Institut Français au Portugal* (Coimbra)
BEPB	*Bulletin des Études Portugaises et Brésiliennes* (Paris). Superseded the *Bulletin des Études Portugaises et de l'Institut Français au Portugal* beginning with vol. XXXIII–XXXIV (1972–73)
BHS	*Bulletin of Hispanic Studies* (Liverpool)
Ch.	Chapter
CILH	*Cuadernos para Investigación de la Literatura Hispánica* (Madrid)
CL	*Comparative Literature* (Eugene, Oregon)
CoL	*Colóquio/Letras* (Lisboa)
col., cols	column(s)
comp.	compiler(s), compiled by
CSIC	Consejo Superior de Investigaciones Científicas.
DA(I)	*Dissertation Abstracts* (Ann Arbor, Michigan): *International* beginning with vol. XXX (1969–70), no. I.
dir.	director, directed by
ed.	edition, editor(s), edited by
EIP	*Estudos Italianos em Portugal* (Lisboa)

EPA	*Estudos Portugueses e Africanos* (Campinas)
EP:HLSP	*Estudos portugueses: Homenagem a Luciana Stegagno Picchio*. Série especial: Memória e Sociedade. Lisboa: DIFEL, 1991. *Review*: a. Maria Luisa Cusati, *Annali dell'Instituto Universitario Orientale–Sezione Romanza*, XXXV (1993), 241–48.
EUNSA	Ediciones Universidad de Navarra, S.A.
GVB	*A Gil Vicente Bibliography (1940–1975)*. London: Grant & Cutler, 1980.
HR	*Hispanic Review* (Philadelphia)
JHP	*Journal of Hispanic Philology* (Tallahassee, Florida)
L–BR	*Luso–Brazilian Review* (Madison)
MGSL	*Minas Gerais Suplemento Literário* (Belo Horizonte)
MLR	*Modern Language Review* (Cambridge)
n.d.	no date
n.p.	no place
n. pub.	no publisher
no., nos	number(s)
NRFH	*Nueva Revista de Filología Hispánica* (México, D.F.)
org.	organizer(s), organized by
QP	*Quaderni Portoghesi* (Pisa)
RaI	*Rassegna Iberistica* (Milano)
rev.	revised
RevL	*Revista Lusitana* (Lisboa)
RFLUL	*Revista da Faculdade de Letras da Universidade de Lisboa*
RFR	*Revista de Filología Románica* (Madrid)
RPhi	*Romance Philology* (Berkeley)
trans.	translation, translator(s), translated by
TV	*Temas vicentinos: Actas do colóquio em torno da obra de Gil Vicente (Teatro de Cornucópia, 1988)*. Diálogo: Série Compilação. Lisboa: Ministério da Educação, Instituto de Cultura e Língua Portuguesa, 1992
vol., vols	volume(s)

A Gil Vicente Bibliography

BIBLIOGRAPHIES

B1. Azevedo Filho, Leodegário A. de. "A edição crítica de textos portugueses." In his *Uma visão brasileira da literatura portuguesa*. Colecção Almedina, XI. Coimbra: Almedina, 1973, pp. 151–74.

On Gil Vicente, pp. 156–58. It appeared originally in *Ocidente*, LXXXIII (1972), 90–100 (see *GVB*, no. B18).

B2. *Letterature iberiche (spagnola, catalana, ispanoamericana, portoghese, brasiliana)*. A cura di Stefano Arata. Introduzione di Carmelo Samonà. Strumenti di Studio. Guide Bibliografiche. Milano: Garzanti, 1992. 457 pp.

On Gil Vicente, pp. 86–87 (by Stefano Arata) and 333–34 (by Mariagrazia Russo).

B3. *Manual bibliographico portuguez de livros raros, classicos e curiosos*. Coordenado por Ricardo Pinto de Mattos, revisto e prefaciado pelo Snr. Camillo Castello Branco. Porto: Livraria Portuense, 1878. Edição revista por Joaquim Ferreira. Porto: Manuel Barreira, 1970. xvi+640 pp.

Section on Gil Vicente on pp. 326–31. Also: Amsterdam: Gérard Th. van Heusden, 1971, 582 pp.

B4. *Manual del librero hispanoamericano. Bibliografía general española e hispanoamericana desde la invención de la imprenta hasta nuestros tiempos con el valor comercial de los impresos descritos por Antonio Palau y Dulcet*. Segunda edición corregida y aumentada por el autor. Tomo XXVI revisado y añadido por Agustín Palau. Barcelona: Antonio Palau Dulcet/ Oxford: Dolphin Book Co., 1975. 485 pp.

Section on Gil Vicente on pp. 349–54.

B5. *Portuguese Literature from its Origins to 1990: A Bibliography Based on the Collections of Indiana University*. Comp. Hugo Kunoff. Metuchen, NJ & London: Scarecrow Press, 1994. 497 pp.

Section on Gil Vicente on pp. 133–40.

B6. Reichenberger, Kurt & Roswitha. *Das spanische Drama im Goldenen Zeitalter: ein bibliographisches Handbuch/El teatro español en los siglos de Oro: inventario de bibliografías*. Teatro del Siglo de Oro: Bibliografías y Catálogos, II. Kassel: Edition Reichenberger, 1989. xiv+319 pp.

Section on Gil Vicente on pp. 73–74 (items 321–34).

B7. *Spanish Literature, 1500–1700: A Bibliography of Golden Age Studies in Spanish and English, 1925–1980*. Comp. William W. Moseley, Glenroy Emmons, Marilyn C. Emmons. Bibliographies and Indexes in World Literature, III. Westport, Conn. & London: Greenwood Press, 1984. lxiii+765 pp.

Section on Gil Vicente on pp. 666–70.

Reviews:

a. Daniel Eisenberg, *JHP*, IX (1985), 255–56.

b. Thomas A. O'Connor, *BCom*, XXXVIII (1986), 258–60.

B8. Stathatos, C. C. "Anglo–American Contributions to the Study of Gil Vicente: A Bibliography (1940–1975)." *Sillages*, 5 (1977), 127–56.

B9. Stathatos, C. C. "Editions and Adaptations of Gil Vicente's Works (1940–1975)." *Segismundo*, 23–24 (1976), 87–110.

B10. Stathatos, C. C. "French Contributions to the Study of Gil Vicente: A Bibliography (1942–1975)." *L–BR*, XV (1978), 105–16.

B11. Stathatos, C. C. *A Gil Vicente Bibliography (1940–1975)*. With a Preface by Thomas R. Hart. Research Bibliographies & Checklists, XXX. London: Grant & Cutler, 1980. 132 pp.

Reviews:

a. J. B. Spieker, *Hispanic Journal*, V, 1 (Fall 1983), 224.

b. David Mackenzie, *BHS*, LXI (1984), 64–65.

B12. Stathatos, C. C. "Gil Vicente Studies." *L–BR*, XX (1983), 119–38.

B13. Stathatos, C. C. "Gil Vicente Studies (1985–1990)." *L–BR*, XXIX, 2 (Winter 1992), 99–111.

B14. Stathatos, C. C. "Supplement to *A Gil Vicente Bibliography (1940–1975)*." *Segismundo*, 35–36 (1982), 9–25.

See also below, nos 183.9, 352.

I
EDITIONS AND ADAPTATIONS

A. *COMPLETE WORKS*

1. *Copilaçam de todalas obras de Gil Vicente.* Introdução e normalização do texto de Maria Leonor Carvalhão Buescu. 2 vols. Biblioteca de Autores Portugueses. Lisboa: Imprensa Nacional–Casa da Moeda, 1983 [1984]. xxv + 516, 715 pp.

I: *Obras de devação* (pp. 19–352), *Comédias* (pp. 357–509). II: *Tragicomédias* (pp. 13–322), *Farsas* (pp. 327–603), *Trovas e cousas miúdas* (pp. 607–67), *Apêndice* (*Auto da Festa*), pp. 673–704. This edition is based on the *Copilaçám* of 1562.

Reviews:
a. A. R., *Brotéria*, CXXI (1985), 115.
b. See no. 353.

See also below, nos. 178–83.

B. *COLLECTIONS AND ANTHOLOGIES*

a. *Drama*

2. *O natal português. Textos tradicionais. Gil Vicente. Fr. Agostinho da Cruz. Gomes Leal. António Feijó. António Nobre. Augusto Gil. Herculano. Júlio Dinis. Ramalho Ortigão. Eça de Queiroz. Fialho de Almeida. Raúl Brandão. Carlos Malheiro Dias. Aquilino Ribeiro. Miguel Torga.* Selecção e prefácio de Vitorino Nemésio. Lisboa: Edições Dois Mundos, 1944. xv + 187 pp.

Selections from the *Auto da feira* (pp. 31–33) and the *Auto de Mofina Mendes* (pp. 35–48).

3. *Poetas quinhentistas: Gil Vicente, Bernardim Ribeiro, Sá de Miranda, Luís de Camões.* Prefácios, revisão e notas de Eduardo Pinheiro. Textos Escolares Figueirinhas, IV. Porto: Figueirinhas, [1948?]. 102 pp.

Includes the text of the *Auto da Alma* (based on Mendes dos Remédios's edition of 1907): pp. 11–44.

4. *Gil Vicente e Camões (excertos)*. Comentário e notas de Eduardo Pinheiro. Porto: Livraria Simões Lopes, 1949. 258 pp.

Pp. 5–16: "Gil Vicente: breve resenha da sua vida e obras." Pp. 19–55: text of the *Auto da Alma*. Pp. 57–66: notes.

5. *Textos literários—V ano: Gil Vicente, Luís de Camões: "Auto da Alma," sonetos e canções*. Introdução e notas por José da Silva. Porto: Sociedade de Papelaria, [1953?]. 102 pp.

Pp. 5–13: introduction to the *Auto da Alma*. Pp. 15–55: text of the play. Pp. 59–71: notes and commentary.

6. *Textos literários do século XVI*. Selecta organizada de acordo com o programa oficial do VI ano dos liceus. Ed. Beatriz Mendes de Paula Silva and Maria Ema Tarracha Ferreira. Lisboa: Aster, [1960?]. 637 pp.

Ch. I (pp. 15–210): in addition to selections from many plays, it includes the complete text of *Visitaçám* (pp. 19–22) with a column by column verse translation in Portuguese by Afonso Lopes Vieira; the almost complete texts of *Quem tem farelos?* (pp. 116–32), *Inês Pereira* (pp. 133–60), *O velho da horta* (pp. 161–78). Also generous portions of the *Auto pastoril português* (pp. 23–34) and *Auto de Mofina Mendes* (pp. 48–63).

7. *Antologia luso–brasileira*. Curso secundário. Ed. Wagner Ribeiro. São Paulo: Editôra Coleção F.T.D., 1964. 406 pp.

Excerpts from the *Auto da feira* (pp. 323–25).

8. Ferreira, Delson Gonçalves. *Língua e literatura luso–brasileira*. 7th rev. and expanded edition. Belo Horizonte: Bernardo Álvares, 1967. 537 pp.

Excerpts from the *Auto da Barca do Inferno* (pp. 143–46).

9. *Novíssima antologia da língua portuguêsa: coletânea de excertos dos principais poetas e prosadores da língua portuguêsa, dos primórdios do idioma à época atual*. Bibliografias, textos, comentários. Para todos os cursos de ensino de grau médio. Ed. Domingos Paschoal Cegalla. 2d ed. Rio de Janeiro: J. Ozon, [1967?]. 548 pp.

Excerpts from *Inês Pereira* (pp. 21–28).

10. Martínez–Almoyna, J. and A. Viera de Lemos. *La lengua española en la literatura portuguesa*. Prólogo por Luís de Pina. Madrid: IMNASA, 1968. 618 pp.

On Gil Vicente, pp. 177–78 (biographical sketch), pp. 410–18 (selections from *Dom Duardos, Auto dos Reis Magos, Comédia do viúvo*).

11. Silva, Adalberto Prado e. *Nova biblioteca da língua portuguêsa*. II: *Literatura portuguêsa*. São Paulo: Formar, 1968, pp. 48–51.

Excerpt from the scene of Todo o Mundo e Ninguém (*Auto da Lusitânia*).

12. *Tesoro breve de las letras hispánicas. Serie castellana*. II: *De "La Celestina" a Cervantes*. Ed. Guillermo Díaz–Plaja. Colección Novelas y Cuentos. Sección Cultura. Serie Historia de la Literatura. Madrid: Magisterio Español, 1968. 457 pp.

Pp. 183–84: introductory note. Pp. 184–87: selection from the *Auto da Barca da Glória*.

13. Vicente, Gil. *Três autos e uma farsa*. Texto fixado e anotado por António Manuel Couto Viana. Biblioteca Básica Verbo, LX. [Lisboa]: Verbo, 1971. 151 pp.

Auto da Alma (pp. 7–35). *Auto da Barca do Inferno* (pp. 37–71). *Auto de Mofina Mendes* (pp. 73–100). *Farsa de Inês Pereira* (pp. 101–42). Notes on pp. 143, 145–46, 147–48, 149–51, respectively.

14. *Antología de teatro del siglo XVI*. Introducción de Federico Carlos Sainz de Robles. Madrid: Círculo de Amigos de la Historia, 1972. 316 pp.

Includes the text of the *Tragicomédia de Dom Duardos* (pp. 73–134). No mention of which text has been followed nor of an editor.

15. *Selecta gil–vicentina (para uso do povo português)*. Ed. José Pereira Tavares. Porto: Lello & Irmão, 1973. 232 pp.

Selections from Gil Vicente's works arranged under the following headings: I: O povo (pp. 13–107). II: Religião e lirismo (pp. 111–46). III: A grandeza de Portugal (pp. 149–62). IV: Crítica e sátira (pp. 165–220). V: "Cousas de folgar" (pp. 223–30).

16. *Antología de la literatura española*. III: *Teatro de los siglos XVI y XVII*. Ed. José María Díez Borque. Madrid: Guadiana, 1975. 627 pp.

Ch. IV (pp. 79–106): introduction by the editor on pp. 79–84. Selections from the *Auto da sibila Cassandra* (pp. 85–90), *Auto dos Quatro Tempos* (pp. 91–92), *Auto da Barca da Glória* (pp. 93–95) and *Dom Duardos* (pp. 96–106).

17. *Literatura portuguêsa em curso.* Ed. Dirce Côrtes Riedel, Beatriz Vieira de Rezende, Nilza Maria Leal Silva, and Renato Cordeiro Gomes. Rio de Janeiro: Livraria Francisco Alves Editôra, 1975. 453 pp.

Excerpts from *Mofina Mendes* (pp. 354–56) and *Auto da feira* (pp. 357–60). Also, Rio de Janeiro: Reper Editôra, 1970, pp. 344–47, 348–51.

18. Gralheiro, Jaime. *Na barca com mestre Gil. Recreação dramática. Texto para um espectáculo de teatro popular centrado em Gil Vicente.* Lisboa: Caminho, 1978. 158 pp.

A two–act play recreating Gil Vicente and his circumstance, based on several of Vicente's works. Gil Vicente himself is a character in the play.
Review:
a. Osório Mateus, *CoL*, 58 (November 1980), 84.

19. *Teatro de Gil Vicente.* Clássicos da Língua Portuguesa. [Lisboa]: Círculo de Leitores, 1978. 169 pp.

No mention of an editor. The texts are apparently based on the *editio princeps*. Includes: *O velho da horta* (pp. 9–30); *Auto da Barca do Inferno* (pp. 31–54); *Auto da Alma* (pp. 55–77); *Farsa de Inês Pereira* (pp. 79–108); *Farsa do Juiz da Beira* (pp. 109–32); *Diálogo dos judeus sobre a ressurreição* (pp. 133–41); *Auto da feira* (pp. 143–69).

20. Barroso Gil, Asunción, Alfonso Berlanga Reyes, María Dolores González Cantos, María Consuelo Hernández Jiménez, and Jesús Toboso Sánchez. *Introducción a la literatura española a través de los textos: Aportación a una metodología del comentario de textos.* Colección Fundamentos, LXV. Vol. I. Madrid: Istmo, 1979. 529 pp.

Selection from the *Auto da sibila Cassandra* (pp. 222–29) and commentary (pp. 229–34).

21. *Clássicos portugueses. Século XVI. Antologia literária comentada.* I: *Teatro de Gil Vicente.* Ed. Mário Fiúza. 3d ed. Porto: Porto Editora/ Coimbra: Livraria Arnado / Lisboa: Fluminense, 1980. 259 pp.

In addition to a Preface (pp. 5–18), it includes the abridged texts of the *Auto da Barca do Inferno* (pp. 21–51), *Auto da Barca do Purgatório* (pp. 53–84), *Auto da Alma* (pp. 85–125), *Auto da feira* (pp. 127–58), *Exortação da guerra* (pp. 161–79), *Farsa chamada "Auto da Índia"* (pp. 183–202), *Quem tem farelos?* (pp. 203–21), and *Farsa de Inês Pereira* (pp. 223–58).

22. Díez Rodríguez, Miguel, María Paz Díez Taboada, and Luis de Tomás Vilaplana. *Literatura española: textos, crítica y relaciones*. I: *Edad Media y Siglos de Oro*. Madrid: Alhambra, 1980. xv+582 pp.

Selection from the *Auto pastoril castelhano* (pp. 350–54).

23. *El teatro del siglo XV: Antología de Gómez Manrique, Juan del Encina, Lucas Fernández, Torres Naharro y Gil Vicente*. Ed. Aurelio Labajo, Carlos Urdiales, and Trini González. Colección Primera Biblioteca de Literatura Española, VIII. Madrid: Coculsa, 1980. 48 pp.

On Gil Vicente, pp. 41–47 (excerpt from *Dom Duardos* on pp. 42–47).

24. *É menino ou menina?: Textos de Gil Vicente*. Dramaturgia de Hélder Costa. Lisboa: Didáctica, 1981. 78 pp.

"Um espectáculo que teve por base uma dramaturgia concebida a partir do encadeamento de 'cenas' extraídas de várias peças vicentinas cuja figura central é a Mulher." Includes also: "*É menino ou menina?* e a crítica" (pp. 65–68); "*É menino ou menina?*: música de Orlando Costa com anotação de Eduardo Pais Mamede" (pp. 69–78)—musical scores with lyrics.

25. G., C. de. "Lembrança lírica do Natal na poesia cristã dos autos de Gil Vicente." *Revista de Teatro*, 440 (October, November, December 1981), 21–22.

The author adapts a few passages (from the *Auto da Fé* and *Mofina Mendes*) which have to do with the birth of Christ.

26. *Gil Vicente. Textos selecionados, estudo histórico–literário, biografia e atividades de compreensão e criação*. Seleção de textos, notas, estudos biográfico, histórico e crítico e exercícios por Álvaro Cardoso Gomes. Literatura Comentada. São Paulo: Abril Educação, 1982. 112 pp.

In addition to supplementary material, it includes the texts of the *Auto da Barca do Inferno* (pp. 10–38), *Auto da Alma* (pp. 39–61), *Auto de Inês Pereira* (pp. 62–94), and the scene of "Todo o Mundo e Ninguém" from the *Auto da Lusitânia* (pp. 95–97).

27. *Teatro español del siglo XVI: Lucas Fernández, Torres Naharro, Gil Vicente, Cervantes*. Ed. Alfredo Hermenegildo. Colección Clásicos Universales, VIII. Serie Clásicos Hispánicos. Madrid: Sociedad General Española de Librería, 1982. 278 pp.

Includes the *Tragicomédia de Dom Duardos* (introduction on pp. 115–28, text on pp. 129–91). The text is based on the *Copilaçám* of 1562 with some corrections from the *Copilaçám* of 1586.
Review:
a. Jerónimo Herrera Navarro, *CILH*, 6 (1984), 261–62.

28. *Teatro de Gil Vicente*. Ed. Gilberto Moura. Biblioteca Ulisseia de Autores Portugueses, XII. Lisboa: Ulisseia, 1983. 178 pp.
   Auto da Índia (pp. 45–62); *Auto da Barca do Inferno* (pp. 63–93); *Auto da Barca do Purgatório* (pp. 95–119); *Farsa de Inês Pereira* (pp. 121–57); notes (pp. 161–62, 163–68, 169–70, 171–73, respectively).
   Review:
a. O[sório] M[ateus], *CoL*, 94 (November 1986), 117.

29. Vicente, Gil. *Teatro*. Estudio preliminar, edición y notas de Thomas R. Hart. Colección Temas de España, CXXXIX. Madrid: Taurus, 1983. 201 pp.
   Contents: Estudio preliminar, Criterios de esta edición, Bibliografía, Lista de abreviaturas (pp. 7–44). *Auto pastoril castellano* (pp. 47–58). *Auto de la sibila Casandra* (pp. 59–80). *Auto de los cuatro tiempos* (pp. 81–99). *Auto de la Barca de la Gloria* (pp. 101–25). *Tragicomedia de Don Duardos* (pp. 127–86). Glosario, Notas explicativas, Cronología (pp. 187–99). The texts of the first four plays are based on the *Copilaçám* of 1562 (as reproduced in facsimile in 1928), whereas that of *Don Duardos* is based on the *Copilaçám* of 1586.
   Review:
a. Charlotte Stern, *HR*, LIII (1985), 484–86.

30. *Antologia do teatro de Gil Vicente*. Seleção, introdução, notas e glossário de Cleonice Berardinelli. 3ª edição. Em convênio com o Instituto Nacional do Livro, Fundação Nacional Pró–Memória. Rio de Janeiro: Nova Fronteira, 1984. 444 pp. (First and second ed., 1971 and 1974, by Grifo Editores).
   Includes selections from several plays and the complete texts of the *Auto da Barca do Inferno* (pp. 53–90), *Auto da Barca do Purgatório* (pp. 91–120), *Auto da Alma* (pp. 121–51), *Breve sumário da história de Deus* (pp. 153–91), *Auto da feira* (pp. 193–230), *Auto da Índia* (pp. 231–50), *Velho da horta* (pp. 251–76), *Quem tem farelos?* (pp. 277–300), *Inês Pereira* (pp. 301–47), and the "Carta de Gil Vicente ao Rei D. João III, sobre o sermão que pregou aos frades de Santarém" (pp. 401–7).

31. *Os Autos das Barcas de Gil Vicente.* Com um prefácio, notas e glossário de Augusto C. Pires de Lima. Colecção Portugal. Porto: Domingos Barreira, 1985. 201 pp.

Auto da Barca do Inferno (pp. 47–85), *Auto da Barca do Purgatório* (pp. 87–120), *Auto da Barca da Glória* (pp. 121–58).

32. *Vicente, Gil. *Os Autos das Barcas.* Apresentação em banda desenhada por José Ruy. [Lisboa]: Editorial Notícias, 1986. 64 pp.

33. *As Barcas (Las Barcas).* Edición y notas de Armando López Castro. León: Universidad de León, Servicio de Publicaciones, 1987. 154 pp.

Contents: Introducción, Criterios de esta edición, Bibliografía (pp. 7–59). *Auto da Barca do Inferno* (pp. 63–101). *Auto da Barca do Purgatório* (pp. 103–28). *Auto de la Barca de la Gloria* (pp. 129–54).

34. Mateus, Osório. "Cinco autos de Gil Vicente: práticas de reconhecimento." Dissertação de doutoramento, Faculdade de Letras da Universidade Clássica de Lisboa, 1987. 280 pp.

Contents: I: Introdução (pp. 3–20). II: Autos (*Martinho*, pp. 22–36. *Índia*, pp. 37–75. *Cortes*, pp. 76–123. *Devisa*, pp. 124–82. *Tormenta* ["Carta que Gil Vicente mandou de Santarém a el–Rei D. João III"], pp. 183–201). III: Aparatos (*Martinho*, pp. 203–04. *Índia*, pp. 205–07. *Cortes*, pp. 208–12. *Devisa*, pp. 213–15. *Tormenta*, p. 216). IV: Bibliografias (*Martinho*, pp. 218–27. *Índia*, pp. 228–44. *Cortes*, pp. 245–57. *Devisa*, pp. 258–70. *Tormenta*, pp. 271–77). V: Conclusão (p. 279). Índice (p. 280).

35. *Teatro renacentista.* Edición de Miguel Ángel Pérez Priego. Biblioteca Crítica de Autores Españoles, LVIII. Barcelona: Plaza & Janés, 1987. 344 pp.

Includes introduction to and bibliography on Gil Vicente (pp. 29–42 and 79–80, respectively) and the text of the *Auto de la sibila Casandra*, based on the *editio princeps* (pp. 159–88).

36. Vicente, Gil. *Os Autos das Barcas.* Introdução, leitura do texto, notas e tradução do *Auto da Barca da Glória* de J. Tomaz Ferreira. 6ª edição. Livros de Bolso Europa–América, LV. Mem Martins: Europa–América, [1987]. 163 pp.

Auto da Barca do Inferno (pp. 45–78). *Auto da Barca do Purgatório* (pp. 79–107). *Auto da Barca da Glória* (original text on pp. 109–37; Portuguese translation on pp. 139–63).

37. *Teatro de Gil Vicente*. Apresentação e leitura de António José Saraiva. Edição revista. [Lisboa]: Dinalivro, 1988. 398 pp.

In addition to selections from several plays, it includes the complete texts of *Quem tem farelos?* (pp. 69–89), *Auto da Barca do Inferno* (pp. 91–125), *Auto da Alma* (pp. 135–62), *Inês Pereira* (pp. 163–204), and *Auto da feira* (pp. 265–99).

38. Vicente, Gil. *Auto da Índia. Farsa de Inês Pereira*. Texto integral. Apresentação em banda desenhada por José Ruy. [Lisboa]: Editorial Notícias, 1988. 46 pp.

Auto da Índia on pp. 3–22. *Inês Pereira* on pp. 23–46.

39. Moreira, Vasco and Hilário Pimenta. *Novas propostas de abordagem*. 9° ano unificado, 3° ano curso geral. Porto: Porto Editora, 1990. 119 pp.

Includes the complete text of the *Auto da Barca do Inferno* (pp. 7–45).

40. Nunes, Carmen and Maria Leonor Sardinha. *O eco dos descobrimentos na literatura portuguesa*. A Caminho da Universidade. Lisboa: Replicação, 1990. 123 pp.

Pp. 35–43 include relevant excerpts from the *Auto da Barca do Inferno*, *Inês Pereira*, *Exortação da guerra*, *Triunfo do Inverno* and, principally, *Auto da Índia*.

41. *Teatro renacentista: Juan del Encina, Diego de Ávila, Lucas Fernández, Bartolomé de Torres Naharro, Gil Vicente*. Ed. Alfredo Hermenegildo. Colección Austral, A: Literatura, CLXXI. Madrid: Espasa–Calpe, 1990. 306 pp.

Includes the *Tragicomédia de Dom Duardos* (introduction, based on that of no. 27, on pp. 213–26, text, based on that of the 1562 *Copilaçám*, on pp. 227–88).

42. *Antología de la literatura española: Renacimiento y Siglo de Oro*. Ed. Bárbara Mujica. New York: John Wiley & Sons, 1991. x+625 pp.

Includes: introduction to Gil Vicente (pp. 426–28) and the text of the *Auto da Barca da Glória* (pp. 428–41).

43. *Espirituais portugueses: antologia.* Selecção e prefácio de Dalila Pereira da Costa & Quirino de Santa Victória. Colecção Lusíada, III. Lisboa: Fundação Lusíada, 1991. 229 pp.

Excerpts from *Dom Duardos* on pp. 95–99.

Review:

a. José Augusto Mourão, *CoL*, 134 (October–December 1994), 156.

44. Vicente, Gil. *Auto da Alma e Auto da feira.* Ed. J. Tomaz Ferreira. Livros de Bolso Europa–América, DXXXXI. Mem Martins: Europa–América, 1991. 126 pp.

Auto da Alma on pp. 45–72. *Auto da feira* on pp. 81–121.

45. Vicente, Gil. *Auto da Índia. Auto dos físicos. A Farsa do velho da horta.* Adaptação de Sara Vaz. Colecção Reler Gil Vicente, II. Lisboa: Edições Ledo, 1993. 107 pp.

Auto da Índia (pp. 3–35). *Auto dos físicos* (pp. 37–69). *Velho da horta* (pp. 71–107). Very modernized prose texts. Speeches in Spanish are translated into Portuguese.

46. Vicente, Gil. *Quem tem farelos? Farsa de Inês Pereira. O Juiz da Beira.* Adaptação de Mariana Gomes. Colecção Reler Gil Vicente, I. Lisboa: Edições Ledo, 1993. 134 pp.

"Carta proloquial" de Orlando Vitorino (pp. 5–16). *Quem tem farelos?* (pp. 17–47). *Inês Pereira* (pp. 49–98). *Juiz da Beira* (pp. 99–134). Very modernized prose texts. Speeches in Spanish are translated into Portuguese.

47. *Literatura española: una antología.* I: *De los orígenes hasta 1700.* Ed. David William Foster, Daniel Altamiranda, Gustavo Óscar Geirola, Carmen de Urioste. Garland Reference Library of the Humanities, MDCCCLXXI. New York & London: Garland Publishing, 1995. xi+887 pp.

Includes the *Auto pastoril castellano* (on pp. 526–41), based on the text in Thomas R. Hart's edition of Vicente's *Obras dramáticas castellanas* (see *GVB*, no. 16).

Review:

a. David Hook, *BHS*, LXXIII (1996), 449–50.

See also below, nos 153, 571, 591.

b. *Poetry*

48. *Poesía de la Edad Media y poesía de tipo tradicional.* Ed. Dámaso Alonso. Buenos Aires: Losada, 1942. 588 pp.

Thirteen lyrics (pp. 343–52). First appeared as *Poesía española. Antología. Poesía de la Edad Media y poesía de tipo tradicional.* Madrid: Signo, 1935. 574 pp.

49. *Pequeña antología: poesías españolas.* Ed. Manuel Salas. New York: F.S. Crofts & Co., 1946. xv+190 pp. (Reprint of the 1940 ed.).

Four lyrics (pp. 3–6).

50. *Antología de la poesía lírica española.* Ed. Enrique Moreno Báez. Madrid: Revista de Occidente, 1952. lxiii+565 pp.

Three lyrics (pp. 122–23).

51. *Antología de la literatura española (siglos X–XX).* Ed. Martín de Riquer. Colección Lope de Vega. Barcelona: Teide, 1953. 275 pp.

Four lyrics (pp. 77–78).

52. Nin–Culmell, Joaquin. *Trois poèmes (Tres poemas) de Gil Vicente pour chant et piano.* Paris: Éditions Max Eschig, 1955. 7 pp.

Musical scores for "¿Por dó pasaré la sierra?" (*Triunfo do Inverno*), pp. 1–3; "Ro, ro, ro" (*Sibila Cassandra*), pp. 3–5; "¿Cuál es la niña / que coge las flores?" (*Velho da horta*), pp. 5–7.

53. *Poesía de España y América.* Ed. Carlos García Prada. Vol. I. Madrid: Ediciones Cultura Hispánica, 1958. 370 pp.

Five lyrics (pp. 160–63).

54. *Ocho siglos de poesía en lengua española.* Ed. Francisco Montes de Oca. Colección Sepan Cuantos, VIII. México: Porrúa, 1961. xxx+554 pp. (Later editions also).

Seven lyrics (pp. 102–4).

55. *Cancionero tradicional (selección).* Ed. José Hesse. Temas de España, XVII. Madrid: Taurus, 1963. 149 pp.

Two lyrics (pp. 49, 100–101).

56. *Antología literaria de autores españoles.* Ed. Antonio Vilanova. Barcelona: Teide, 1964. 798 pp.

    Eight lyrics (pp. 133–35). Introduction (pp. 132–33).

57. *Colectânea de versos portugueses do século XII ao século XX.* Ed. João Cabral do Nascimento. Lisboa: Minerva, 1964. 221 pp.

    Includes "Ao conde de Vimioso" ("Senhor, a longa esperança / mui curto prazer ordena"), pp. 26–27.

58. *Cien de las mejores poesías españolas.* Ed. Eugenio Florit. New York: Las Américas, 1965. 250 pp.

    Two lyrics (pp. 37–38).

59. *Los cien poetas mejores de la lírica castellana: antología.* Ed. Rafael Morales. Madrid: Ediciones Giner, 1967. 937 pp.

    Ten lyrics (pp. 145–51).

60. Ward, Philip. *Spanish Literary Appreciation.* London: University of London Press, 1969. 144 pp.

    Text of "Dicen que me case yo" (*Sibila Cassandra*), p. 69, and analysis of it, p. 70.

61. DaCosta, Luísa. *De mãos dadas, estrada fora...: Antologia de textos.* Ilustrações de Jorge Pinheiro. Porto: Figueirinhas, 1970. 103 pp.

    Pp. 99–100: introduction on Gil Vicente. Pp. 101–3 ("Figurinhas de presépio antigo"): three lyrics and Paulo Quintela's Portuguese translation of "Ro, ro, ro" (*Sibila Cassandra*).

62. *Flores del romancero.* Ed. Amelia Agostini de del Río. Englewood Cliffs, New Jersey: Prentice–Hall, 1970. viii+276 pp.

    Includes the "Romance de Flérida y Don Duardos" (pp. 174–75).
    Review:
    a. Colin Smith, *HR*, XLI (1973), 559–61.

63. *Libro de oro de la poesía en lengua castellana (España y América).* Ed. María Luz Morales. Obras Maestras de la Literatura Universal. Vol. I. Barcelona: Juventud, 1970. 591 pp.

    Four lyrics (pp. 135–38).

64. *Spanish Poetry of the Golden Age.* Ed. Milton A. Buchanan. 2d ed. Toronto: University of Toronto Press, 1970. 149 pp. (Reprint of the 1947 rev. ed. First ed., 1942).
Three lyrics (pp. 31–32).

65. *Antología de poetas del siglo XVI.* Introducción de Federico Carlos Sainz de Robles. Madrid: Círculo de Amigos de la Historia, 1972. 313 pp.
Thirteen lyrics (pp. 131–38).

66. *Enciclopedia histórico–antológica de las más famosas obras en lengua castellana.* Redactada por un equipo de colaboradores literarios y gráficos bajo la presidencia de fray Justo Pérez de Urbel, con la asesoría de Tomás Borrás Bermejo y la dirección de Alberto Vassallo de Mumbert. Prólogo–Presentación de Joaquín de Entrambasaguas. La Tijera Literaria. Vol. I. Madrid: Siglo Ilustrado, 1972. x+320 pp.
Eight lyrics (p. 261).

67. *Floresta de lírica española.* Ed. José M. Blecua. 3ª ed. aumentada. Biblioteca Románica Hispánica, VI: Antología Hispánica, 9. Vol. I. Madrid: Gredos, 1972. 330 pp. (First ed., 1957, 2d, 1963).
Four lyrics (pp. 85–86).

68. *Antología de albas, alboradas y poemas afines en la Península Ibérica hasta 1625.* Ed. Dionisia Empaytaz. Colección Nova Scholar. Madrid: Playor, 1976. 213 pp.
One lyric (p. 162).

69. *Lírica hispánica de tipo popular: Edad Media y Renacimiento.* Ed. Margit Frenk Alatorre. Letras Hispánicas, LX. Madrid: Cátedra, 1977. 292 pp.
Includes thirty–nine lyrics. First published in 1966 by the Universidad Nacional Autónoma de México.
Review:
a. María Teresa López García–Berdoy, *CILH*, 2–3 (1980), 506–08.

70. *Las cien mejores poesías españolas.* Ed. Enrique Díaz–Canedo. Colección Ideas, Letras y Vida. México: Compañía General de Ediciones, 1980. 161 pp.
Two lyrics (pp. 145–46).

71. Namorado, Joaquim. "Nos bastidores do palco de mestre Gil." *O Instituto*, CXL–CXLI (1980–81), 204–13.

Seven poems inspired in Gil Vicente's work. "O diabo sem máscara" (pp. 204–06). "Pecados de frei António do Paço" (p. 207). "O diabo que pergunta no martírio de Santa Eufémia" (p. 208). "O diabo disfarçado de gente" (p. 209). "Pranto por Maria Parda" (pp. 210–11). "O bom pastor" (p. 212). "Os cavaleiros" (p. 213).

72. *Panorama de la poesía española en castellano. I: De la Edad Media al Renacimiento (siglos XI–XVI)*. Selección e introducciones por Bartolomé Mostaza Rodríguez. Madrid: Ediciones Rioduero, 1981. lvi+521 pp.

Eight lyrics (pp. 298–300).

73. Reckert, Stephen. "Las poesías del *Auto pastoril castellano* (edición, comentario y notas)." In *Homenaje a Eugenio Asensio*. Ed. Luisa López Grigera & Augustin Redondo. Madrid: Gredos, 1988, pp. 379–89.

Provides the text (normalized but not modernized) of the play's four lyric poems with textual notes and analyses.

74. *Cancionero tradicional*. Edición, introducción y notas de José María Alín. Clásicos Castalia, CXC. Madrid: Castalia, 1991. 587 pp.

Includes twenty–four lyrics by Gil Vicente on pp. 160, 162–64, 166–67, 177–79, 181–83, 186–88, 191–92 (Nos 146–47, 154–55, 161–65, 185–88, 192–97, 201–3, 208–10, respectively).

75. Vicente, Gil. *Lírica*. Edición de Armando López Castro. Letras Hispánicas, CCCLXX. Madrid: Cátedra, 1993. 253 pp.

Contents: Introducción (pp. 7–56). Esta edición (pp. 57–60). Bibliografía (pp. 61–68). Lírica (pp. 69–230). Glosario (pp. 231–40). Ejemplificaciones musicales (pp. 241–45). Índice de primeros versos (pp. 247–51).

See also below, nos 129, 133, 200, 312, 314, 452–53, 585, 607.

c. *Drama and Poetry*

76. *Primavera y flor de la literatura hispánica*. Ed. Dámaso Alonso, Eulalia Galvarriato de Alonso, Luis Rosales. Vol. I. Madrid: Selecciones del Reader's Digest, 1966. xxvi+534 pp.

Seven lyrics (pp. 132–35); selection from *Dom Duardos* (pp. 154–58).

77. *Antología de la poesía en lengua española (siglos XVI y XVII)*. Centro de Estudios Literarios. Lecturas Universitarias, I. México: Universidad Nacional Autónoma de México, 1971. 222 pp.

Excerpts from *Sibila Cassandra* (pp. 12–16) and *Dom Duardos* ("En el mes era de abril"), pp. 16–17.

78. *Antologia da poesia portuguesa (séc. XII–séc. XX). I (sécs. XII–XVI): Da poesia trovadoresca galego–portuguesa ao Renascimento*. Ed. Alexandre Pinheiro Torres. Porto: Lello & Irmão, 1977. vii+1522 pp.

Pp. 755–59: introduction on Gil Vicente. Pp. 761–68: ten lyrics. Pp. 768–69: "Ao conde de Vimioso." Pp. 770–72: "Romance que fez quando foi levantado por rei El–Rei Dom João o terceiro, de gloriosa memória." Selections from the *Auto da Lusitânia* (the scene of Todo o Mundo e Ninguém, pp. 791–95), *Mofina Mendes* (p. 796), *Auto da Cananeia* (pp. 797–99), *Auto da Fé* (p. 799), *Exortação da guerra* (pp. 800–804), *Auto da Fama* (pp. 805–9), *Côrtes de Júpiter* (pp. 809–10), *Romagem de agravados* (pp. 810–11), *Auto das fadas* (pp. 812–14), *Auto pastoril português* (pp. 814–15), and *Triunfo do Inverno* (p. 816).

Reviews:

a. Mário Martins, *Itinerarium*, XXIV (1978), 211–12.

b. Gerald M. Moser, *Hispania*, LXI (1978), 1008.

79. *The Spanish Traditional Lyric*. Ed. John G. Cummins. Oxford: Pergamon Press, 1977. xi+179 pp.

Pp. 140–44: extracts from the *Tragicomédia pastoril da Serra da Estrêla*. Other lyrics on pp. 17, 27, 31, 32, 53, 81, 103–4.

Review:

a. Patrick Gallagher, *BHS*, LVIII (1981), 77–78.

80. *Santa Maria nos poetas portugueses do século XVI*. Selecção e prólogo do P. Moreira das Neves. Fátima: Santuário, 1979. 108 pp.

Includes excerpts from *Mofina Mendes* (pp. 21–28), *Auto da feira* (p. 29), *Auto pastoril português* (pp. 30–31), *Auto da Alma* (pp. 32–33), "Orações dos grandes de Portugal a Nossa Senhora, depois de enterrado el–Rei" (p. 34), *Sibila Cassandra* (p. 35).

C. INDIVIDUAL PLAYS

Monólogo do vaqueiro (1502)

See above, nos 1, 6, and below, nos 127, 180.9.

Auto de São Martinho (1504)

81. *Vicente, Caldas, 1504*. Edição de Osório Mateus. Concepção gráfica de Ana Jota. Caldas da Rainha: Casa da Cultura, 1985. 4 pp.

82. Pestana, Sebastião. *O "Auto de São Martinho" de Gil Vicente*. Lisboa: Instituto Português do Património Cultural, 1985. 126 pp.

See also above, nos 1, 34, and below, no. 178.4.

Auto da Índia (1509)

83. *Farsa chamada Auto da Índia*. Realização didáctica de Luís Amaro de Oliveira. Com sínteses críticas, análise literária, planos de estudo. Direcção de leitura, ficha de leitura. Porto: Porto Editora/Coimbra: Arnado/Lisboa: Fluminense, 1975. 79 pp. (Also later reprints).

84. *Auto da Índia*. Precedida do texto fac–similado da primeira edição (1562). 2ª ed. escolar com introdução, notas, glossário, questionário ideológico e ficha de leitura por Júlio Martins, Cecília Soares, Jaime da Mota. Lisboa: Didáctica, 1979. 77 pp. (First ed., 1975).

85. *Auto da Índia*. Com introdução, anotações e comentários de A. Ambrósio de Pina e José Cardoso. Porto: Porto Editora, 1980. 107 pp.

86. *O Auto da Índia de Gil Vicente*. Apresentação crítica, transcrição, notas e linhas de leitura de Osório Mateus. 2ª ed. Textos Literários, VIII. Lisboa: Comunicação, 1984. 83 pp. (First ed.: Seara Nova / Comunicação, 1979).
   Review:
   a. Carlos Alberto Iannone, *Boletim Informativo do Centro de Estudos Portugueses da Universidade de São Paulo*, 2ª Série, 8 (January–December 1980), 43–45.

87. *Auto da Índia. Farsa*. Edição didáctica de Mário Fiúza. Porto: Porto Editora/Coimbra: Arnado/Lisboa: Fluminense, 1986. 111 pp. (First ed., 1975, second, 1979).

88. *Auto da Índia*. Introdução, comentário, síntese e glossário de Manuel dos Santos Alves. 3ª edição. Lisboa: Universitária Editora, 1990. 68 pp. (First ed.: Francisco Franco, 1977).

Includes a translation into Portuguese of the Spaniard's speeches (pp. 52–57).

89. *Auto da Índia de Gil Vicente*. Apresentação crítica, fixação do texto, notas e sugestões para análise literária de Manuel Simões. Textos Literários, LX. Lisboa: Comunicação, 1991. 74 pp.

See also above, nos 1, 21, 28, 30, 34, 38, 40, 45, and below, nos 125, 178.5.

Auto pastoril castelhano (1509)

90. Pestana, Sebastião. *O "Auto pastoril castelhano" de Gil Vicente*. Introdução que contém: métrica, rimas, vocabulário rimado e sequências vocálicas para o estudo da escansão. Texto fac–similado da Copilaçam de 1562. Texto fixado, variantes e sua responsabilidade, vocabulário total do *Auto*, devidamente estudado. Bibliografia. Lisboa: Pestana, 1978. 322 pp.

See also above, nos 1, 22, 29, 47, and below no. 179.5.

Auto dos Reis Magos (1510)

91. *Auto dos Reis Magos*. Introdução, texto fac–similado, texto fixado, variantes, vocabulário, bibliografia por Sebastião Pestana. Lisboa: Pestana, 1979. 247 pp.

See also above, nos 1, 10, and below, no. 180.7.

Auto da Fé (1510)

See above, nos 1, 25, 78, and below, no. 179.7.

O velho da horta (1512)

See above, nos 1, 6, 30, 45, and below, no. 181.9.

Auto dos Quatro Tempos (1513)

See above, nos 1, 16, 29, and below, no. 181.1.

Auto da sibila Cassandra (1513)

92. Ayuntamiento de Barcelona. Museo de Industrias y Artes Populares. *Representación del "Auto de la sibila Casandra" de Gil Vicente*. Barcelona: Archivo Histórico de la Ciudad, 1941. 55 pp.
  Contains: "Cuatro palabras explicativas" por Luis Masriera (pp. 7–8); the text of the play (pp. 9–24); "Música del maestro Planás" (pp. 27–38); Documentos gráficos de la representación (pp. 41–48); and Comentarios de la prensa (pp. 51–55).

See also above, nos 1, 16, 20, 29, 35, 77, and below, nos 122, 182.7.

Exortação da guerra (1514)

93. *Exortação da guerra*. Introdução, comentário, síntese e glossário de Manuel dos Santos Alves. Lisboa: Livraria Popular, 1979. 69 pp.

94. *Exortação da guerra*. Para o ensino unificado. Anotações de Albano Monteiro Soares. Porto: Porto Editora, 1980. 67 pp.

See also above, nos 1, 21, 40, 78, and below, no. 182.4.

Quem tem farelos? (1515)

95. *Quem tem farelos?*. Edição de Joaquim Ferreira. Porto: Domingos Barreira, 1977. 95 pp.

96. *Farsa de "Quem tem farelos?"* Edição didáctica. Comentário e anotações de Angelina Vasques Martins. Porto: Porto Editora, 1979. 112 pp.

97. *Farsa de "Quem tem farelos?"* Introdução, comentário, síntese e glossário de Manuel dos Santos Alves. Lisboa: Francisco Franco, 1979. 72 pp.

98. *Farsa de "Quem tem farelos?"* Para o ensino secundário unificado. Anotações de Albano Monteiro Soares. Porto: Porto Editora, 1979. 68 pp.

99. *Quem tem farelos?* Apresentação crítica, transcrição, notas e sugestões para análise literária de Vanda Anastácio. Textos Literários, XLII. Lisboa: Comunicação, 1985. 90 pp.
   Review:
   a. O[sório] M[ateus], *CoL*, 94 (November 1986), 117.

See also above, nos 1, 6, 21, 30, 37, 46, and below, no. 178.8.

Auto de Mofina Mendes (1515)

100. *Auto de Mofina Mendes: mistério.* Texto integral de acordo com o da edição de 1562. Prefácio, anotações e comentário por Mário Fiúza. Porto: Porto Editora, 1978. 120 pp.

See also above, nos 1–2, 6, 13, 17, 25, 78, 80, and below, no. 180.2.

Auto da Barca do Inferno (1517)

101. *Auto da Barca do Inferno: moralidade.* Texto integral e crítico. Para o ensino secundário. 3ª edição didáctica, anotada e comentada por Mário Fiúza. Porto: Porto Editora, 1981. 135 pp. (First ed., 1975).

102. *Auto da Barca do Inferno.* Apresentação crítica, notas, glossário e sugestões para análise literária de Maria Idalina Resina Rodrigues. Textos Literários, XXVII. Lisboa: Comunicação, 1982. 114 pp.
   Review:
   a. P. L., *Brotéria*, CXX (1985), 228 [very brief].

See also above, nos 1, 8, 13, 19, 21, 26, 28, 30–33, 36–37, 39–40, and below, no. 183.1.

Auto da Alma (1518)

103. *Auto da Alma*. Edição de Feliciano Ramos. 2ª ed. Braga: Livraria Cruz, 1976. 87 pp.

104. *Auto da Alma*. Apresentação crítica, notas, sugestões para análise literária e apêndice documental de Maria Idalina Resina Rodrigues. Textos Literários, XV. Lisboa: Comunicação, 1980. 117 pp.

105. *Auto da Alma*. Com introdução, anotações e glossário de A. Ambrósio de Pina. 2ª ed. Porto: Porto Editora, 1980. 80 pp. (First ed., 1974).

See also above, nos 1, 3–5, 13, 19, 21, 26, 30, 37, 44, 80, and below, nos 183.4, 571.

Auto da Barca do Purgatório (1518)

See above, nos 1, 21, 28, 30–33, 36, and below, no. 183.2.

Auto da Barca da Glória (1519)

See above, nos 1, 12, 16, 29, 31–33, 36, 42, and below, no. 183.3.

Auto da Fama (1520)

See above, nos 1, 78, and below, no. 179.8.

Côrtes de Júpiter (1521)

See above, nos 1, 34, 78, and below, nos 178.9, 591.

Comédia de Rubena (1521)

106. *A comédia de Rubena*. Fixação do texto com tradução das falas em castelhano e introdução de Agostinho Domingues e Santiago Real Peña. Amares: Câmara Municipal de Amares, 1988. 111 pp.
   Review:
   a. José Camões, *CoL*, 121–122 (July–December 1991), 262–63.

See also above, no. 1.

Auto das ciganas (1521)

See above, no. 1, and below, no. 178.6.

Tragicomédia de Dom Duardos (1522)

107. Alonso, Dámaso. "Gil Vicente: *Tragicomedia de Don Duardos*." In his *Obras completas*. VIII: *Comentarios de textos*. Madrid: Gredos, 1985, pp. 273–479.
    Originally published in 1942 (see *GVB*, nos 124 & 301). It includes: Plan (pp. 277–78). La poesía dramática en la *Tragicomedia de Don Duardos* (pp. 279–94). *Tragicomedia de Don Duardos* (pp. 295–358). Nota editorial (pp. 359–61). Problemas del castellano vicentino (pp. 363–90). Abreviaturas y notas (pp. 391–94). Notas (pp. 395–461). Adiciones y correcciones (pp. 462–67). Índice alfabético de las notas (pp. 469–79). See also "La Generación de 1927 y el gusto por Góngora, por el cancionero tradicional y por Gil Vicente" (pp. 699–701, in the same volume).

See also above, nos 1, 10, 14, 16, 23, 27, 29, 41, 43, 76–77.

Auto de Inês Pereira (1523)

108. *A Farsa de Inês Pereira de Gil Vicente*. Contada aos jovens por Irene Fernandes. N.p.: n. pub., n.d. No pagination.
    Photocopy of a typescript.

109. **Farsa de Inês Pereira*. Edição de Leonel Abrantes. Luanda, Angola: n. pub., 1973.

110. *Farsa de Inês Pereira*. Coordenação, apresentação, comentários e notas de Carlos Camposa. Colecção Escolar Atlântico, II. Trofa: Livraria Sólivros de Portugal, 1983. 93 pp.

111. *Auto de Inês Pereira de Gil Vicente*. Apresentação crítica, transcrição do texto, notas e sugestões para análise literária de Cristina Almeida Ribeiro. Textos Literários, LXII. Lisboa: Comunicação, 1992. 119 pp.
    On pp. 41–60, it includes a facsimile of the text of the play as it appears in a pamphlet in the Biblioteca Nacional of Madrid.

112. *Farsa de Inês Pereira de Gil Vicente*. Estudo, análise, notas, vocabu-lário e questionários de Albano Monteiro Soares. Para o ensino secundário. 2ª edição. Porto: Porto Editora, 1993. 102 pp. (First ed., 1979).

See also above, nos 1, 6, 9, 13, 19, 21, 26, 28, 30, 37–38, 40, 46, and below, no. 181.3.

Auto pastoril português (1523)

See above, nos 1, 6, 78, 80, and below, no. 180.6.

Tragicomédia de Amadis de Gaula (1523)

See above, no. 1.

Comédia do viúvo (1524)

113. *Comedia del viudo*. Edizione, introduzione e note a cura di M[aría] L[uisa] Tobar. Messina: Peloritana, 1977. 79 pp.

See also above, nos 1, 10, and below, no. 180.1.

Frágua de Amor (1524)

See above, no. 1, and below, no. 181.2.

Farsa dos físicos (1524)

See above, nos 1, 45, and below, no. 181.7.

O Juiz da Beira (1525 or 1526)

See above, nos 1, 19, 46, and below, no. 179.10.

Templo de Apolo (1526)

See above, no. 1, and below, no. 179.2.

Auto da feira (1526)

114. *Auto da feira*. Prefácio e anotações de Joaquim Ferreira. Porto: Domingos Barreira, n.d. 112 pp.

115. *Auto da feira*. Introdução, comentário, síntese e glossário de Manuel dos Santos Alves. Lisboa: Francisco Franco, 1977. 90 pp.

116. *Auto da feira*. Apresentação crítica, notas, glossário e sugestões para análise literária de Artur Ribeiro Gonçalves. Textos Literários, XXXIX. Lisboa: Comunicação, 1984. 89 pp.
   Reviews:
   a. Silvina Rodrigues Lopes, *CoL*, 89 (January 1986), 101.
   b. O[sório] M[ateus], *CoL*, 94 (November 1986), 117.

117. *Auto da feira*. Introdução e edição interpretativa de Luís F. Lindley Cintra, seguido de "O *Auto da feira* e o Saque de Roma" por João Nuno Alçada igualmente responsável pela selecção dos documentos complementares. Biblioteca de Bolso, XLII. Lisboa: Dom Quixote, 1989. 107 pp.
   Review:
   a. Maria Ema Tarracha Ferreira, *CoL*, 121–122 (July–December 1991), 261–62.

118. *Auto da feira*. Comentário e anotações didácticas de Angelina Vasques Martins. Coimbra: Arnado, 1994. 144 pp.

See also above, nos 1–2, 7, 17, 19, 21, 30, 37, 44, 80.

Nau de amores (1527)

See above, no. 1.

Comédia sobre a divisa da cidade de Coimbra (1527)

119. *Comédia sobre a divisa da cidade de Coimbra*. Con una introducción y notas. Ed. Daniel Rangel–Guerrero. Romance Monographs, XXXVIII. University, Mississippi: Romance Monographs, 1980. 82 pp.

Revised version of his doctoral dissertation for the University of Oregon (1967). See *DA*, XXVIII (1967–68), 2219A–2220A, and *GVB*, no. 153.

Reviews:

a. Joseph L. Laurenti, *Hispania*, LXIV (1981), 475–76.

b. Charlotte Stern, *HR*, L (1982), 486–88.

See also above, nos 1, 34, and below, no. 178.10.

Farsa dos almocreves (1527)

See above, no. 1, and below, no. 183.5.

Tragicomédia pastoril da Serra da Estrêla (1527)

See above, nos 1, 79, and below, no. 183.6.

Breve sumário da história de Deus (1527)

See above, nos 1, 30, and below, no. 180.3.

Diálogo sobre a ressurreição de Cristo (1527)

See above, nos 1, 19, and below, no. 180.5.

Auto das fadas (1527)

See above, nos 1, 78, and below, no. 179.4.

Auto da festa (1527 or 1528)

See above, no. 1, and below, no. 182.1.

O triunfo do Inverno (1529)

See above, nos 1, 40, 78.

O clérigo da Beira (1529 or 1530)

See above, no. 1, and below, no. 179.6.

Auto da Lusitânia (1532)

See above, nos 1, 11, 26, 78.

Romagem de agravados (1533)

See above, nos 1, 78, and below, no. 180.10.

Auto da Cananeia (1534)

See above, nos 1, 78, and below, no. 182.2.

Floresta de enganos (1536)

See above, no. 1.

Obra da geração humana (attributed to Gil Vicente by I. S. Révah)

120. *Auto da geração humana atribuído a Gil Vicente*. Adaptado, para representação, por António Lopes Ribeiro. Lisboa: Casa Portuguesa, 1978. 111 pp.

Includes an introduction ("*Obra da geraçã humana*: uma bela 'Moralidade' quinhentista") by Justino Mendes de Almeida (pp. 9–17), a facsimile reproduction of the first sixteenth–century edition of the play (pp. 21–67) and Ribeiro's adaptation (pp. 71–111).

See also below, no. 182.3.

Auto de Deus Padre e Justiça e Misericórdia (attributed to Gil Vicente by I. S. Révah)

See below, no. 183.7.

D. *MISCELLANEOUS WORKS*

121. Reckert, Stephen. "A paráfrase vicentina do *Miserere* (edição, notas e comentário)." *RFLUL*, 5ª Série, 13–14 [*Homenagem a José V. de Pina Martins*] (December 1990), 441–53.

A normalized but not modernized edition of Gil Vicente's "Salmo de *Miserere mei, Deus*" (a paraphrase of Biblical Psalm 51 based on Savonarola's *Miserere*) with textual notes and commentary.

See also above, nos 1, 30, 34, 57, 78, 80, and below, nos 179.1, 179.3, 180.4, 180.8, 181.8, 182.10, 266, 536.

II
TRANSLATIONS

A. *DRAMA*

English

122. *El auto de la sibila Casandra*. Bilingual edition with an introduction by Mary Borelli. Valencia: ECIR, E. López Mezquida, 1970 [1971]. 87 pp.
    Pp. 7–29: introduction. Pp. 32–81: text and line by line prose translation on facing pages.

123. *Don Duardos*. Translated with an introduction by Mary Borelli. Columbia, South Carolina: n. pub., 1976. vi+45 pp.
    Prose translation.

See also below, no. 172.

French

124. *Théâtre espagnol du XVIe siècle*. Dir. Robert Marrast. General Introduction by Jean Canavaggio. Bibliothèque de la Pléiade, CCCV. Paris: Gallimard, 1983. lxxxiv+1090 pp.
    Includes Paul Teyssier's prose translations of *Auto da sibila Cassandra* (pp. 203–15), *Auto da Barca da Glória* (pp. 219–34), *Tragicomédia de Dom Duardos* (pp. 237–69). Also his biographical sketch of Gil Vicente and bibliographical note (pp. 880–83), and his notes to the plays (pp. 884–88, 889–96, and 896–905, respectively).

Italian

125. Ceccucci, Piero and Brunello de Cusatis. *Cultura e società nel Portogallo del XVI secolo*. Perugia: Università degli Studi di Perugia, 1984. 129 pp.
    Includes: "*Auto dell'India* di Gil Vicente. Saggio introduttivo, traduzione e note di Brunello de Cusatis" (pp. 51–129). Original text and facing–page Italian prose translation on pp. 80–113.

126. *Vicente, Gil. *Trilogia delle Barche*. Trans. Gianfranco Contini. Torino: Einaudi, 1992. First appeared in *Teatro religioso del Medioevo fuori d'Italia. Raccolta di testi dal secolo VII al secolo XV*. Ed. Gianfranco Contini. Milano: Bompiani, 1949, pp. 323–72 (see *GVB*, no. 191).

Portuguese

127. Fonseca, Gondin da. *Poemas da angústia alheia*. Traduções em verso de: Oscar Wilde, Edgar Poe, Arvers, Rimbaud, Verlaine, Kipling, T. S. Eliot, T. E. Lawrence, Dante, Frei Luís de Sousa, Gil Vicente, Gonçalves Dias, S. Francisco de Assis. Confrontadas com os textos originais. 4ª ed. Rio de Janeiro: Livraria São José, 1966. 177 pp.

Includes the original Spanish text with facing–page Portuguese verse translation of the complete *Monólogo do vaqueiro* (pp. 138–46).

See also above, nos 6, 36, 45–46, 88, 106.

Spanish

128. *Auto da Índia de Gil Vicente*. Trans. María Josefa Postigo Aldeamil and Denis M. Canellas de Castro Duarte. Madrid: Universidad Complutense, 1984.

B. POETRY

English

129. *An Anthology of Spanish Poetry from the Beginnings to the Present Day, Including Both Spain and Spanish America*. Comp. and ed. John A. Crow. Baton Rouge and London: Louisiana State University Press, 1979. xxxv+220 pp.

Includes the original texts and verse translations of "¡Sañosa está la niña!" (George Ticknor), "Dicen que me case yo" (John Bowring), and "Muy graciosa es la doncella" (John A. Crow)—all from *Sibila Cassandra*—on p. 55 (see *GVB*, no. 216).

130. *The Best of Spanish Literature in Translation*. Ed. Seymour Resnick and Jeanne Pasmantier. New York: Frederick Ungar, 1976. xv+304 pp.

Includes (p. 63) verse translations of "Muy graciosa es la doncella" (Alice Jane McVan) and "Dicen que me case yo" (George Ticknor), both from *Sibila Cassandra* (see *GVB*, nos 197, 203, 205, 212–16).

131. Campbell, Roy. *Portugal*. London: Max Reinhardt, 1957. Reprinted, Chicago: Henry Regnery, 1958. x+206 pp.

On Gil Vicente, pp. 128–32. Includes the author's verse translations of "Todo o Mundo e Ninguém" (*Auto da Lusitânia*), pp. 129–31, the closing scene with the four knights (*Auto da Barca do Inferno*), pp. 131–32, and "Remando vam remadores" (*Auto da Barca do Purgatório*), p. 132 (see *GVB*, nos 200–201).

132. *The Catholic Anthology: The World's Great Catholic Poetry*. Ed. Thomas Walsh. Rev. ed. New York: Macmillan, 1947. 584 pp. (First ed., 1927. Rev. ed., 1932. Several subsequent reprints).

Includes the editor's verse translations of "Blanca estais colorada" (*Auto da feira*) and "Muy graciosa es la doncella" (*Sibila Cassandra*) on pp. 132 and 133 respectively. Also Aubrey F. G. Bell's verse renderings of "Remando vam remadores" (*Auto da Barca do Purgatório*) and "A ti dino de adorar" (*Auto dos Quatro Tempos*), on pp. 132 and 133 respectively (see *GVB*, no. 204).

133. *Nine Centuries of Spanish Literature/Nueve siglos de literatura española: A Dual–Language Anthology*. Ed. Seymour Resnick and Jeanne Pasmantier. New York: Dover Publications, 1994. xviii+462 pp.

Includes the original text and Alice Jane McVan's verse translation of "Muy graciosa es la doncella" (on facing pages 112–13) and the original text with George Ticknor's verse translation of "Dicen que me case yo" (on facing pages 114–15). Both lyrics are from the *Sibila Cassandra* (see above, no. 130). The volume is a slightly corrected version of *Highlights of Spanish Literature: A Bilingual Anthology* (New York: Ungar, 1963), 463 pp. (see *GVB*, no. 203).

See also below, nos 534, 574, 577A, 607.

French

134. *Anthologie de la poésie portugaise du XII⁵ au XX⁵ siècle*. Ed. Isabel Meyrelles. [Paris]: Gallimard, 1971. 382 pp.

Includes Paul Teyssier's verse translation of Maria Parda's plaint (pp. 51–55) from the homonymous work.

Portuguese

See above, no. 61.

C. DRAMA AND POETRY

Italian

135. *Antologia delle letterature portoghese e brasiliana.* Ed. Cesco Vian. Letteratura Universale (a cura di Luigi Santucci), XX. Milano: Fratelli Fabbri, 1969. 399 pp.

"Gil Vicente, drammaturgo e lirico del Rinascimento" (pp. 19–91): includes verse translations of the *Auto da Barca do Inferno* (pp. 19–51) and *Auto de Inês Pereira* (pp. 51–89), both from: Gil Vicente, *Teatro,* trans. Enzio di Poppa Vòlture, 2 vols. (Firenze: Sansoni, 1953–54), vol. I, pp. 179–207 and vol. II, pp. 567–605 respectively (see *GVB*, no. 189). It also includes Piero Raimondi's verse translations of "Los amores de la niña" (*Auto da Lusitânia*), pp. 89–90, "¿Por dó pasaré la sierra?" (*Triunfo do Inverno*), p. 90, and "Muy graciosa es la doncella" (*Sibila Cassandra*), pp. 90–91: all three from *Orfeo: il tesoro della lirica universale interpretato in versi italiani,* ed. Vincenzo Errante and Emilio Mariano (Firenze: Sansoni, 1961), pp. 374, 375, 375, respectively (see *GVB*, no. 221).

III
CRITICAL STUDIES

A. *BOOKS, MONOGRAPHS, THESES, AND PAMPHLETS*

136. *Almada Negreiros e o Auto da Alma*. Évora: Centro Dramático de Évora, 1992. 32 pp.
    Contents: "Apresentação," by Dr. José Teixeira (p. 9). "Gil Vicente 'visto' por Almada Negreiros," by Vitor Pavão dos Santos (pp. 11–14). Auto da Alma (1965)—Descrição dos trajos (pp. 17–18). Auto da Alma—Figurinos (pp. 19–25). Notas de encenação de Almada Negreiros (pp. 26–29). Auto da Alma—Fotografias (1965), pp. 30–32. See below, no. 144.

137. Araújo, Matilde Rosa. *Gil Vicente*. Colecção Educativa, CXV: Série R (Grandes Portugueses), 5. [Lisboa]: Ministério da Educação e Cultura/ Direcção Geral da Educação Permanente, 1974 [1975]. 173 pp.
    Presents Gil Vicente's life and works to a young audience.

138. *Bomfim, Eneida do Rego. "Vocábulos e expressões referentes ao vestuário nos autos de Gil Vicente." Tese de mestrado, Departamento de Letras e Artes, Pontifícia Universidade Católica do Rio de Janeiro, 1973.

139. Calderón Calderón, Manuel. "La lírica de tipo tradicional de Gil Vicente." Doctoral thesis, Universidad de Barcelona, 1992. 529 pp.
    Contents: Introducción (pp. 7–22). I: Métrica (pp. 23–69). II: Música y coreografía (pp. 70–123). III: Estilo (pp. 124–252). IV: Temas (pp. 253–342). V: Tipos humanos (pp. 343–87). VI: Conclusión (pp. 388–93). VII: Apéndice (pp. 394–407). VIII: Corpus (pp. 408–67). IX: Bibliografía (pp. 468–529). Analyzes the formal, stylistic, and thematic characteristics of Gil Vicente's traditional type poetry and assesses its differentiating traits and its function within the dramatic context in which it occurs. From the point of view of metrics, Vicente's *cantigas*, *villancicos*, and *romances* show archaic traits in their structure, rhyme, and method of composition. This poetry is generally sung polyphonically and is accompanied by dances, such as the *folía* and the *morisca*, which refer to the carnival tradition. Poetry, song, and music perform multiple inter-related functions, either as dynamic elements of the dramatic action or as

symbols of the theme or the relations among the characters. In terms of content, in the secular love poetry, one finds themes, topics, and motifs belonging to a long tradition in Romance poetry and in the *canción de mujer*. In terms of style, there is frequent use of plurilingualism both in the religious *villancicos* and in the compositions of a humorous tone, assigned to negroes and gypsies.

140. *Carneiro, Alexandre Soares. "Notas sobre as origens do teatro de Gil Vicente." Tese de mestrado, Universidade Estadual de Campinas, 1992.

141. Carneiro, F[rancisco] Gonçalves. *O Teatro Universitário e as carapuças de Mestre Gil: resposta a uma crítica do "Notícias de Chaves".* Chaves: A Nova Tipografia, 1951. 21 pp.

In an article ("Jardim–Escola João de Deus") published in *Notícias de Chaves*, 29 (27 January 1951), Francisco Subtil objects to calling Gil Vicente's theater "clássico," since Vicente was a medieval man. Carneiro responds by defining the term *clássico* and concludes: "clássico pela sua formação e pelo seu humanismo, Gil Vicente produziu uma obra que é, sem dúvida, das mais representativas da língua portuguesa: uma obra clássica."

142. *Carter, Janet E. *The Concept of Allegory and Gil Vicente's "Auto da Alma".* Acta Portugaliensia, I. Johannesburg: Ernest Oppenheimer Institute for Portuguese Studies, University of the Witwatersrand, 1982.

143. Carvalho, Ilka Valle de. "Estrutura e 'mensagem' de *Inês Pereira*." Doctoral dissertation, University of California, Santa Barbara, 1981. 206 pp. See *DAI*, XLIII (1982–83), 2360–A.

Carvalho examines the play both as a dramatic and theatrical structure and as a literary text which reflects its sociohistorical milieu. She also analyzes its characters and attempts to explain its meaning.

144. Cid, Isabel. *Gil Vicente e a sua época*. Évora: Centro Dramático de Évora, 1992. 65 pp.

Contents: Prólogo (pp. 9–10). Apontamentos sobre a vida e obra de Gil Vicente (pp. 11–12). Cronologia (pp. 13–22). Catálogo das obras expostas (pp. 23–49). Catálogo de obras sobre Gil Vicente existentes na biblioteca [de Évora] que não foram expostas (pp. 51–65). This work is bound together, end to end, with no. 136.

145. Costa, Dalila Pereira da. *Gil Vicente e sua época*. Lisboa: Guimarães Editores, 1989. 198 pp.

Contents: I: *Uma transição* (Um testemunho. Duas correntes: medieval e renascentista. Teocentrismo e antropocentrismo. *Scientia experimentalis. Regnum hominis.* O Humanismo. *Ressuscitare*), pp. 11–45. II: *Uma concepção da vida* (O existencialismo cristão português. Os "secretos divinos". *Memento mori.* O Bem e o Mal. Obras, Fé e Graça. Omnipotência divina e livre arbítrio, astros e fortuna. Predestinação e liberdade. Um tema peninsular: a vida é sonho. O Anjo no teatro vicentino), pp. 49–101. III: *O poeta–dramaturgo áulico* (A rainha D. Leonor e o teatro didáctico. Humanismo, Pré–Reforma e Reforma. Acção e contemplação. A mística do norte. Uma obra conduzida em várias frentes. Teatro religioso e teatro profano. Uma arte laica de corte. A música na corte e no teatro vicentino. Realismo e simbolismo), pp. 105–59. IV: *Uma temática arcaica* (O Vate português. Ritos escatológicos nas *Barcas*. O fantástico infernal na *Barca da Glória*. Ritos cíclicos das estações no *Triunfo do Inverno*. Cybele, deusa dos cultos orientais no *Auto da Lusitânia*), pp. 163–96.

146. Cruz, Maria Leonor García da. *Gil Vicente e a sociedade portuguesa de quinhentos: leitura crítica num mundo "de cara atrás" (as personagens e o palco da sua acção)*. Construir o Passado, XXI. Lisboa: Gradiva, 1990. 276 pp.

Contents: A *condenação do mundo* (pp. 13–20): 1: A corcovada Justiça e os seus "negros" servidores (pp. 21–32); 2: A Corte e o domínio da falsidade, da lisonja e da "aderência" (pp. 32–52); 3: A falta de fé e a crise de valores morais e espirituais (pp. 52–116); 4: A ambição, a cobiça e a usura (pp. 116–23); 5: A honra e a soberba ou o culto das aparências (pp. 123–35); 6: O "medrar" como objectivo social e económico de todas as camadas sociais (pp. 135–46); 7: Todo o Mundo e Ninguém (pp. 146–48). *O alerta de um "louco" pregador* (pp. 149–51): 1: O reforço da fé e da missão espiritual do clero (pp. 151–217); 2: Revalorização da hierarquia jurídica e tripartida da sociedade para restabelecimento da ordem social e espiritual (pp. 218–52); 3: A justificação da Expansão portuguesa no mundo (pp. 253–65). Conclusão ou os sinais preconizadores de tensões e perseguição (pp. 267–69). Bibliografia (pp. 271–76).

Review:

a. F. Pires Lopes, *Brotéria*, CXXXI (1990), 118.

147. Fernandes, Irene. *Subsídios para a descodificação de "A Farsa de Inês Pereira" de Gil Vicente*. N.p.: n. pub., 1989. (Photocopy of a typescript).

Contents: Introdução (pp. 1–3). Investigação analítica (pp. 4–30). A crítica vicentina (pp. 31–33). *A Farsa de Inês Pereira*—uma nova didáctica (p. 34). Conclusão (p. 35). Notas à *Farsa de Inês Pereira* (pp. 36–37). Bibliografia (p. 38). Text of *Inês Pereira* (no pagination provided).

148. Fonseca, Maria Amália Ortiz da. *Gil Vicente. Auto da Alma*. Apontamentos, XLVII. Mem Martins: Europa–América, 1991. 92 pp.
Contents: A produção literária de Gil Vicente (pp. 7–8). O *Auto da Alma* na biografia do autor (pp. 9–10). O *Auto da Alma* no contexto cultural (pp. 11–15). O *Auto da Alma* no contexto histórico nacional (pp. 16–20). O *Auto da Alma* no contexto histórico europeu (pp. 21–24). Estrutura da obra (pp. 25–29). Arquitectura e encenação (pp. 30–73). A Moralidade em Gil Vicente (pp. 74–87). A Moralidade no *Auto da Alma* (pp. 88–89). Sugestões de trabalho (p. 90). Bibliografia (pp. 91–92).

149. Fonseca, Maria Amália Ortiz da. *Gil Vicente. Auto da feira*. Apontamentos, XLVI. Mem Martins: Europa–América, 1991. 121 pp.
Contents: A produção literária de Gil Vicente (pp. 7–8). O *Auto da feira* na biografia do autor (pp. 9–11). O *Auto da feira* no contexto cultural (pp. 12–17). O *Auto da feira* no contexto histórico nacional (pp. 18–23). O *Auto da feira* no contexto histórico europeu (pp. 24–28). Estrutura da obra (pp. 29–36). Arquitectura e encenação (pp. 37–102). A Moralidade em Gil Vicente (pp. 103–15). A Moralidade no *Auto da feira* (pp. 116–18). Sugestões de trabalho (p. 119). Bibliografia (pp. 120–21).

150. Fonseca, Maria Amália Ortiz da. *Gil Vicente. Auto da Índia*. Apontamentos, LXIV. Mem Martins: Europa–América, 1991. 89 pp.
Contents: A produção literária de Gil Vicente (pp. 7–8). O *Auto da Índia* na biografia do autor (pp. 8–10). O *Auto da Índia* no contexto cultural (pp. 11–15). O *Auto da Índia* no contexto histórico nacional (pp. 15–21). O *Auto da Índia* no contexto histórico europeu (pp. 21–24). Estrutura da obra (pp. 25–32). Arquitectura e encenação (pp. 32–75). A sátira social em Gil Vicente (pp. 76–84). A sátira social no *Auto da Índia* (pp. 84–86). Sugestões de trabalho (p. 87). Bibliografia (pp. 88–89).

151. Fonseca, Maria Amália Ortiz da. *Gil Vicente. Farsa de Inês Pereira*. Apontamentos, XIX. Mem Martins: Europa–América, 1990. 70 pp.

Contents: A produção literária de Gil Vicente (pp. 5–6). A *Farsa de Inês Pereira* na biografia do autor (pp. 7–9). A *Farsa de Inês Pereira* no contexto cultural (pp. 10–14). A *Farsa de Inês Pereira* no contexto histórico nacional (pp. 15–20). A *Farsa de Inês Pereira* no contexto histórico europeu (pp. 21–25). Estrutura da obra (pp. 26–28). Arquitectura e encenação (pp. 28–60). A sátira social em Gil Vicente (pp. 61–64). A sátira social na *Farsa de Inês Pereira* (pp. 65–67). Sugestão de trabalho (p. 68). Bibliografia (pp. 69–70).

152. Garay, René Pedro. *Gil Vicente and the Development of the Comedia.* North Carolina Studies in the Romance Languages and Literatures, CCXXXII. Chapel Hill: University of North Carolina Press, 1988. xix+220 pp.

Originally his doctoral dissertation for Vanderbilt University, Nashville, Tennessee, 1984: see *DAI*, XLV (1984–85), 3633A–34A. *Contents:* Introduction: Gil Vicente's Comic Renaissance Drama (pp. 1–8). I: Comic Theory Before the Sixteenth Century (pp. 9–33). II: The Development of the *Comédia* Form in the Iberian Peninsula (pp. 35–74). III: The Scope of the Vicentine Secular Perspective (pp. 75–109). IV: The *Comédia de Rubena* (pp. 111–74). V: The *Comédia do Viúvo* (pp. 175–216). Argues that greater emphasis ought to be given to Gil Vicente's *comédia* and to his having initiated, together with Torres Naharro, the most important dramatic current of the Hispanic dramatic tradition: the *comedia* of the Spanish Golden Age. An analysis of the *Comédia de Rubena* and the *Comédia do viúvo* shows that Vicente has formulated a concept of *comédia* which is structurally more significant to later manifestations of comic forms than his earlier *autos*.

Reviews:

a. David J. Hildner, *L–BR*, XXVII, 1 (Summer 1990), 115–17.

b. Jack H. Parker, *BCom*, XLII (1990), 161–63.

c. Paul Teyssier, *ACCP*, XXVIII (1990), 599–603.

d. Esther de Pablo, *Romance Quarterly*, XXXVIII (1991), 113–14.

e. Maureen Ihrie, *Hispania*, LXXV (1992), 556–57.

153. *Gil Vicente.* Coordenação de António Manuel Couto Viana. Colaboração de Maria Emília Simões Assunção, Maria Adelaide Couto Viana and Maria Stella Afonso. Gigantes da Literatura Universal, IV. Lisboa: Verbo, 1983. 135 pp.

Contents: Gil Vicente por ele próprio (p. 5). O teatro pré–vicentino (pp. 6–7). A vida (pp. 9–21). Os contemporâneos (pp. 22–23). Os acontecimentos da época (p. 24). Gil Vicente de perto (pp. 25–30). Cronologia (pp. 30–32). Os escritores do seu tempo (p. 32). As obras (pp. 33–48). A arte da época (pp. 49–56). Antologia (pp. 57–88). As personagens (pp. 89–104). Os descobrimentos portugueses (pp. 105–20). Gil Vicente e a crítica (pp. 121–32). Algumas notas (p. 132). Principais edições (p. 133). Principais traduções (p. 133). Gil Vicente hoje (p. 134).

154. *Gil Vicente.* Porto: Escola de Artes Decorativas Soares dos Reis, 1966. 57 pp.
    Contents: Abertura (p. 5). Biografia (pp. 7–17). Religiosidade (pp. 19–28). Crítica social (pp. 29–38). Um diálogo sobre Gil Vicente (pp. 39–54). Colaboração artística (p. 55). Orientação e execução (p. 57). "Os alunos, sob a orientação dos respectivos professores, debruçaramse mais atentamente sobre a vida e obra de Gil Vicente surgindo assim pequenas composições escritas a que eles próprios deram vida com as suas interpretações... Outros alunos deram o contributo dos desenhos e arranjo gráfico... Homenagem de um grupo de jovens portugueses de hoje a um grande português de sempre."

155. *Gil Vicente. Comédia de Rubena.* Teatro de Cornucópia. [Lisboa]: Livros Cotovia, 1991. 43 pp.
    Program of the staging of the play. Lacks pagination. Includes: "Este espectáculo" by Luís Miguel Cintra, pp. [2–3]. "As edições da *Comédia de Rubena*," p. [4] and "Uma Introdução à *Comédia de Rubena*," pp. [4–8], both from the Introduction to Giuseppe Tavani's critical edition of the play (Roma: Ateneo, 1965), trans. by A. B. "A unidade dramática da *Comédia de Rubena*," pp. [8–13], from Thomas R. Hart's "The Dramatic Unity of Gil Vicente's *Comédia de Rubena*," *BHS*, XLVI (1969), 97–108, trans. by M. J. G. "A *Comédia de Rubena*: uma hipótese de relação com os milagres de Nossa Senhora," pp. [13–16], from Yvonne David–Peyre's "La *Comédia de Rubena*. Une pièce insolite de Gil Vicente," *BEP*, XXXII (1971), 11–27, trans. by M. J. G. "Imagens de diabos, bruxas, vida, morte e destino na Europa de Gil Vicente," pp. [16–22], by João Nuno Alçada (with an Appendix of relevant texts trans. by A. B. on pp. [23–25]). "A igreja católica e a igreja diabólica em Gil Vicente: a propósito do *Auto das fadas*," pp. [26–28], from João Nuno Alçada's "Charivari, Rébus e heresia na fala do Diabo picardo do *Auto das fadas*," *QP*, 15–24 (1984–88), 51–147. "As canções e a técnica dramática," pp. [42–43], from the Introduction to Thomas R. Hart's edition of Gil Vicente, *Teatro* (Madrid: Taurus, 1983), trans. by L. B.

156. Gonçalves, Maria José and António Eusebio. *Auto da Barca do Inferno de Gil Vicente*. Apontamentos, I. Mem Martins: Europa–América, 1987. 50 pp.

Contents: A produção literária de Gil Vicente (pp. 7–8). O *Auto da Barca do Inferno* na biografia do autor (pp. 9–10). O *Auto da Barca do Inferno* no contexto intelectual (pp. 11–13). O *Auto da Barca do Inferno* no contexto histórico nacional (pp. 15–16). O *Auto da Barca do Inferno* no contexto histórico europeu (pp. 17–19). O *Auto da Barca do Inferno* e a sua estrutura (p. 21). Arquitectura e encenação (pp. 23–44). A sátira social em Gil Vicente (p. 45). A sátira social no *Auto da Barca do Inferno* (pp. 47–48). Sugestões de trabalhos (p. 49). Bibliografia (p. 50).

157. *Gouveia, M. Margarida de Miranda Barbosa C. de. "A *Tragicomédia de Dom Duardos*. Génese, tema e estrutura do auto vicentino." Tese de dissertação de licenciatura em Filologia Românica, Universidade de Coimbra, 1971.

158. Hart, Thomas R. *Gil Vicente: "Casandra" and "Don Duardos"*. Critical Guides to Spanish Texts, XXIX. London: Grant & Cutler & Tamesis Books, 1981. 88 pp.

Hart examines the two plays in terms of sources (*Guarino mezquino* for *Cassandra*, *Primaleón* for *Dom Duardos*), texts, dates, staging, language and style, and imagery. He also discusses characterization in *Cassandra* and Vicente's masterful manner of transforming parts of a romance of chivalry, *Primaleón*, into one of his best plays, *Dom Duardos*. In an Appendix (pp. 78–88), Hart has transcribed the two chapters of *Primaleón* (98 and 101), which served as source for *Dom Duardos*.

Reviews:

a. Alice R. Clemente, *Modern Language Studies*, XIII, 3 (Summer 1983), 133–34.

b. Nigel Griffin, *MLR*, LXXVIII (1983), 942–43.

c. Antonio Dueñas, *Cuadernos Hispanoamericanos*, 414 (December 1984), 176–77.

159. Keates, Laurence. *O teatro de Gil Vicente na Corte*. Terra Nostra, V. Lisboa: Teorema, 1988. 131 pp.

The author's translation into Portuguese of his *The Court Theatre of Gil Vicente* (Lisboa: Livraria Escolar, 1962), 154 pp. Originally his M.A. thesis for the University of Birmingham, 1959. *Contents*: I: Gil Vicente na Corte (pp. 11–29). II: As bases culturais de Gil Vicente (pp.

31–46). III: Antecedentes teatrais e prototeatrais (pp. 47–73). IV: Gil Vicente empresário (pp. 75–89). V: Uma breve análise do teatro vicentino (pp. 91–114). VI: Conclusão e observações (pp. 115–24). Apêndice: Lista cronológica das peças de Gil Vicente (pp. 125–26). Bibliografia seleccionada (pp. 127–30).

160. *Lopes, Francisco Fernandes. *A música nos autos de Gil Vicente.* Lisboa: Divulgação Musical, 1940.

161. Moseley, William W. *A Concordance to the Spanish in the Complete Works of Gil Vicente.* Ann Arbor: Monograph Series, Xerox University Microfilms, 1977. 2 vols. x + 1001 pp.

162. *Noronha, Maria da Penha Sandoval. "O fidalgo em Gil Vicente." Tese de mestrado, Faculdade de Filosofia, Letras e Ciências Humanas, Universidade de São Paulo, 1978.

163. Oliveira, Joaquim de. *Gil Vicente nasceu em 1470: arquitectura literária para a biografia do ourives–poeta e criador do teatro português.* [Lisboa]: Author, 1975. 500 pp.
On the basis of internal evidence, Oliveira concludes that Gil Vicente was born in 1470 in Guimarães de Tavares (Beira). He argues for the identification of the dramatist with the goldsmith and he attacks the traditionally held view that the Queen Dona Leonor was the founder and protectress of the Portuguese theater. Oliveira includes a detailed description of the *custódia de Belém* and shows that Dona Catarina was responsible for the publication of the *Copilaçám*. He attacks the commemorations of Vicente's death and birth (1936, 1965) and objects to the application of the term *revisteiro* to Gil Vicente. He claims that Vicente's death created a vacuum in the Portuguese theater, for he had no real continuators. Oliveira views Vicente as tolerant toward the Jews. He discusses astrology and medicine in Vicente's works. He shows that Canto V of the *Lusíadas* was inspired in the *Triunfo do Inverno.* Some of these ideas had been expressed previously in several articles (see *GVB*, nos 273, 507, 564, 706, 773).

164. Palla, Maria José. *Do essencial e do supérfluo: estudo lexical do traje e adornos em Gil Vicente.* Imprensa Universitária, XCVII. Lisboa: Estampa, 1992. 260 pp.

The author's Portuguese version of her doctoral thesis in French (Sorbonne, 1991). *Contents*: Introdução (pp. 21–25). I: O traje (1. Generalidades, pp. 29–37. 2. Inventário e descrição, pp. 39–86. 3. Fiação e trabalhos de agulha, pp. 87–97. 4. As cores do traje, pp. 99–112. 5. A simbologia do traje, pp. 113–33). II: O corpo (6. As cores do corpo humano, pp. 137–49. 7. Pêlos e cabelos, pp. 151–78). III: Os acessórios (8. Os acessórios do traje, pp. 181–85. 9. Adornos e jóias, pp. 187–93. 10. As armas, pp. 195–201. 11. Os instrumentos de música, pp. 203–18). Conclusão (pp. 219–24). Anexos (pp. 225–31). Bibliografia (pp. 233–54). Índice analítico (pp. 255–60).

165. Ramsay, Elizabeth Grace. "A Computer–Assisted Literary Analysis of the *Barcas* of Gil Vicente." Doctoral dissertation, Catholic University of America, Washington, D.C., 1984. 277 pp. See *DAI*, XLV (1984–85), 3655–A.

Analyzes lexical and syntactical patterns in the *Barcas* and concludes that the first two (*Auto da Barca do Inferno* and *Auto da Barca do Purgatório*) are written in a highly colloquial style, whereas the *Auto da Barca da Glória* is characterized by a more elevated, literary tone.

166. Reckert, Stephen. *Espírito e letra de Gil Vicente*. Temas Portugueses. Lisboa: Imprensa Nacional–Casa da Moeda, 1983. 290 pp.

A revised version of his *Gil Vicente: espíritu y letra*. I: *Estudios*, Biblioteca Románica Hispánica, IV: Textos, 10 (Madrid: Gredos, 1977)—see *GVB*, no. 285A. In the Portuguese version, the diplomatic text of *Dom Duardos* has been omitted, and an entirely new chapter (IX: "Critérios para a edição de textos vicentinos," pp. 257–77) has been added. This chapter is a revised version of a paper presented at the Colloquium on Portuguese Textual Criticism in the Centro Cultural Gulbenkian (Paris, October 1981) and subsequently published in *ACCP*, XX (1984), 393–409. In it, the author advises respect not only for the spirit but also for the letter of Gil Vicente's work, for failure to respect the letter may lead to a distortion of the spirit.

Reviews:

a. P. L., *Brotéria*, CXVII (1983), 595.

b. Thomas R. Hart, *MLN*, IC (1984), 393–94.

c. Paul Teyssier, *BEPB*, XLIV–XLV (1983–85), 517–18.

d. See no. 353.

167. Reckert, Stephen. *O essencial sobre Gil Vicente*. Colecção Essencial, X. Lisboa: Imprensa Nacional–Casa da Moeda, 1985. 60 pp.
A shorter version of the first two sections of his *Espírito e letra de Gil Vicente* (see no. 166 above).
Review:
a. O[sório] M[ateus], *CoL*, 93 (September 1986), 131.

168. Reis, João da Encarnação. *Panorâmica vicentina dos alvores do quinhentismo (uma leitura metódica do poeta dramaturgo)*. Coimbra: Livraria Minerva, 1992. 113 pp.
Contents: Alimentação (pp. 9–20). Amor (pp. 21–29). Casa, mobiliário, objectos e actividades domésticas (pp. 31–34). Higiene e doença (pp. 35–37). Actividades económicas (pp. 39–43). Costumes (pp. 45–48). Diabo e Inferno (pp. 49–51). Linguagem vicentina (pp. 53–56). Judeus (pp. 57–60). Mar (pp. 61–67). Descobrimentos (pp. 69–70). Moeda e medidas (pp. 71–75). Música e diversões (pp. 77–81). Provérbios (pp. 83–85). Religião (pp. 87–92). Vestuário e adornos (pp. 93–100). Tipos sociais (pp. 101–7). Bibliografia (p. 111).

169. Ribeiro, Maria Aparecida. *Gil Vicente e a nostalgia da ordem*. Rio de Janeiro: Livraria Eu e Você Editora, 1984. 112 pp.
Originally her doctoral thesis for the Universidade Federal do Rio de Janeiro (1980). *Contents:* Introdução (*O problema. A metodologia. O corpus*), pp. 15–26. O texto vicentino (*A ordem e a desordem* [Paço: parasitismo, aderência & cia. Roma: luxúria & simonia. Pero & Inês: ignorância & ociosidade. Todo–o–Mundo X Ninguém: a melancolia]; *O resgate da ordem* [A corrosão. A festa]), pp. 27–98. Conclusão, pp. 99–100. Bibliografia, pp. 101–7. Notas, pp. 108–12. For the ideas expressed here, see nos 326–27 below.
Review:
a. P. L., *Brotéria*, CXXII (1986), 112.

170. Santos, Fernando Eduardo. *Gil Vicente, moralizador de consciências*. Paços de Ferreira: Câmara Municipal de Paços de Ferreira, 1994. 43 pp.
"Conferência proferida em Freamunde, em 11 de Dezembro de 1965, com ilustrações cénicas a cargo do Grupo Teatral Freamunde, integrada nas comemorações do V Centenário do Nascimento de Gil Vicente." General discussion of Gil Vicente's social and ecclesiastical criticism with reference to several plays.

171. Saraiva, José H[ermano]. *Testemunho social e condenação de Gil Vicente*. Comunicação apresentada à Classe de Letras da Academia das Ciências de Lisboa em 15 de Maio de 1975. [Lisboa]: [Author], 1975. 72 pp.

Contents: I: O testemunho vicentino (pp. 7–20). II: Um exemplo: *A Romagem dos agravados* (pp. 21–48). III: Acusação e condenação de Gil Vicente (pp. 49–72). Saraiva believes that some of Gil Vicente's plays are social studies in theater language rather than plays with social aspects. He therefore advocates a more sociosemantic reexamination of them. He proceeds to examine the *Romagem de agravados*, the last social play, in this light and at length. Saraiva claims that, following the staging of the now lost *Jubileu de amores* in Antwerp (1531), Vicente incurred the disfavor of the royal court, from which he disappeared for three years. Some of his later plays are allegorical attempts to defend himself against the injustice done to him. Saraiva also questions the attribution of *Dom Duardos* to Gil Vicente.

172. Smolen, Marian Leanna. "Bilingualism as Semiotic Code in the Theatrical Code Systems of the Theater of Gil Vicente." Doctoral thesis, Arizona State University, 1990. vi+166 pp.

Contents: I: Introduction: A Statement of Premises (pp. 1–18). II: Bilingualism as Part of the Theatrical Sign System in *Quem tem farelos?* and *Auto da Índia* (pp. 19–59). III: Linguistic Codes in the *Auto do Inferno, Auto do Purgatório* and *Auto da Glória*: Their Relationship to Dramatic Structure (pp. 60–89). IV: The Use of Dialects and Other Subcodes in *Inês Pereira* and *Juiz da Beira* (pp. 90–118). V: Conclusions (pp. 119–32). Bibliography (pp. 133–42). Appendix: Gil Vicente's *Who Has Bran?* [prose translation of *Farelos*] (pp. 143–66). Smolen studies how Vicente has integrated the use of Spanish and Portuguese into a complex system of linguistic and nonlinguistic theatrical codes.

173. *Suárez, José Ignacio. "Bakhtinian Theory and the Codification of Gil Vicente's Comic Modes." Doctoral thesis, University of New Mexico, 1981.

174. Suárez, José Ignacio. *The Carnival Stage: Vicentine Comedy Within the Serio–Comic Mode*. Rutherford, New Jersey: Fairleigh Dickinson University Press, 1993. 172 pp.

Contents: Introduction (pp. 15–31). The Origins of Peninsular Drama (pp. 32–46). The Serio–Comic Genres: A Brief Overview (pp.

47–72). The Basic Characteristics of the Menippean Satire and Their Application to Vicentine Comedy (pp. 73–153). Notes (pp. 155–62). Select Bibliography (pp. 163–68). Index (pp. 169–72). Application of Bakhtinian critical theories to Gil Vicente's works. Gil Vicente is a continuator of the serio–comic tradition and, therefore, a precursor to Rabelais.

Reviews:

a. George D. Greenia, Hispania, LXXVII (1994), 818–19.
b. Thomas R. Hart, MLR, XC (1995), 220–21.
c. Luís de Sousa Rebelo, Portuguese Studies, XI (1995), 216–17.
d. David J. Hildner, L–BR, XXXIII, 1 (Summer 1996), 154–55.

175. Teles, Maria J[osé], M[aria] Leonor Cruz, and S[usana] Marta Pinheiro. O discurso carnavalesco em Gil Vicente no âmbito de uma história das mentalidades. Apresentação de Fernando António Baptista Pereira. Colecção Estudos–Ensaios, I. Lisboa: GEC Publicações, 1984. 146 pp.

A detailed study of the carnivalesque aspects of Gil Vicente's discourse, with particular attention to vocabulary and figures of speech, and with an analysis of the characters who use this mode of expression. The authors conclude by placing Vicente's work in its cultural, mental and ideological context, viewing it as the meeting point of medieval structures and Renaissance modes of thought so closely associated with the great debate of ideas in the first half of the sixteenth century.

176. Teyssier, Paul. Gil Vicente—O autor e a obra. Trans. Álvaro Salema. Biblioteca Breve, LXVII. Série Literatura. Lisboa: Instituto de Cultura e Língua Portuguesa, Ministério da Educação e das Universidades/Amadora: Bertrand, 1982. 177 pp.

Contents: O autor e o seu texto (pp. 9–29). Os autos: elaboração e análise (pp. 31–105). Os autos: comentários gerais (pp. 107–40). Esboço de interpretação global (pp. 141–73). Bibliografia (pp. 175–77).

Review:

a. Osório Mateus, CoL, 73 (May 1983), 97–98.

177. Tobar, María Luisa. Gil Vicente y la comedia. Università degli Studi di Messina, Facoltà di Magistero, Instituto di Lingue e Letterature Romanze. Messina: Peloritana Editrice, 1980. 180 pp.

Contents: Introducción (pp. 9–20). Gil Vicente y la teoría de la comedia (pp. 21–55). Estructura de las comedias (pp. 57–96). Cambio de personalidad y disfraz en la comedia (pp. 97–146). Conclusión (pp. 147–50). Bibliografía (pp. 153–80). Gil Vicente followed the medieval conception of comedy as put forth by Juan de Mena (*Coronación*) and the Marqués de Santillana (*Comedieta de Ponza*). Tobar proceeds to justify the *Copilaçám* classification of four plays as *comedias* (*Comédia do viúvo, Comédia de Rubena, Comédia sobre a divisa da cidade de Coimbra, Floresta de enganos*). Finally, she analyzes the structure of these plays in terms of their textual division, their prologues, and the comic interludes inserted in them.

178. *Vicente.* Colecção dirigida por Osório Mateus. Lisboa: Quimera, 1988.

Consists of the following ten *cadernos:*

1. Graça Abreu, *Lusitânia* (21 pp.): analysis of the *Auto da Lusitânia* in terms of the formula of play within play.

2. Margarida Vieira Mendes, *Maria Parda* (19 pp.): discussion of the *Pranto de Maria Parda* as a possible theatrical text.

3. Teresa Castro Nunes, *Nau* (15 pp.): analysis of the *Nau de amores.*

4. Osório Mateus, *Martinho* (11 pp.): the complete text of the *Auto de São Martinho* (based on the 1562 *Copilaçám*) interspersed with commentary.

5. Osório Mateus, *Índia* (25 pp.): the complete text of the *Auto da Índia* (based on the 1562 *Copilaçám*) interspersed with commentary.

6. João Nuno Sales, *Ciganas* (18 pp.): the complete text of the *Auto das ciganas* (based on the 1562 *Copilaçám*) interspersed with commentary.

7. Osório Mateus, *Tormenta* (11 pp.): discussion of the "Carta que Gil Vicente mandou de Santarém a el–Rei Dom João" as a dramatic piece.

8. José Camões, *Farelos* (27 pp.): the complete text of *Quem tem farelos?* (based on the 1562 *Copilaçám*) interspersed with commentary.

9. Osório Mateus, *Cortes* (29 pp.): the complete text of *Côrtes de Júpiter* (based on the 1562 *Copilaçám*) interspersed with commentary.

10. Osório Mateus, *Devisa* (35 pp.): the complete text of the *Comédia sobre a divisa da cidade de Coimbra* (based on the 1562 *Copilaçám*) interspersed with commentary.

Review:

a. Maria João Brilhante, *CoL*, 112 (November–December 1989), 114–15.

179. *Vicente.* Colecção dirigida por Osório Mateus. Lisboa: Quimera, 1989.

Consists of the following ten *cadernos*:

1. Osório Mateus, *Pregação* (23 pp.): the complete text of the "Sermão de Abrantes" (based on the 1562 *Copilaçám*) interspersed with commentary.

2. Cristina Firmino, *Templo* (31 pp.): the complete text of the *Templo de Apolo* (based on the 1562 *Copilaçám*) interspersed with commentary.

3. Alina Villalva, *Vasco Abul* (27 pp.): text of the *Processo de Vasco Abul* (from Garcia de Resende's *Cancioneiro geral*), to which Gil Vicente contributed 8 nine–line stanzas, interspersed with commentary.

4. José Camões, *Fadas* (35 pp.): the complete text of the *Auto das fadas* (based on the 1562 *Copilaçám*) interspersed with commentary.

5. María Victoria Navas, *Pastoril castelhano* (23 pp.): the complete text of the *Auto pastoril castelhano* (based on the 1562 *Copilaçám*) interspersed with linguistic commentary.

6. Ângela Correia, *Clérigo* (35 pp.): the complete text of the *Clérigo da Beira* (based on the 1562 *Copilaçám*) interspersed with commentary.

7. Carlos Gouveia, *Fé* (21 pp.): the complete text of the *Auto da Fé* (based on the 1562 *Copilaçám*) on pp. 4–12, followed by commentary on pp. 13–19.

8. Cristina Serôdio, *Fama* (27 pp.): the complete text of the *Auto da Fama* (based on the 1562 *Copilaçám*) interspersed with commentary.

9. Maria João Almeida, *Feira* (23 pp.): analysis of the *Auto da feira*.

10. João Dionísio, *Juiz* (31 pp.): the complete text of the *Juiz da Beira* (based on the 1562 *Copilaçám*) interspersed with commentary.

180. *Vicente*. Colecção dirigida por Osório Mateus. Lisboa: Quimera, 1990.

Consists of the following ten *cadernos*:

1. Alina Villalva, *Viúvo* (39 pp.): the complete text of the *Comédia do viúvo* (based on the 1562 *Copilaçám*) interspersed with commentary.

2. Maria João Brilhante, *Mofina* (35 pp.): the complete text of the *Auto de Mofina Mendes* (based on the 1562 *Copilaçám*) interspersed with commentary.

3. José Moreira, *História de Deos* (35 pp.): complete text of the *Breve sumário da história de Deus* (based on the 1562 *Copilaçám*) interspersed with commentary.

4. José Camões, *Aclamação de João III* (19 pp.): the complete text of "Outro romance de Gil Vicente que fez quando foi levantado por rei

el–Rei Dom João, o terceiro, de gloriosa memória" (based on the 1562 *Copilaçám*) interspersed with commentary.

5. Fátima Silva, *Ressurreição* (23 pp.): the complete text of the *Diálogo sobre a Ressurreição* (based on the 1562 *Copilaçám*) interspersed with commentary.

6. Alexandra Mariano, *Pastoril Português* (27 pp.): the complete text of the *Auto pastoril português* (based on the 1562 *Copilaçám*) interspersed with commentary.

7. Osório Mateus, *Reis* (15 pp.): the complete text of the *Auto dos Reis Magos* (based on the 1562 *Copilaçám*) interspersed with commentary.

8. José Camões, *Morte de Manuel I* (19 pp.): the complete text of "De Gil Vicente à morte do muito alto e esclarecido Rei Dom Manuel, o primeiro do nome" (based on the 1562 *Copilaçám*) interspersed with commentary.

9. Osório Mateus, *Visitação* (11 pp.): the complete text of the *Auto da visitação* (based on the 1562 *Copilaçám*) interspersed with commentary.

10. Ernestina Carrilho, *Romagem* (39 pp.): the complete text of the *Romagem de agravados* (based on the 1562 *Copilaçám*) interspersed with commentary.

181. *Vicente*. Colecção dirigida por Osório Mateus. Lisboa: Quimera, 1991.

Consists of the following ten *cadernos*:

1. José Camões, *Tempos* (31 pp.): introduction to the *Auto dos Quatro Tempos* (on pp. 3–12) followed by the complete text of the play (based on the 1562 *Copilaçám*) on pp. 13–29.

2. João Nuno Sales, *Frágua* (35 pp.): the complete text of the *Frágua de Amor* (based on the 1562 *Copilaçám*) interspersed with commentary.

3. Cristina Almeida Ribeiro, *Inês* (27 pp.): the complete text of the *Auto de Inês Pereira* (based on the individual edition of the play with an occasional reference to the 1562 *Copilaçám*) interspersed with commentary.

4. Isabel Almeida, *Duardos* (27 pp.): analysis of *Dom Duardos*.

5. João Frazão, *Sepultura* (11 pp.): discussion of Gil Vicente's epitaph and drawing of the tombstone as they appear on the last leaf of the *Copilaçám*.

6. Leonor Curado Neves, *Inverno e Verão* (27 pp.): analysis of the *Triunfo do Inverno*.

7. Maria Jorge, *Físicos* (31 pp.): the complete text of the *Farsa dos físicos* (based on the 1562 *Copilaçám*) interspersed with commentary.

8. Maria João Borges, *Miserere* (23 pp.): the complete text of "O salmo de 'Miserere mei, Deus'" (based on the 1562 *Copilaçám*) interspersed with an analysis of the intertextual relationship of this text, Savonarola's *Miserere* and the Biblical psalm.

9. Cristina Almeida Ribeiro, *Velho* (31 pp.): the complete text of the *Velho da horta* (based on the 1562 *Copilaçám*) interspersed with commentary.

10. Maria João Amaral, *Rubena* (31 pp.): analysis of the *Comédia de Rubena*.

182. *Vicente*. Colecção dirigida por Osório Mateus. Lisboa: Quimera, 1992.

Consists of the following ten *cadernos*:

1. José Camões, *Festa* (35 pp.): the complete text of the *Auto da festa* (based on the individual edition) interspersed with commentary.

2. Maria João Pimenta, *Cananea* (35 pp.): the complete text of the *Auto da Cananeia* (based on the 1562 *Copilaçám*) interspersed with commentary.

3. Alves Tavares, *Geração* (43 pp.): the complete text of the *Obra da geração humana* (based on the 1536 individual edition)—which I. S. Révah attributed to Gil Vicente—with a short introduction on pp. 3–7.

4. Luís Martins, *Exortação* (27 pp.): the complete text of the *Exortação da guerra* (based on the 1562 *Copilaçám*) interspersed with commentary.

5. Fátima Iglésias, *Corpus Christi* (11 pp.): Gil Vicente had participated in the Corpus Christi celebrations of 1511 with an *auto*, for which he was paid 5,070 *réis*. Nothing is known about this *auto*.

6. Teresa Amado, *Amadis* (31 pp.): analysis of *Amadis de Gaula*.

7. Margarida Vieira Mendes, *Cassandra* (39 pp.): the complete text of the *Auto da sibila Cassandra* (based on the 1562 *Copilaçám*) interspersed with commentary.

8. Antunes Fonseca, *Entrada dos Reis* (15 pp.): discussion of the festive preparations for Manuel I's return to Lisbon (1521), of which Gil Vicente was in charge.

9. Maria João Brilhante, *Floresta* (35 pp.): analysis of the *Floresta de enganos*.

10. Cameira Gomes, *Trovas* (15 pp.): the complete texts of "Ao conde do Vimioso," "A Filipe Guilhém," the three *trovas* "A Afonso Lopes

Sapaio," and "De Gil Vicente a el–Rei Dom João terceiro" (based on the 1562 *Copilaçám*) with commentaries.

183. *Vicente*. Colecção dirigida por Osório Mateus. Lisboa: Quimera, 1993.

Consists of the following ten *cadernos*:

1. Cardeira Villalva, *Inferno* (39 pp.): provides the complete text, interspersed with commentary, of the *Auto da Barca do Inferno* (based on the 1517 edition but also pointing out readings from the *Copilaçám* of 1562).

2. José Camões, *Purgatório* (39 pp.): analyzes the *Auto da Barca do Purgatório* and provides the complete text of the play (on pp. 17–37), based on the *Copilaçám* of 1562.

3. Ernestina Carrilho, *Glória* (35 pp.): the complete text of the *Auto da Barca da Glória* (based on the 1562 *Copilaçám*) interspersed with commentary.

4. Maria Jorge, *Alma* (35 pp.): the complete text of the *Auto da Alma* (based on the 1562 *Copilaçám*) interspersed with commentary.

5. Ernestina Carrilho, *Almocreves* (31 pp.): the complete text of the *Farsa dos almocreves* (based on the 1562 *Copilaçám*) interspersed with commentary.

6. José Camões, *Serra* (31 pp.): the complete text of the *Tragicomédia pastoril da Serra da Estrêla* (based on that of the 1562 *Copilaçám*) interspersed with commentary.

7. Osório Mateus, *Deos Padre* (35 pp.): the text of the anonymous *Auto de Deus Padre e Justiça e Misericórdia* (which I. S. Révah attributed to Gil Vicente), based on the copy included in a miscellany (R 219 V) in Lisbon's Biblioteca Nacional.

8. Esperança Cardeira, *Jubileu* (11 pp.): discusses the circumstances surrounding the staging, as well as the possible content, of the lost play *Jubileu de Amor* in December 1531 (Brussels), and cites the testimonies of the Italian Cardinal Girolamo Aleandro, André de Resende, Pedro Mascarenhas, and the list of Vicentine pieces—including this play—placed on the 1551 Index.

9. Osório Mateus, *Livro das obras* (15 pp.): provides a detailed bibliographic description of all editions of Vicente's complete works since 1562.

10. João Nuno Sales, *Custódia* (15 pp.): gives a detailed description of the monstrance of Belém and the circumstances surrounding its

creation, and argues in favor of identifying Gil Vicente, the playwright, with Gil Vicente, the goldsmith.

184. Vicente, Gil. *Quem tem farelos?* Braga: Escola Secundária de Sá de Miranda, [1985]. 11 pp.

On the occasion of the mise–en–scène of *Quem tem farelos?* by the Grupo de Teatro da Escola Secundária de Sá de Miranda. Includes: De(bate) numa incógnita com duas partes (pp. 1–4). Teatro pré-vicentino—arremedilhos e momos (p. 5). Notas breves sobre a obra vicentina (pp. 6–7). *Quem tem farelos?* (pp. 7–8). Em jeito de agradeci-mento (pp. 8–9).

B. *CHAPTERS IN BOOKS AND ESSAYS IN COLLECTIONS*

185. Albuquerque, Luís de. "A astrologia e Gil Vicente." In his *Estudos de história*. Vol. I. Coimbra: Acta Universitatis Conimbrigensis, 1974, pp. 1–45.

See *GVB*, no. 639.

186. Alçada, João Nuno. "Apresentação." In *TV*, pp. 7–18.

Discusses Gil Vicente's "archaic modernity," his having maintained a balance between medieval culture and Renaissance values, and introduces the studies contained in the volume (see nos 197–98, 211, 229, 248, 253, 263, 279, 282, 288, 294, 299).

187. Alçada, J[oão] N[uno]. "Pour une possible interprétation de la présence de *Todo o Mundo (Elck)* et *Ninguém (Niemand)* dans l'*Auto da Lusitânia*." In *Non nova, sed nove: Mélanges de civilisation médiévale dédies à Willem Noomen*. Ed. Martin Gosman and Jaap van Os. Gro-ningen: Bouma's Boekhuis, 1984, pp. 11–24.

A much shorter version of no. 433.

188. Alonso Hernández, José Luis. "Notas críticas al *Pranto de Maria Parda* de Gil Vicente (edición de Luciana Stegagno Picchio)." In *EP:HLSP*, pp. 233–58.

The author offers many additions, corrections, and amplifications to Luciana Stegagno Picchio's clarificatory notes to her 1963 edition of

Maria Parda, which attest to the depth of Gil Vicente's knowledge of both folklore and literature.

189. Antunes–Fernandes, Marie–France. "Gil Vicente: un espagnol portugais du début du XVIᵉ siècle." In *Les Cahiers du C.R.I.A.R.*, No. 9: *Langues et identités dans la Péninsule Ibérique*. Études recueillies et présentées par Alain Milhou. Publications de l'Université de Rouen, CXLV. Rouen: Université de Rouen, 1989, pp. 23–50.

   Discusses Gil Vicente as a bilingual dramatist, the conditions which aided the penetration of Spanish into Portugal and Vicente's use of it; Portugal as a cultural satellite of Castile; how Vicente viewed Castilian and Castile; whether he was xenophobic; and whether he was truly Portuguese, to conclude that he was Spanish, in the medieval sense of the term (the notion of Spain as inclusive of Portugal), but he was also fully cognizant of Portugal's singularity.

190. Asensio, Eugenio. "Gil Vicente y su deuda con el humanismo: Luciano, Erasmo, Beroaldo." In *EP:HLSP*, pp. 277–99.

   In the *Barca do Inferno*, Gil Vicente has christianized pagan elements borrowed from Lucian's *Scaphidion* and *Tyrannus*. In *Triunfo do Inverno* and *Romagem de agravados*, respectively, he has borrowed certain comic elements and theatrical situations from Erasmus's *Naufragium* and *Procus et puella*, disregarding the moral instruction which informed the sources. Finally, in *O Juiz da Beira*, Vicente has utilized elements from Filippo Beroaldo's *Declamatio lepidissima ebriosi, scortatoris, aleatoris de vitiositate disceptantium*.

191. Askins, Arthur L.–F. "Notes on Pre–1536 Portuguese Theatrical Chapbooks." In *EP:HLSP*, pp. 301–9.

   Thirteen of Gil Vicente's plays, individually printed, have survived. There is evidence that another five (*Comédia do viúvo*, *Auto da Barca do Purgatório*, *Velho da horta*, *Auto da Índia*, and *O Juiz da Beira*) were individually printed before 1536. They had been brought together with a couple of other sixteenth–century Portuguese plays into a miscellany volume in the library of Fernando Colón (Seville). The volume itself has been lost but the description of its contents has survived.

192. Barata, José Oliveira. "Due momenti del Rinascimento europeo: Ruzante e Gil Vicente." In *Convegno Internazionale di studi sul Ruzante*

(Padova, 26/27/28 maggio 1983). A cura di Giovanni Calendoli e Giuseppe Vellucci. Venezia: Corbo e Fiore Editori, 1987, pp. 37–47.

A comparative study of Gil Vicente and Ruzante in several terms: the sociopolitical milieu in which each functioned, the use—and motives behind it—of rustic speech (*sayagués* and *beirão* in Vicente's case, *pavano* in Ruzante's), and the treatment of the figure of the peasant (Vicente views the peasant through the eyes of a courtier, Ruzante represents the countryside from the perspective of the peasant himself). A version of the essay had appeared before as "O vilão às avessas do seu mundo. Para um estudo do vilão vicentino," *Biblos*, LI (1975), 93–123 (see *GVB*, no. 593A).

193. Barreira, Cecília. "Eros e morte em Gil Vicente." In her *Sete faces ocultas da cultura portuguesa (de Gil Vicente a Pascoaes).* Colecção Átrio/Ensaio. Lisboa: Átrio, 1991, pp. 9–20.

A discussion of the *Barcas* and the *Velho da horta* as paradigms of the imbrication of Death/Eros. Death, punitive and irreversible, is the logical counterpoint to life. Disorder in customs, especially from the sexual point of view, emerges as a primordial sin which leads directly to suffering in hell. Salvation comes only and exclusively (except through express divine will) to those whose innocence cannot be questioned. The *Velho da horta* is the place of punishment of a love which has violated the parameters within which it should appear. The enamored old man breaks the codes of a society that constantly reminds him of his oncoming death.

194. Beau, Albin Eduard. "A estrutura dos Autos de Gil Vicente." In his *Duas conferências inéditas sobre teatro: A estrutura dos Autos de Gil Vicente. Teatro espectáculo, teatro lírico, teatro ideológico.* Edição apresentada por Maria Armanda de Almeida e Sousa. Publicações do Instituto de Estudos Alemães da Universidade de Coimbra. Coimbra: Faculdade de Letras, 1977, pp. 9–39.

Originally given in 1965 (first at Coimbra and later at Lisbon) on the occasion of the fifth centenary of Gil Vicente's birth. The structure of Gil Vicente's plays follows *theatrical* rather than *dramatic* canons. When considered as spectacles, they reveal a tendency toward symmetry and numerical proportions and correspondences in the configuration and grouping of scenes and characters. The recurrence of these elements suggests that they correspond to aesthetic canons which guided the structuring of the plays.

195. Berardinelli, Cleonice. *Estudos de literatura portuguesa.* Temas Portugueses. Lisboa: Imprensa Nacional–Casa da Moeda, 1985. 417 pp.

Includes: "O teatro pré–vicentino em Portugal" (pp. 27–51). "O teatro vicentino" (pp. 53–64), first published in her edition of *Autos de Gil Vicente,* Coleção Nossos Clássicos, CV (Rio de Janeiro: Agir, 1974), pp. 1–17 (see *GVB,* no. 31). "Dois autos de Gil Vicente" (pp. 65–76), first published as "Estudo prévio" in *Dois autos de Gil Vicente (o da Mofina Mendes e o da Alma),* ed. Sousa da Silveira, 3ª ed., Coleção de Estudos Filológicos,III (Rio de Janeiro: Ministério da Educação e Cultura/ Fundação Casa de Rui Barbosa, 1973), pp. xv–xxiii (see *GVB,* no. 10).

Review:

a. Osório Mateus, *CoL,* 89 (January 1986), 112–13.

196. Berardinelli, Cleonice. "A romagem da Fé em alguns autos vicentinos." In *EP:HLSP,* pp. 311–23.

Surveys several plays (principally the *Auto da Fé,* the *Auto pastoril castelhano,* the *Auto da Barca da Glória,* the *Romagem de agravados,* and the *Auto da Cananeia*), which demonstrate Gil Vicente's concept of Christian faith and his attitude toward the Catholic Church.

197. Blanc de Portugal, José. "Schumann e Gil Vicente." In *TV,* pp. 19–26.

Following the Hamburg edition of Gil Vicente's *Obras completas* by Barreto Feio and Gomes Monteiro (1834), E. Geibel translated some of Vicente's songs into German and Robert Schumann put them to music. The musical scores of two of these songs, both from the *Auto da sibila Cassandra,* are reproduced here: *Opus* 138, no. 3 ("O wie lieblich ist das Mädchen!" [Muy graciosa es la doncella]) and *Opus* 138, no. 7 ("Weh, wie zornig ist das Mädchen!" [Sañosa está la niña]).

198. Blasco, Pierre. "O *Auto de Inês Pereira:* a análise do texto ao serviço da história das mentalidades." In *TV,* pp. 27–42.

Gil Vicente's purpose in having created a burlesque and morally warped society and characters in this play was dual: to incite laughter and, at the same time, to convey, negatively, a moral lesson to those Portuguese in the audience who were engaged in the national crusade of territorial expansion under the sign of the cross; to caution them against such moral and material dangers as the play depicts. The article appeared also in French: "La *Farce d'Inès Pereira:* l'analyse du texte au service de l'histoire des mentalités," *Taíra,* 3 (1991), 21–43.

199. Blasco, Pierre. "La *Barque de l'Enfer* de Gil Vicente comme miroir d'une mentalité." In *EP:HLSP*, pp. 339–47.

The *Auto da Barca do Inferno* is addressed to an audience which was directly engaged in the great adventure of discovery and conquest, the king and the nobility. The playwright provides entertainment but, at the same time, a moral lesson designed to fortify them in the enterprise to which they are devoted. By means of the *hidalgo* episode, Gil Vicente wishes to inspire in his audience the fear of Hell and to show, by negative examples, what the true qualities that accompany noble condition are on the social, religious and moral planes.

200. Botelho de Amaral, Vasco. "Expressão do mundo: A obra de Gil Vicente e a descrição objectiva da realidade: Análise de um auto de crítica social." In his *Estudos de apoio ao português*. Porto: Livraria Avis, 1976, pp. 185–96.

Surveys the *Auto da Barca do Inferno* in an effort to show the playwright's stylistic fluency and satiric expression. Also quotes two lyrics, from other plays, as samples of Gil Vicente's masterful use of language.

201. Calderón Calderón, Manuel and Joana Lloret Cantero. "La comunicación no verbal en los autos y en las farsas de Gil Vicente." In *AHLM–III*, pp. 313–17.

On the variety and functional importance of nonverbal means of communication (type and tone of voice, body movement and gestures, movement of characters on stage, choreography, etc.) in Gil Vicente's *autos de devaçám* and *farsas*.

202. Cerqueira, Dorine Daisy Pedreira de. "Gil Vicente e o teatro do absurdo." In *Singularidades de uma cultura plural. XIII Encontro de professores universitários brasileiros de literatura portuguesa (Rio de Janeiro, 30 de julho a 3 de agosto de 1990)*. Ed. Cleonice Berardinelli, Gilda Santos and Teresa Cristina Cerdeira. Rio de Janeiro: Universidade Federal do Rio de Janeiro, 1992, pp. 475–79.

An exposition of the similarities between Judge Azdak of Bertolt Brecht's *Caucasian Chalk Circle* and Pêro Marques of Gil Vicente's *Juiz da Beira*. Both are fools made judges and both pronounce equally absurd sentences. By satirizing these sentences, the dramatists affirm ideal justice—as they understand it—through the absurd.

203. Costa, Aida. "Gil Vicente e o mundo clássico." In her *Temas clássicos*. São Paulo: Cultrix & Secretaria da Cultura, Ciência e Tecnologia do Estado de São Paulo, 1978, pp. 134–49.

Revised version of an article published originally in *Estado de São Paulo. Suplemento Literário*, 457 (4 December 1965), 2 (see *GVB*, no. 644A). Despite its medieval roots, Gil Vicente's theater betrays the presence of the classical world which reached the dramatist via the medieval classical tradition, his indirect knowledge of classical sources through medieval translations and adaptations, and, perhaps, through direct exposure to Roman sources accessible to him thanks to his knowledge of ecclesiastical Latin. These Greco–Roman ingredients (gods and goddesses of the classical antiquity, the figure of the Sibyl, the descent to Hades, the type of the braggart, the term "tragicomedy" as well as certain formal aspects) have been well integrated into Vicente's theater.

Review (of the book):

a. Américo da Costa Ramalho, *CoL*, 52 (November 1979), 96–97.

204. Cunha, Celso Ferreira da. *Estudos de versificação portuguesa (séculos XIII a XVI)*. Civilização Portuguesa, VI. Paris: Fundação Calouste Gulbenkian/Centro Cultural Português, 1982. xxvi+336 pp.

In addition to many references to Gil Vicente throughout, the book includes "Regularidade e irregularidade na versificação do primeiro *Auto das Barcas* de Gil Vicente" (pp. 273–98), which had appeared first in *Studia philologica: homenaje ofrecido a Dámaso Alonso por sus amigos y discípulos*, vol. I (Madrid: Gredos, 1960), pp. 459–79, and subsequently in Celso Cunha's *Língua e verso. Ensaios*, 2ª ed. (Rio de Janeiro: Livraria São José, 1968), pp. 49–76 (see *GVB*, no. 319): it had been thought that Vicente's work reflected the popular Hispanic tradition of irregular versification. Through an analysis of lines in the *Auto da Barca do Inferno* and taking into account certain phonetic factors of Vicente's times, Celso Cunha shows that Vicente's versification is more regular than had been assumed.

Review:

a. Elsa Gonçalves, *CoL*, 80 (July 1984), 109–11.

204A. Delgado Morales, Manuel. "El mito platónico del carro alado y el teatro de Gil Vicente y Juan del Encina." In *Dramaturgia española y novohispana (siglos XVI–XVII)*. Ed. Lillian von der Walde and Serafín González García. Fondo Ruiz de Alarcón y el Teatro de su Tiempo, I.

Iztapalapa: Universidad Autónoma Metropolitana, Unidad Iztapalapa, 1993, pp. 103–18.

Several of Gil Vicente's plays reveal the affinity of the playwright's thought with the Neoplatonism of his time in his renunciation of the material and the search for the ideal.

205. Dias, Graça Silva. "Cultura e sociedade na infância e adolescência de Camões." In *Empire in Transition: The Portuguese World in the Time of Camões*. Ed. Alfred Hower and Richard A. Preto–Rodas. Gainesville: University Presses of Florida, 1985, p. 155–63.

In the *Auto de Mofina Mendes*, the protagonist is the allegory of the subversion of the moral values which ought to characterize Christian monarchs. Gil Vicente rises against any attempt at subversion, against anything which may call the traditional values of order and hierarchy to question. His reaction is rooted in his Christian mode of living and his position at court which led him to adopt the values and aspirations of one of the two hegemonic classes.

Reviews (of the book):

a. T. F. Earle, *Portuguese Studies*, III (1987), 216–17.

b. Marian L. Smolen, *Hispania*, LXXI (1988), 77.

206. Escudero Martínez, Carmen. "La estructura especular dramática (a propósito de Gil Vicente y Jardiel Poncela)." In *Critique sociale et conventions théâtrales (domaine ibérique). Colloque International (1–3 décembre 1988)*. Cahiers de l'Université, XX. Pau: Université de Pau et des Pays de l'Adour, 1989, pp. 69–77.

Gil Vicente achieved the fusion of reality and fiction by having direct audience participation in certain plays (*Comédia do viúvo, Auto das ciganas*) and by employing a mirror structure: in the initial scenes of *Dom Duardos*, he reproduced on stage the court hall in which the spectators sat, so that they might be transported into the dramatic fiction and think that they were really witnessing the fictional events represented on stage. Although, in general terms, the dramatic works of Enrique Jardiel Poncela bear little or no resemblance to those of Vicente, he too employed a similar mirror structure to bridge reality and fiction: in the first scenes of *Eloísa está debajo de un almendro*, the set is a neighborhood cinema where the actors are watching a film while being watched by the real audience.

207. Fernandes, Manuel Correia. "Da actualidade do teatro vicentino." In *Estudios sobre literatura y arte dedicados al Profesor Emilio Orozco Díaz.*

Ed. A. Gallego Morell, Andrés Soria, Nicolás Marín. Vol. I. Granada: Universidad de Granada, 1979, pp. 319–32.

Fernandes compares Gil Vicente's *Autos das Barcas* with Bertolt Brecht's *Die Ausnahme und die Regel*, in order to prove his claim that the former's work has withstood the test of time and remains quite modern. Both are allegorical pieces. Vicente's intention is social criticism whereas Brecht's is didactic. Vicente's approach in interpreting society is analytical, as he exposes the errors of each group that the characters represent (attitudes), whereas Brecht's is synthetical for he exposes collective errors (situations). Vicente's characters are representative of social groups whereas Brecht's are interpretative of social classes. Fernandes concludes by listing nine points of contact between Vicente's theater and Brecht's.

208. Figueiredo, Fidelino de. "Gil Vicente e Lope." In his *Últimas aventuras*. Rio de Janeiro: A Noite, [1941], pp. 262–68.

The Gil Vicente who influenced Lope de Vega is the author of the *obras de devação*.

209. Frèches, Claude–Henri. "L'Économie du salut dans la trilogie des *Barques*." In *Mélanges à la mémoire d'André Joucla–Ruau*. Études Littéraires, II. Vol. II. Aix–en–Provence: Éditions de l'Université de Provence, 1978, pp. 723–36.

The trilogy of the *Barcas* is both a satirical and an edifying work. Gil Vicente views the question of salvation in the most traditionally orthodox fashion. He stresses the necessity and power of baptism and the Eucharist, and warns against sacrilegious and incomplete confession. In his view, there can be no salvation without faith and works, but faith and the Church, together with hope, allow the sinner to avoid damnation merited by bad works.

210. Frenk Alatorre, Margit. *Estudios sobre lírica antigua*. Literatura y Sociedad, XV. Madrid: Castalia, 1978. 339 pp.

Numerous references to Gil Vicente. Among other studies, it includes: "Dignificación de la lírica popular en el Siglo de Oro" (pp. 47–80): first published in the *Anuario de Letras*, II (1962), 27–54. "Supervivencias de la antigua lírica popular" (pp. 81–112): from *Studia philologica: homenaje ofrecido a Dámaso Alonso por sus amigos y discípulos*, I (Madrid: Gredos, 1960), 51–78. "Problemas de la antigua lírica popular" (pp. 137–53): from *Filología*, XIII (1968–69), 175–90. "Refranes cantados y cantares proverbializados" (pp. 154–71): from *NRFH*, XV (1961), 155–68.

"Sobre los textos poéticos en Juan Vásquez, Mudarra y Narváez" (pp. 175–203): from *NRFH*, VI (1952), 33–56. "Quién maora ca mi sayo" (pp. 212–20): from *NRFH*, XI (1957), 386–91 (a philological interpretation of a *villancico* which occurs in the *Triunfo do Inverno*). "Glosas de tipo popular en la antigua lírica" (pp. 267–308): also from *NRFH*, XII (1958), 301–34. See *GVB*, nos 666–67, 772.

211. Galhoz, Maria Aliete. "*Topoi* da inanidade e brevidade da vida na fala de Job do *Breve Sumário da História de Deus* de Gil Vicente—Símiles comparativos." In *TV*, pp. 73–80.

Examines the *topoi* of the vanity and brevity of life as expressed in the speech of Job of Gil Vicente's *Breve sumário da história de Deus*, in João de Deus's "A vida" and in the "Sofrimento" of Camilo Gomes da Silva (popular Brazilian poet) and finds that in all three cases there is a common existential/religious component.

212. Groult, Pierre. "El diablo picardo de Gil Vicente." In his *Literatura espiritual española: Edad Media y Renacimiento*. Trans. and ed. Rodrigo A. Molina. Biblioteca de Hispanismo, IV. Madrid: Fundación Universitaria Española, 1980, pp. 191–204.

Originally published in French in *BEP*, XVI (1952), 79–95 (see *GVB*, no. 769): discusses the lines in the dialect of Picardy found in Gil Vicente's *Auto das fadas*, and concludes that the dramatist's use of this dialect, in spite of accidental or intentional slips, is original and suitable to his purpose of inciting laughter.

Review (of the book):

a. A[lphonse] Vermeylen, *Les Lettres Romanes*, XXXVII (1983), 123–24.

213. Hart, Thomas R. "Poetry and Politics in Gil Vicente's Theatre." In *Studies in Portuguese Literature and History in Honour of Luís de Sousa Rebelo*. Ed. Helder Macedo. Colección Támesis: Série A: Monografías, CXXXXVII. London: Tamesis Books, 1992, pp. 53–61.

The differences that separate Gil Vicente's festival plays from the English masques devised by Ben Jonson and Inigo Jones are viewed in terms of scenery (elaborate stage machinery in the masques, verbal description in the festival plays), classical learning (quite absent from the festival plays), and political criticism (less central and deliberate in Vicente's plays).

Review (of the volume):
a. N. J. Lamb, *BHS*, LXXII (1995), 245–46.

214. Hart, Thomas R. "Teatro vicentino y teatro valenciano." In *Actas del cuarto congreso internacional de hispanistas celebrado en Salamanca, Agosto de 1971.* Ed. Eugenio de Bustos Tovar. Salamanca: Asociación Internacional de Hispanistas / Consejo General de Castilla y León / Universidad de Salamanca, 1982, vol. I, pp. 751–56.

Compares the little play inserted by Luis Milán in his *El cortesano* with Gil Vicente's festival plays, and finds that they all share a reliance upon a hinge, which is their most important link to the tradition of the court masque. Juan Fernández de Heredia's *Coloquio de las damas valencianas*—very different from Milán's play—reminds one of Vicente's farces, although the characters in the latter are more fully individualized. As a playwright, Vicente is superior to both Valencians. His superiority lies in the greater conceptual richness of his theater. A version of the article in English with footnotes appeared in *MLN*, LXXXVII (1972), 307–15 (see *GVB*, no. 541).

215. Hart, Thomas R. "The Unity of Gil Vicente's *Auto da Mofina Mendes.*" In *Studies in Honor of Bruce W. Wardropper.* Ed. Dian Fox, Harry Sieber, and Robert Ter Horst. Juan de la Cuesta Hispanic Monographs: *Homenajes*, VI. Newark, Delaware: Juan de la Cuesta, 1989, pp. 135–46.

Both the friar's speech, which opens the play, and the episode of Mofina Mendes have often been seen as out of keeping with the rest of the play. Hart, however, shows that both are integral parts of it: the monks that the friar ridicules and Mofina Mendes herself stand in contrast to Virgin Mary, the first for their interest in personal profit and their attempts to foretell the future, the second for her lack of prudence and her self-interest.

Review (of the volume):
a. Glen F. Dille, *BHS*, LXVIII (1991), 514.

216. Henríquez Ureña, Pedro. "Portugués y castellano: Gil Vicente." In his *Estudios de versificación española.* Publicaciones del Instituto de Filología Hispánica "Doctor Amado Alonso." Buenos Aires: Universidad de Buenos Aires, 1961, pp. 86–91.

The essay can also be found in his *La versificación irregular en la poesía castellana.* Junta para Ampliación de Estudios e Investigaciones

Científicas. Centro de Estudios Históricos. Madrid: Revista de Filología Española, 1920, pp. 104–9 (originally his doctoral dissertation for the University of Minnesota, 1918). A second edition (Publicaciones de la Revista de Filología Española, IV. Madrid: Librería Hernando) appeared in 1933. Cites examples of irregular versification from several Spanish and Portuguese plays of Gil Vicente. Other passing references also.

217. Hess, Rainer. "Gil Vicente. *Tragicomedia de Don Duardos*." In *Das spanische Theater vom Mittelalter bis zur Gegenwart*. Ed. Volker Roloff and Harald Wentzlaff–Eggebert. Düsseldorf: Schwann–Bagel, 1988, pp. 36–52.

An examination of the play in several respects leads to the conclusion that Gil Vicente is not a modern, psychological playwright. His time imposed style on him. The play is a dramatization of a thesis; it can indeed be viewed as an *exemplum* of man's powerlessness in the face of love, even death. The playwright has succeeded with a tragicomedy rich in international motifs, inner dramatic patterns, symmetrical correspondences, and linguistic refinements.

218. Houwens Post, H[endrik]. "Gil Vicente est-il érasmiste?" In *L'Humanisme portugais et l'Europe. Actes du XXIe colloque international d'études humanistes (Tours, 3–13 juillet 1978)*. Ed. Jean–Claude Margolin and José V. de Pina Martins. Centre d'Études Superieures de la Renaissance, Université de Tours. Paris: Fondation Calouste Gulbenkian/ Centre Culturel Portugais, 1984, pp. 643–54.

Lists several characteristic traits that Erasmus and Gil Vicente have in common, but lets the reader decide the answer to the question in the title.

Review (of the book):
a. R. Clive Willis, *BHS*, LXV (1988), 197.

219. Infantes, Víctor. "Notas sobre una edición desconocida de la *Tragicomedia de Don Duardos* (Sevilla, Bartolomé Pérez, 1530)." In his *En el Siglo de Oro: estudios y textos de literatura áurea*. Scripta Humanistica, LXXXVIII. Potomac, Maryland: Scripta Humanistica, 1992, pp. 85–123.

In about February 1530, the Sevillian printer Bartolomé Pérez used sixty-one lines from the middle of *Dom Duardos* to fill the last page of a broadsheet titled *Nuevas de Italia venidas de Boloña a Madrid*. Infantes theorizes that Bartolomé Pérez proceeded to print the entire *Dom*

Duardos from a manuscript version, and that this Seville edition circulated widely in the Peninsula. He compares the fragment of the broadsheet with the corresponding parts of the 1562 and 1586 editions, and finds it to be closer to that of 1586. The 1586 edition of the play, he argues, ultimately derived from the supposed Seville edition. The study was originally published, with a facsimile of the broadsheet, in *ACCP*, XVII (1982), 663–701.

Review (of the book):
a. Nadine Ly, *NRFH*, XLIII (1995), 492–98.

220. Keates, Laurence. "Las *Barcas* de Gil Vicente—¿la síntesis medieval más perfecta?" In *AHLM–III*, pp. 253–58.

In the *Barcas*, Gil Vicente interweaves and gives dramatic form to several themes and motifs: death and judgment, fools, dance of death, and political and church ranks.

221. Keates, Laurence. "Gil Vicente's *Auto da Alma*: A Triptych." In *Catholic Tastes and Times: Essays in Honour of Michael E. Williams.* Ed. Margaret A. Rees. Leeds: Trinity and All Saints' College, 1987, pp. 233–46.

A reading of the play as an allegorical triptych: the preparation of the Soul for its journey through life, the paradigmatic journey itself (with the Soul's constant conflict between good and evil), and the Soul's arrival at the inn whose innkeeper is the Holy Mother Church.

222. Lafer, Celso. "O judeu em Gil Vicente." In his *Gil Vicente e Camões (dois estudos sobre a cultura portuguesa do século XVI)*. Coleção Ensaios, L. São Paulo: Ática, 1978, pp. 19–101.

Gil Vicente makes a distinction between the pre– and post–Christ Jew. He believes that, since the latter did not accept or understand Christ, he is religiously an imperfect being and therefore unworthy of the Lord's grace (as shown in the *Auto da Barca do Inferno* and the *Diálogo sobre a ressurreição*). In Vicente's farces, the Jew is portrayed like any other member of Portuguese society (as in *Inês Pereira, Juiz da Beira, Auto da Lusitânia*). On other occasions, Vicente defends the Jew against attacks of intolerance (see his "Sermão" and the "Carta a D. João III"). This essay had been published individually in 1963 (São Paulo: Conselho Estadual de Cultura)—see *GVB*, no. 261.

Reviews:
a. E. d'A. Magalhães, *Revista Camoniana*, II (1979), 127–29.

b. Stephen Reckert, *CoL*, 52 (November 1979), 95–96.

223. Laitenberger, Hugo. "Gil Vicente, 'dramaturgo navideño'." In *Edad Media y Renacimiento: continuidades y rupturas*. Estudios reunidos y presentados por J[ean] Canavaggio y B[ernard] Darbord. Centre de Recherches en Langues, Littératures et Civilisations du Monde Ibérique et de l'Italie. Caen: Centre de Publications de l'Université de Caen, 1991, pp. 65–87.

An examination of nine Christmas plays (*Monólogo do vaqueiro*, *Auto pastoril castelhano*, *Auto da Fé*, *Auto da sibila Cassandra*, *Auto da Barca do Purgatório*, *Auto dos Quatro Tempos*, *Auto pastoril português*, *Auto da feira*, and *Auto de Mofina Mendes*), which span Gil Vicente's dramatic career, shows that the original balance between *docere* and *delectare* gradually disappears. In the last plays of this genre, especially those staged in the reign of João III, the doctrinal element has lost ground to satire, both anticlerical and antipapal.

224. Lapa, M[anuel] Rodrigues. "Ainda, e sempre, o nosso Mestre Gil." In his *As minhas razões: "Memórias de um idealista que quis endireitar o mundo…"*. Coimbra: Coimbra Editora, 1983, pp. 149–69.

First published in *Vértice*, XXV (1965), 699–714 (see *GVB*, no. 489). Gil Vicente was not a mere closet intellectual, a poet of abstract poetry, the mouthpiece of the ideology of the court. He was a writer involved with the people, concerned with their problems and the injustices they suffered. He defended the humble and the truth, without fear of consequences; he defended the Jews at a time when King João III was seeking to establish the Inquisition in Portugal.

225. Leite, Ana Cristina, and Paulo Pereira. "São João verde, o Selvagem e o Gigante em Gil Vicente—apontamento iconológico." In *EP:HLSP*, pp. 371–84 plus 3 plates on pp. 385–87.

In the portrayal of the character of the Wild Man (in the *Triunfo do Inverno*, *Auto da festa*, *Dom Duardos*, *Divisa da cidade de Coimbra*), Gil Vicente has combined traits from popular tradition and literary culture as well as iconography.

226. López Castro, Armando. "Las cantigas paralelísticas de Gil Vicente." In *AHLM–II*, pp. 175–85.

Gil Vicente's plays are full of songs, some simply picked up from oral tradition, others elaborated by the dramatist on the basis of original *estribillos*, and others composed by the dramatist himself. These songs cannot be separated from the tradition of which they form part, namely the Iberian popular lyric poetry. Perhaps, without recourse to the old traditional poetry, Gil Vicente would not have been the accomplished playwright he was.

226A. López Castro, Armando. "La lírica de Gil Vicente." In *Actas del III congreso de la Asociación Hispánica de Literatura Medieval (Salamanca, 3 al 6 de octubre de 1989)*. Ed. María Isabel Toro Pascua. Vol. I. Salamanca: Biblioteca Española del Siglo XV, Departamento de Literatura Española e Hispanoamericana, 1994, pp. 517–24.

Gil Vicente has achieved in his theater a harmonious synthesis of drama, poetry, and music.

227. Márquez Villanueva, Francisco. "*Os judeus casamenteiros* de Gil Vicente." In *Les Cultures ibériques en devenir: Essais publiés en hommage à la mémoire de Marcel Bataillon (1895–1977)*. Paris: Fondation Singer–Polignac, 1979, pp. 375–79.

Gil Vicente's choice of Jewish matchmakers (Latão and Vidal) in *Inês Pereira* (1523) was nothing extraordinary, since Jews had been traditionally entrusted with similar functions. Religious syncretism was still alive in 1523. Even in Spain, religious intolerance took a long time to reach general proportions.

228. Martins, José V. de Pina. "Humanismo cristão e erasmismo: Gil Vicente e Sá de Miranda." In his *Humanismo e erasmismo na cultura portuguesa do século XVI. Estudo e textos*. Série Histórica & Literária, XI. Paris: Fundação Calouste Gulbenkian/Centro Cultural Português, 1973, pp. 27–32.

Gil Vicente's satire of the external aspects of religion and faith does not reflect Erasmus, but rather a humanistic heritage which makes the dramatist's work more vivid, without placing it within the confines of humanism. Other passing references also.

229. Martins, Mário. "A árvore de Jessé e a canção final do *Auto da feira*." In *TV*, pp. 81–86.

In the final *cantiga* of the *Auto da feira*, Gil Vicente uses elements from the many representations of the genealogical tree of Jesse (in the Bible, in liturgy, in poetry, in the miniatures and engravings of the *Livros de horas* and breviaries, and in medieval Portuguese architecture).

230. Martins, Mário. *Estudos de cultura medieval*. Vol. III. Lisboa: Edições Brotéria, 1983. 438 pp.

Includes: "O Pai–Nosso na Idade Média portuguesa, até Gil Vicente" (pp. 289–319): surveys the variant glosses of *Pater Noster* in several Portuguese writers, including Gil Vicente's in the *Auto da Cananeia* (pp. 314–18). "A visão de Túngulo ou Tundalo, no *Breve sumário da história de Deus*" (pp. 321–31): in seven free verses, Gil Vicente's genius has succeeded in synthesizing, in this play, the infernal landscape and torments of *A visão de Túngulo*, a twelfth–century Irish legend, translated both into Latin and twice into medieval Portuguese.

Review:

a. A. Ruela, *Brotéria*, CXVII (1983), 109–10.

231. Martins, Mário. "Gil Vicente e as gravuras dos Livros de Horas." Appendix to his *Introdução histórica à vidência do tempo e da morte*. II: *Do teatro pós–vicentino até Vieira, Bernardes e frei António das Chagas*. Colecção Filosofia, XXVI. Braga: Livraria Cruz, 1969, pp. 244–76.

Explores the possibility that several ingredients of Gil Vicente's works were inspired by illustrations in the Books of Hours. Vicente's anticlericalism also may have been derived from the same sources. The volume includes other references to Vicente (pp. 27–30, 149–52, *et passim*).

232. Mateus, Osório. "La censura de los impresos y el teatro de Gil Vicente." Trans. María Victoria Navas. In *Le Théâtre sous la contrainte: Actes du colloque international réalisé à Aix–en–Provence les 4 et 5 décembre 1985*. Aix–en–Provence: Université de Provence, Centres de Recherches Latino–Américaines et Luso–Afro–Brésiliennes, 1988, pp. 19–30.

Also appeared as "Vicente, 'indicia'," *RFLUL*, 5ª Série, 5 (April 1986), 57–66. Examines the effects of censorship—Inquisitional and lay—on the *Auto da Barca do Inferno*, by comparing the corresponding passages of the text of the 1517 individual edition with those of Vicente's complete works (1562 and 1586) as well as later editions. Also provides examples of the changes Afonso Lopes Vieira effected, for patriotic reasons, in his adaptation of the play (1911).

Reviews (of the volume):

a. Luiz Francisco Rebello, *CoL*, 108 (March–April 1989), 117–18.

b. Frank Dauster, *HR*, LVIII (1990), 251–54.

233. Mateus, Osório. "Fiat simile." In *EP:HLSP*, pp. 389–91.

By the year 2002, which will mark the fifth centenary of the beginning of Gil Vicente's dramatic career, a new facsimile edition of Vicente's works—based on all extant copies of the *editio princeps* and employing modern editorial technologies—should be published.

234. Mateus, Osório. "Scilicet." In *Estudos portugueses: Homenagem a António José Saraiva*. Diálogo: Série Compilação. Lisboa: Instituto de Cultura e Língua Portuguesa/Faculdade de Letras da Universidade de Lisboa, 1990, pp. 427–32.

The best edition of Gil Vicente's works in the twentieth century still is the 1928 facsimile reproduction of the 1562 *Copilaçám*, in spite of its errors. Almost all we know of Vicente's dramatic production comes only from a few pre–1562 editions of plays and from the *Copilaçám* of 1562. All these printed texts came after the theater: they are documents of lost theatrical events. A new general project—aiming at the monographic and chronological analysis of Vicente's dramatic production—should be undertaken. Each play should be treated individually, since each play is itself and its circumstances. There should be a new reading of Vicente's works. To this end, direct knowledge of the *Copilaçám* and the extant individual editions is indispensable. A new facsimile of the *Copilaçám* is urgently needed.

235. Mateus, Osório. "Talvez assim." In *Actas do terceiro congresso da Associação Internacional de Lusitanistas (Universidade de Coimbra,18 a 22 de junho de 1990)*. Coimbra: Associação Internacional de Lusitanistas, 1992, pp. 95–97.

Describes the Vicente collection (see nos 178–83), which Mateus himself directed, and the editorial procedures followed.

236. Mateus, Osório. "Vicente anónimo castelhano." In *Os estudos literários: (entre) ciência e hermenêutica. Actas do primeiro congresso da Associação Portuguesa de Literatura Comparada. II: Faculdade de Letras, Universidade de Lisboa, 16 e 17 março 1989*. Lisboa: Associação Portuguesa de Literatura Comparada, 1990, pp. 131–36.

Mateus compares Gil Vicente's *Auto de moralidade*, the first printed version of the *Auto da Barca do Inferno* (1517), with the anonymous *Tragicomedia alegórica del parayso y del infierno* (Burgos, 1539)—presumably one of several Spanish translations of Vicente's play—in terms of their texts and the engravings which accompany them. The question is raised whether Vicente himself was also responsible for the engraving of the *Auto de moralidade*. If so, this would be an argument in favor of identifying Vicente, the dramatist, with Vicente, the goldsmith.

237. Mateus, Osório. "Vicente 1562." In *Homenagem a Eduardo Lourenço. Colectânea de estudos. Organização das Secções de Português e Espanhol da Universidade de Nice.* Diálogo: Série Compilação. Lisboa: Ministério da Educação, Instituto de Cultura e Língua Portuguesa/Nice: Universidade de Nice, 1992, pp. 159–65.

Mateus describes the *Copilaçám* of 1562, its contents and the circumstances surrounding its publication, pointing out that it is not by any means a complete register of Vicente's works. Finally, he lists the known extant copies of it and their current locations.

238. McGinniss, Cheryl Folkins. "La danza literaria como símbolo de metamorfosis: empleo y sentido en el teatro de Juan del Encina y Gil Vicente." Doctoral dissertation, Case Western Reserve University, 1977. vii + 110 pp. (See *DAI*, XXXVIII [1977–78], 1437–A).

Ch. III: "La danza del teatro castellano vicentino: tránsito a lo moral" (pp. 70–101): *Auto pastoril castellano* (pp. 72–79), *Comedia del viudo* (pp. 79–84), *Auto de la sibila Casandra* (pp. 84–97), Notas (pp. 98–101). Dance serves consistently as a symbol of important changes in characterization or scene.

239. Mendes, João. *Homens e problemas. I: Autores portugueses.* Ed. Alves Pires, S. J. Colecção Presenças, XXXIII. Lisboa: Verbo, 1983. 393 pp.

Includes: "Gil Vicente sobrerrealista" (pp. 11–67), originally published in *Brotéria*, LXXXVI (1968), 329–50, 456–75 (see *GVB*, no. 649): Vicente's work is characterized by a conflicting world view which reflects the distinction the dramatist made between the harmonious heavenly world and the chaotic earthly one (see the "Carta que Gil Vicente mandou de Santarém a El–Rei D. João III"). These two opposing worlds finally merge in the *Auto dos Quatro Tempos*. "Comemoração de Gil Vicente" (pp. 68–82), from *Brotéria*, LXXXI (1965), 111–20 (see *GVB*, no. 492): Gil Vicente is very pessimistic about justice among humans. This pessimism is exorcised by the presence of Virgin Mary, intermediary between heaven and earth, adorned with three fundamental attributes: light, height, and royal majesty. "*Gil Vicente e o fim do teatro medieval*" (pp. 83–91), from *Brotéria*, LXXXII (1966), 676–83 (see *GVB*, no. 291.1): a review of the second edition of A. J. Saraiva's book (see *GVB*, no. 291).

"Um estudo sobre Gil Vicente" (pp. 92–96), from *Brotéria*, LVII (1953), 201–05: a review of the section on Gil Vicente of A. J. da Costa Pimpão's *História da literatura portuguesa* (see no. 479). "Sobre Histórias da literatura portuguesa" (pp. 347–83): includes reviews of A. J. Saraiva and Óscar Lopes, *História da literatura portuguesa* (pp. 347–54), from *Brotéria*, LXII (1956), 205–10 (see *GVB*, no. 461.2); João Gaspar Simões, *História da poesia portuguesa* (pp. 354–63), from *Brotéria*, LX (1955), 433–41 (see *GVB*, no. 463); A. J. Saraiva, *Para a história da cultura em Portugal* (pp. 375–83), from *Brotéria*, LXXIV (1962), 689–95 (see *GVB*, no. 363.1).

240. Mendes, Margarida Vieira. "Encina e Vicente: disparates." In *AHLM–III*, pp. 347–54.

In the treatment of nonsense, Gil Vicente follows, with some variations, his model, Juan del Encina. The fundamental difference between the two can be found in the thematic unity which characterizes Vicente's text (see the prologue to the *Templo de Apolo*).

241. Mendes, Margarida Vieira. "Gil Vicente: o génio e os géneros." In *Estudos portugueses: Homenagem a António José Saraiva*. Diálogo: Série Compilação. Lisboa: Instituto de Cultura e Língua Portuguesa/Faculdade de Letras da Universidade de Lisboa, 1990, pp. 327–34.

Mendes comments on the inadequacy of the several attempts to classify Gil Vicente's works—those based on their theatrical character, whether functional, morphological, or structural—and provides tentatively a list of several formative factors as an alternative.

242. Michaëlis de Vasconcelos, Carolina. "Este es Calbi orabi." In her *Dispersos: originais portugueses*. I: *Vária*. Lisboa: Edição da Revista "Ocidente," 1969, pp. 448–62.

Originally appeared in the *RevL*, XVIII (1915), 1–15. A discussion of the Arabic song *Calbi orabi* ("o meu coração é o de um árabe") which appears in *Dom Duardos* and is mentioned in the *Comédia de Rubena*. Michaëlis concludes that it is the corrupt representative of an Arabic *anexim*.

243. Moreira, Vasco and Hilário Pimenta. *Propostas de abordagem*. 9° ano unificado, 3° ano curso geral. Porto: Porto Editora/Coimbra: Arnado/Lisboa: Fluminense, 1986. 149 pp.

Analysis of scenes from the *Auto da Barca do Inferno* (pp. 9–65).

244. Moser, Fernando de Mello. "Gil Vicente and the Late Medieval Mysteries: Facts and Conjectures." In *Atti del IV colloquio della Societé Internationale pour l'Étude du Théâtre Médiéval (Viterbo, 10–15 luglio 1983)*. Ed. M. Chiabò, F. Doglio and M. Maymone. Viterbo: Centro Studi sul Teatro Medioevale e Rinascimentale, 1984, pp. 111–20.

Parallels between the *Auto de Mofina Mendes* and the Wakefield Master's *Prima Pastorum*, the *Breve sumário da história de Deus* and *N'Town* plays show that Gil Vicente used several sources in common with other playwrights of Mystery plays and that he was directly or indirectly aware of what was being done outside the Iberian Peninsula.

245. Navas Sánchez–Élez, María Victoria. "La lengua de Juan del Encina en el *Auto pastoril castellano* de Vicente." In *Actas del I congreso internacional de historia de la lengua española (Cáceres, 30 de marzo–4 de abril de 1987)*. Ed. M. Ariza, A. Salvador, and A. Viudas. Vol. II. [Madrid]: Arco, 1988, pp. 1315–28.

The great number of linguistic and semantic similarities between Juan del Encina's *Églogas* and Gil Vicente's *Auto pastoril castelhano* show that indeed the first were a source for the second, but not the only source. There also exist other antecedent works (the *Coplas de Mingo Revulgo*, Fray Íñigo de Mendoza's *Vita Christi*, the *Song of Songs*, etc.) to which Vicente is indebted.

246. Navas Sánchez–Élez, María Victoria. "*O Velho da horta*, de Gil Vicente." In *Homenaje a Alonso Zamora Vicente. III, 1: Literaturas medievales. Literatura española de los siglos XV–XVII*. Ed. Pedro Peira, Pablo Jauralde, Jesús Sánchez Lobato, Jorge Urrutia. Madrid: Castalia, 1988 [1991], pp. 253–64.

Rodrigo de Cota's *Diálogo entre el Amor y un viejo* (1511) and the anonymous late fifteenth or early sixteenth–century *Interlocutores senex et amor mulierque pulchra forma* (better known as *Diálogo del viejo, el Amor y la hermosa*) served as literary sources for Gil Vicente's play (1512). From the first, Vicente borrowed the general theme and some motifs; the second helped him to arrive at the format he gave the *Velho*.

247. Nemésio, Vitorino. "Gil Vicente, floresta de enganos." In his *Quase que os vi viver*. Venda Nova: Bertrand, 1985, pp. 13–58.

A symbolic journey into the forest that is Gil Vicente's work, with the purpose of systematizing critically Vicente's poetic and dramatic message.

The essay was originally published in book form in 1941 (see *GVB*, no. 272).

Review (of the volume):

a. Ofélia Paiva Monteiro, *CoL*, 95 (January–February 1987), 127.

247A. Palla, Maria José. "'La nave va'– La Barque à la fin des temps chez Gil Vicente." In *Fin des temps et temps de la fin dans l'univers médiéval*. Sénéfiance, XXXIII. Aix–en–Provence: Centre Universitaire d'Études et de Recherches Médiévales d'Aix, 1993, pp. 329–42.

The trilogy of the *Barcas* represents three stages in the Christian history of man: the stage of inclemency (*Auto da Barca do Inferno*), the stage of promise (*Auto da Barca do Purgatório*), and the stage of salvation (*Auto da Barca da Glória*).

248. Palla, Maria José. "O parvo e o mundo às avessas em Gil Vicente—algumas reflexões." In *TV*, pp. 87–94, plus plates (pp. 97–99).

A schematic discussion of the *parvo* and the topos of *mundus inversus* as they appear in several of Gil Vicente's plays. The *parvo* is the direct descendant of the medieval French *sot* or *fou*, who were intimately linked to the Roman Saturnalia, the medieval carnival, and other manifestations of the *mundus inversus* topos. Other possible sources for Vicente are Sebastian Brant's *Das Narrenschiff* and Erasmus's *Encomium moriae*, with both of which Vicente must have been familiar. Though there are several types of *parvos* in Vicente's works, they all share a common denominator: a mania for animals, for eating and sleeping, and for speaking in an incoherent, hyperbolic, and, usually, scatological fashion. In concluding, Palla wonders whether Vicente was himself his king's fool and whether his last play, the *Floresta de enganos*, was really a metaphor for his own circumstance.

249. Palla, Maria José. "La Sorcière et l'entremetteuse dans le théâtre de Gil Vicente." In *Théâtre et spectacles hier et aujourd'hui: Moyen Âge et Renaissance. Actes du 115ᵉ congrès national des Sociétés Savantes (Avignon, 1990): Section d'histoire médiévale et de philologie*. Paris: Editions du CTHS [Comité des Travaux Historiques et Scientifiques], 1991, pp. 165–75.

Discusses sorcery and its practices, surveys several sorceresses and procuresses in Gil Vicente's theater (Genebra Pereira of the *Auto das fadas*, Brísida Vaz of the *Auto da Barca do Inferno*, Branca Gil of the *Velho da horta*, the Feiticeira and the Beata of the *Comédia de Rubena*, Cezília of the *Clérigo da Beira*), points out their linguistic peculiarities (the use of intervocalic –d– in second–person plural verb forms), and explains the symbolism in their names.

250. Parker, J[ack] H[orace]. "Medievalism in Gil Vicente." In *Studies in Honor of Gerald E. Wade*. Ed. Sylvia Bowman, Bruno M. Damiani, Janet W. Díaz, E. Michael Gerli, Everett Hesse, John E. Keller, Luis Leal, Russell P. Sebold. Studia Humanitatis. Madrid: Porrúa Turanzas, 1979, pp. 179–86.

Maintains that Gil Vicente was thoroughly medieval in all his literary activities.

251. Pavão, J. Almeida. "Evolução da 'moralidade' medieval no teatro vicentino." In *Afecto às letras: Homenagem da literatura portuguesa contemporânea a Jacinto do Prado Coelho*. Org. David Mourão–Ferreira, Luís Filipe Lindley Cintra, Maria Alzira Seixo, Maria de Lourdes Belchior Pontes, Urbano Tavares Rodrigues. Temas Portugueses. Lisboa: Imprensa Nacional–Casa da Moeda, 1984, pp. 259–66.

Several of Gil Vicente's moralities show great originality in the treatment of the genre: a handling of old forms insufflated with a new spirit. This is revealed not only in Vicente's experiential knowledge—acquired and enriched through observation and analysis of the problems of his time—but also in a remodeling of structures which bring Portuguese theater to the level of its true essence in terms of spectacle as well as drama.

Review (of the volume):
a. A. B., *Brotéria*, CXX (1985), 352.

252. Pedroso, Ana. "O bucolismo: das *Églogas* de Juan del Encina ao teatro natalício de Gil Vicente." In *AHLM–II*, pp. 117–20.

In his *Églogas*, Juan del Encina combined the two pastoral traditions, the sacred and the secular. Gil Vicente's shepherds are reminiscent of those of Juan del Encina's and share the same features (ingenuousness, simplicity, and religiosity). With Gil Terrón of the *Auto pastoril castelhano*, however, Gil Vicente distances himself from his model: unlike the typical shepherds, Gil Terrón prefers a contemplative life and views things differently.

253. Pereira, Paulo. "Gil Vicente e a contaminação das artes. O teatro na arquitectura—O caso do Manuelino." In *TV*, pp. 101–23, plus plates (pp. 127–37).

A study of the interplay of Gil Vicente's theater, popular and literary cultures and the plastic arts in the first decades of the sixteenth century. Vicente's successful blending of motifs and personages from popular culture and literary and iconographic sources leads the author to pose the possibility that the dramatist (in his additional capacities of goldsmith, *Mestre da Balança*, and *Vedor das obras em prata e ouro* of the Mosteiro dos Jerónimos and the Hospital Real de Todos–os–Santos) played a more active role in the design of certain works of art.

254. *Pestana, Sebastião. "Comentários ao 'Segundo Auto das Barcas—Purgatório' de Gil Vicente." In *Serta gratulatoria in honorem Juan Régulo*. I: *Filología*. La Laguna: Universidad de La Laguna, 1985, pp. 577–90.

255. Pinto, Milton José. "A mitologia vicentina das *Barcas*: ensaios de interpretação I." In *Estruturalismo e teoria da linguagem*. Textos de Michel Foucault, Luiz Costa Lima, Antônio Sérgio Mendonça, Milton José Pinto, Mário Guerreiro. Apresentação de Luiz Felipe Baêta Neves & Antônio Sérgio Mendonça. Coleção Epistemologia e Pensamento Contemporâneo, I. Petrópolis: Vozes, 1971, pp. 195–202.

A semantic analysis of the *Barcas*. This essay—a revised version of the last part of Pinto's "*Barcas* vicentinas: ideologia de uma época," *Vozes*, LXIII (1969), 245–52 (see *GVB*, no. 726)—forms part of a longer essay: "Elementos para uma teoria de interpretação semântica dos discursos" (pp. 180–215).

256. Porto, Carlos. *Em busca do teatro perdido, 1958–1971*. 2 vols. Colecção Movimento, I. Lisboa: Plátano, 1973, 287, 308 pp.

Vol. I includes: "Espectáculo vicentino" (pp. 100–103): review of Carlos Avilez's staging of the *Auto da feira, Auto da Índia*, and the *Barcas* (Teatro Experimental do Porto, 1965)—first published in the *Jornal de Letras e Artes*, 181 (17 March 1965). "*Breve sumário da história de Deus* de Gil Vicente" (pp. 178–79): review of Carlos Avilez's staging of the play (Teatro Experimental de Cascais, December 1970)—first published in the *Diário de Lisboa* (3 December 1970). Briefer mentions in vol. II also: pp. 243, 262, 266.

257. *Prestes, A. Quadri. "As peças teatrais de Gil Vicente como fonte para o conhecimento histórico." In *Memória da III semana da história. 17 a*

21/VIII/1981. Franca, São Paulo: Universidade Estadual Paulista/ Instituto de História e Serviço Social, 1982.

258. Raimundo, Jacques. "Latim e português na fala dos negros." In *Miscelânea de estudos à memória de Cláudio Basto.* Organizada por Hermínia Basto. Porto: Imprensa Portuguesa, 1948, pp. 267–85.

An examination of the peculiarities of the Latin and Portuguese spoken by African negroes in Gil Vicente's *Clérigo da Beira, Frágua de Amor,* and *Nau de amores.*

259. Ramalho, Américo da Costa. *Estudos sobre o século XVI.* 2d expanded ed. Temas Portugueses. Lisboa: Imprensa Nacional–Casa da Moeda, 1983. xii+416 pp. (First ed.: Paris: Fundação Calouste Gulbenkian/Centro Cultural Português, 1980).

Includes: "Alguns aspectos do cómico vicentino" (pp. 95–124): first published in *Biblos,* XLI (1965), 5–33 (see *GVB,* no. 598): discusses several aspects of comedy in Gil Vicente's works: comic characters, situations, satire, language (plays on words, parody of heraldry, mythology, songs, juridical terminology, prayers, the Spanish and Portuguese of negroes, Jews, gypsies, the broken Latin, Italian, and French). "Mestre Anrique da *Farsa dos físicos* de Gil Vicente" (pp. 153–74): first published in *Humanitas* (Coimbra), XXV–XXVI (1973–74), 91–113: on pp. 153–62, Ramalho identifies Mestre Anrique of Vicente's play with a *converso* from Trapani, Sicily, named Próspero before his conversion. The remaining pages include the facsimile text of a letter to Próspero by his compatriot Cataldo Sículo and other documents which support Ramalho's identification. Anselmo Braamcamp Freire (see *GVB,* no. 234) had thought that the Mestre Anrique of the play was the Mestre Anrique who served as physician to D. Manuel. Alberto da Rocha Brito (see *GVB,* no. 147), on the other hand, had claimed that Mestre Anrique was really Henrique de Cuellar, the first professor of medicine of the University of Coimbra. Their identifications affected their dating of Vicente's play: Braamcamp Freire placed it in 1512 and Rocha Brito in 1520. Ramalho accepts as most probable the date proposed by Augusta Faria Gersão Ventura (1524—see *GVB,* no. 757). "Ainda o latim de Gil Vicente" (pp. 175–77): from *Humanitas* (Coimbra), XXIII–XXIV (1971–72), 473–75: a note, based on the *Frágua de Amor,* which shows that Gil Vicente's knowledge of Latin should not be underestimated. There are several other references to Vicente in the book.

Reviews:

a. Fernando Castelo–Branco, *Humanitas*, XXXI–XXXII (1979–80), 343–44.
b. Jean Aubin, *BEPB*, XLII–XLIII (1981–82), 246–49.
c. Sebastião Pinho, *ACCP*, XVII (1982), 939–42.
d. Luís de Sousa Rebelo, *CoL*, 67 (May 1982), 96–98.

260. Ramos Ortega, Francisco. "Tradición e innovación en el *Auto de la Barca de la Gloria* de Gil Vicente." In *Atti del IV colloquio della Societé Internationale pour l'Étude du Théâtre Médiéval (Viterbo, 10–15 luglio 1983).* Ed. M. Chiabò, F. Doglio and M. Maymone. Viterbo: Centro Studi sul Teatro Medioevale e Rinascimentale, 1984, pp. 121–27.

In this play, Gil Vicente shows conservatism in the form and innovation in the content. He follows medieval tradition by basing the play's dramatic configuration on the sort of radial structure which characterizes the *Representación de los Reyes Magos.* He innovates by incorporating Erasmian ideas, especially by affirming that salvation is possible through faith alone.

261. Raposo, Hipólito. "Aos estudantes de Lisboa: palavras ditas em récita escolar no Teatro Nacional Almeida–Garrett, em Lisboa, aos 2 de junho de 1937." In his *Oferenda.* Lisboa: Empresa Nacional de Publicidade, 1950, pp. 168–76.

General statements about Gil Vicente and his work. Other references on pp. 18–19, 118–19, 135, 235. Originally published in the *Centenário de Gil Vicente* (+1537–1937): *livro em que se contêm as obras do poeta representadas nas récitas vicentinas, de gala, escolares e populares, realizadas em Lisboa e províncias, acompanhadas das palavras que então foram ditas, e mandado publicar pelo Ministério da Educação Nacional.* Lisboa: Imprensa Nacional, 1937, pp. 19–23.

262. Reckert, Stephen. "Cavalaria, cortesia e desmi(s)tificação (o modelo ibérico)." In *Cavalaria espiritual e conquista do mundo.* Ed. Y. K. Centeno. Gabinete de Estudos de Simbologia. Lisboa: Instituto Nacional de Investigação Científica, 1986, pp. 23–40.

An analysis of two Vicentine works, *Sibila Cassandra* and *Dom Duardos*, inspired by romances of chivalry in Spanish (*Guarino mezquino* and *Primaleón*, respectively). The structure of the first rests on a polarity—understood as symmetry and as dialectics. Regarding the visual, musical and choreographic aspects, symmetry is perfect. But, so far as the dialectics between Solomon and Cassandra is concerned, the other female characters ally themselves automatically with the male side in an effort to censure their niece's whim in letting such a good match get away from her. In *Dom Duardos*, chivalry and courtliness converge, though already purified of all that is mere literature and not poetry. Above all a poet, Gil Vicente personifies a unique and ephemeral moment which allowed the synthesis of certain apparently opposed but complementary phenomena: Middle Ages and Renaissance, verbal and plastic arts, religious and secular drama, etc.

263. Reckert, Stephen. "Gil Vicente e a génese da 'comédia espanhola'." In *TV*, pp. 139–50.

An examination of the structural rhythm of what the author considers Gil Vicente's masterpiece, *Dom Duardos*. Vicente's *comédia*, by virtue of its dramatic structure—precursor of the Spanish *comedia* of the Siglo de Oro—and its underlying irony and psychological and symbolic subtlety, was extremely innovative for its historic moment. But it proved ephemeral, for it disappeared shortly along with the Portuguese royal court, the only physical space possible for a Portuguese *comédia*. And Vicente is remembered as a writer of *autos*, never of *comédias*.

264. Reckert, Stephen. "Gil Vicente y la configuración de la *comedia*." In *Literatura en la época del emperador*. Ed. Víctor García de la Concha. Acta Salmanticensia: Academia Literaria Renacentista, V. Salamanca: Universidad de Salamanca, 1988, pp. 165–80.

The configuration of Vicentine *comedia*, as exemplified by *Don Duardos*, is not limited to its own constitutive rhythm, since this rhythm reflects the playwright's vital circumstance and concerns. The play is a synthesis of chivalry and *courtoisie* and of a host of other complementary phenomena.

265. Reckert, Stephen. "A sintaxe dramática de *O Velho da Horta*." In *EP:HLSP*, pp. 401–10.

An analysis of the five lyrics inserted in the play enables us to penetrate its hidden center and discover its plan. This plan can be summarily defined as "know thyself."

266. Rocha, Andrée Crabbé. "Gil Vicente." In her *A epistolografia em Portugal*. Coimbra: Livraria Almedina, 1965, pp. 71–76.

Discusses Gil Vicente's two letters to D. João III (one included in the prologue to the *Copilaçám* and the other, concerning the 1531 earthquake, sent to the king from Santarém): pp. 71–74. The same discussion appeared also in *Dionysos*, X, 12 (September 1965), 27–28, under the title "Duas cartas de Gil Vicente" (see *GVB*, no. 793). On pp. 74–76 the text of the second letter is reproduced.

267. Rodrigues, Maria Idalina Resina. "Dos salmantinos a Gil Vicente: as celebrações do Natal." In *AHLM–I*, pp. 107–35.

Rodrigues examines the similarities between two plays of Lucas Fernández (*Égloga o farsa del nascimiento de Nuestro Redemptor Jesucristo* and *Auto o farsa del nascimiento de Nuestro Señor Jesucristo*) and Gil Vicente's *Auto pastoril castelhano* and *Auto dos Reis Magos*, and those between some of Juan del Encina's plays and Vicente's *Auto da visitação*. She then proceeds to study how Vicente treated the Nativity theme in the *Auto pastoril português*, *Auto da feira*, *Auto da Barca do Purgatório*, *Auto da Fé*, *Auto da sibila Cassandra*, *Auto de Mofina Mendes*, and *Auto dos Quatro Tempos*.

268. Rodrigues, Maria Idalina Resina. *Estudos ibéricos: da cultura à literatura: pontos de encontro. Séculos XIII a XVII*. Diálogo: Série Fronteiras Abertas. Lisboa: Instituto de Cultura e Língua Portuguesa, Ministério da Educação, 1987. 433 pp.

Includes: "*Auto da Barca do Inferno*: os textos e os públicos" (pp. 79–99): surveys the various editions of the play intended for the student, the casual reader, and the theatergoer, and finds them wanting in several respects, especially their fidelity to the Vicentine texts. Admitting that a single edition designed for these three groups is an impossibility, she proposes a set of norms which should guide the editor of a student edition. Finally, she advises that the 1518 text of the play should be used as a basis. The same essay had appeared in *Actes du colloque international de critique textuelle portugaise (Paris, 20–24 octobre 1981)*. Paris: Fondation Calouste Gulbenkian/Centre Culturel Portugais, 1986, pp. 131–46. "Gil Vicente e Lope de Vega: um tema e duas perspectivas" (pp. 101–13): examines Gil Vicente's and Lope de Vega's dramatic recreation of the same Biblical theme, God's history (in the *Breve sumário da história de Deus* and *La creación del mundo*, respectively). She finds that Vicente opts for situations which point to a future free of the need for punishment, whereas Lope retains, in human conduct, the signs of an active past. This essay appeared twice before as "O *Breve sumário da história de Deus* e *La creación del mundo*: um tema e duas perspectivas," in *Brotéria*, CXI (1980), 251–61, and in *Lope de Vega y los orígenes del teatro español. Actas del I congreso internacional sobre Lope de Vega*, ed. Manuel Criado de Val (Madrid: EDI–6, 1981), pp. 233–40.

269. Rodrigues, Maria Idalina Resina. "A nave que parte e a cidade que fica. A propósito da *Nao d'Amores* de Gil Vicente." In *EP:HLSP*, pp. 411–34.

The first part of the *Nao d'amores*—a play designed as part of the festivities welcoming D. João III and Dona Catarina to Lisbon in 1527—presents a paradisiac Lisbon peopled with noble and, even, supernatural characters who seek the Ilha da Ventura. With the appearance of Frei Martinho, who has turned crazy through love, we are transported into a different, more realistic Lisbon with a more popular set of citizens.

270. Roig, Adrien. "Los españoles en el teatro de Gil Vicente." In *Actas Irvine–92. [XI congreso de la] Asociación Internacional de Hispanistas. III: Encuentros y desencuentros de culturas: desde la Edad Media al siglo XVIII*. Ed. Juan Villegas. Irvine: University of California, 1994, pp. 129–38.

Spanish characters abound in Gil Vicente's theater. Apart from the rustics—imitations of the creations of Juan del Encina and Lucas Fernández—there are wild men, low and villainous men, and humbug seducers, all depicted with profound contempt. On the contrary, the dramatist praises the great historical achievements of Spain although he affirms the preeminence of Portugal.

271. Roig, Adrien. "Tempestade sobre a rota da Índia em *Triunfo do Inverno* de Gil Vicente." In *A abertura do mundo: Estudos de história dos descobrimentos europeus em homenagem a Luís de Albuquerque*. Vol. I. Lisboa: Presença, 1986, pp. 69–88.

First appeared in French in *Quadrant*, 2 (1985), 5–31. *Tragicomédia do Inverno e Verão* is a more appropriate title to the whole play than *Triunfo do Inverno*. The scene of the storm occupies the center of the play. The storm represents the totality of forces which act jointly against the ship, center of the action. In a world upside down, the storm serves to reveal the truth, ascribing to each crew member his true merit. The storm offers Gil Vicente the opportunity to denounce, before the king and the royal court, the flagrant abuses in the distribution of posts: the promotion of the unfit at the expense of true merit. But the serious issues are underlying. This play is more farce than tragedy, since it was designed to celebrate a happy event (the birth of Princess Isabel) and entertain.

272. San Miguel, Ángel. "Le [sic] evolución del espacio escénico ideal en la obra en castellano de Gil Vicente." In *Edad Media y Renacimiento: continuidades y rupturas*. Estudios reunidos y presentados por J[ean] Canavaggio y B[ernard] Darbord. Centre de Recherches en Langues, Littératures et Civilisations du Monde Ibérique et de l'Italie. Caen: Centre de Publications de l'Université de Caen, 1991, pp. 145–59.

The stage directions and references in the dialogue show the kind of stage settings Gil Vicente had in mind for his plays in Spanish. In the first phase of his production in Spanish (the Christmas cycle plays), the settings are rural. The dramatist generally follows in this respect his Spanish models, Juan del Encina and Lucas Fernández. In the second phase, which coincides with the *Auto da Barca da Glória*, Vicente demonstrates his capacity and interest in the creation of a whole series of spatial and visual scenic elements which constitute a departure from his Spanish models and which bring his scenography to new heights. In the third phase, in the tragicomedies of *Dom Duardos* and *Amadis de Gaula*, Vicente shares with Juan del Encina the deruralization and ennoblement of the place in which the dramatic action unfolds: the pastoral cabin is replaced by palatial halls.

273. Saraiva, António José. "Estética dos *autos de devoção*." In his *Poesia e drama: Bernardim Ribeiro. Gil Vicente. Cantigas de amigo*. Lisboa: Gradiva, 1990, pp. 145–78.

Originally published in *RFLUL*, V (1938), 272–98. The application of medieval aesthetic criteria to Gil Vicente's *autos de devoção* reveals that the dramatist is an essentially medieval spirit. It can be said that Gil Vicente, a medieval man displaced into the sixteenth century, is gradually reintegrating himself into the Middle Ages in proportion as his creative genius is becoming freer and its expression more spontaneous.

274. Sena, Jorge de. *Estudos de literatura portuguesa—I*. Obras de Jorge de Sena. Lisboa: Edições 70, 1981. 258 pp.

Includes: "Sobre Gil Vicente," (pp. 29–33): originally published in *O Estado de São Paulo. Suplemento Literário*, (14 January 1961): argues that Gil Vicente's work needs to be liberated from critical tendencies such as the *eruditismo historicista* and the *filosofismo politizante*, and to be considered in its aesthetic dimension. "Sobre Gil Vicente, a propósito de um centenário hipotético," (pp. 35–40): first published in *O Tempo e o Modo*, 33 (December 1965), 1136–40 (see *GVB*, no. 498): questions the value of commemorative centenaries which leave fundamental questions unanswered. Apropos of the fifth centenary of Vicente's birth (1965), Sena claims that no one is really interested in studying him, in understanding him, in elucidating him. Many ill–founded claims have been made regarding Vicente's life and art by men who are, by and large, only through hearsay familiar with universal culture.

Reviews:

a. Ofélia Paiva Monteiro, *CoL*, 73 (May 1983), 88–89.

b. João Maia, *Brotéria*, CXXI (1985), 478.

275. Senabre, Ricardo. "Un villancico de Gil Vicente." In *Homenaje a Pedro Sainz Rodríguez.* II: *Estudios de lengua y literatura.* Madrid: Fundación Universitaria Española, 1986, pp. 623–31.

The *villancico* "Halcón que se atreve," which occurs in the *Comédia de Rubena*, is not an autonomous entity. Its allegorical meaning becomes clear only by the larger context of which it forms a part. It is sung by Cismena's needlewomen in order to disabuse Felício of his amorous pursuit.

276. *Silveira, Tasso da. *Gil Vicente e outros estudos portugueses.* Coleção Homens e Idéias, I. São Paulo: S.E. Panorama, 1940. xxxviii+221 pp.

277. Smith, Dawn L. "Staging the *auto sacramental*: Gil Vicente and Calderón at the Chamizal Festival." In *Texto y espectáculo: nuevas dimensiones críticas de la "comedia".* Ed. Arturo Pérez–Pisonero and Ana Semidey–Torres. New Brunswick, New Jersey: SLUSA, 1990, pp. 109–16.

A discussion of how successfully Tiempo Común, a professional group from Caracas, recreated Gil Vicente's *Auto da Barca da Glória*, under the direction of Hugo Márquez, for a modern audience at the Chamizal Festival in March 1987.

278. Sousa, Ronald. "'Vós outros também cantai por vosso uso acostumado': Representation of the Popular in Gil Vicente." In *Literature Among Discourses: The Spanish Golden Age.* Ed. Wlad Godzich and Nicholas Spadaccini. Minneapolis: University of Minnesota Press, 1986, pp. 116–31.

In Gil Vicente's *Auto da Fé*, two culturally, linguistically, and socially differentiated groups are represented: that of the shepherds Bras and Benito and that of Faith, who reflects the culture of the nobility, the one shown to be superior. The conciliation of these two cultural entities, implicit in the play's structure and language, is never achieved. The play's resolution is grounded in cultural divergence, with union only through an authority principle.

Reviews (of the volume):

a. Edward H. Friedman, *Hispania*, LXX (1987), 82–84.

b. Patricia A. McCoy, *Seventeenth–Century News*, VL (1987), 15–16.

c. Paul Julian Smith, *BHS*, LXV (1988), 294–95.

279. Stathatos, C. C. "Exemplos de ironia no *Auto da Índia*." Trans. Manuel João Gomes. In *TV*, pp. 151–58.

Gil Vicente has handled irony expertly to show that, in the world of this play, things are not what they are supposed to be, thus producing the desired comic tone. At the same time, irony has served the playwright well in reinforcing the audience's/reader's impression of Constança's guile and her husband's stupidity.

280. Stathatos, C. C. "Reconsidering the Temporal Unity of Gil Vicente's *Auto da Índia*." In *EP:HLSP*, pp. 475–85.

An examination of all problematic aspects of the *Auto da Índia*'s temporal structure leads to the conclusion that, if it were not for the reference to Christmas, the play's temporal logic would be flawless.

281. Stegagno Picchio, Luciana. *La Méthode philologique: Écrits sur la littérature portugaise*. II: *La Prose et le théâtre*. Trans. Maï Mouniana. Civilização Portuguesa, V, 2. Paris: Fundação Calouste Gulbenkian/ Centro Cultural Português, 1982. 359 pp.

In addition to many references to Gil Vicente throughout, it includes: "Pour une typologie du théâtre portugais" (pp. 45–60), first published in Portuguese in her "Quatro lições sobre o teatro português," *EIP*, 28 (1967), 53–67, and in Italian in her *Ricerche sul teatro portoghese*, Officina Romanica, XIV: Studi e Testi Portoghesi e Brasiliani, 9 (Roma: Ateneo, 1969), pp. 13–34: considers Portuguese theater both on the literary and the social levels; examines its two great stylistic traditions (popular and learned) and discusses the stylistic constants which inform the entire system, paying special attention to the style of Gil Vicente, the emblematic founder of the first tradition. "Considérations sur les textes sayagais de Gil Vicente" (pp. 103–16), first published as "Considerazioni sui testi saiaghesi di Gil Vicente" in *Studi di Letteratura Spagnola*, I (1964), 231–41, and, later, in her *Ricerche*, pp. 65–85: Gil Vicente's adoption of *sayagués* was not a servile acceptance of a foreign language but rather a conscious choice of a linguistic style capable of expressing a definite poetic reality. The *sayagués* texts of Juan del Encina, Lucas Fernández and, especially, Gil Vicente should be studied in comparison with the pastoral and rustic plays of sixteenth–century Europe. "Sayagais, langue rustique portugaise, pavan: considérations sur les langues rustiques dans le théâtre du XVIe siècle" (pp. 117–35), first published as "Saiaghese, lingua rustica portoghese, pavano: considerazioni sulle parlate rustiche nel teatro del Cinquecento" in her *Ricerche*, pp. 87–112, and in *Studi sul teatro veneto fra Rinascimento ed età baroca*, ed. M.T. Muraro (Firenze: C. Olschki, 1971), pp. 273–93: the author surveys the history of *sayagués* (employed by Juan del Encina, Lucas Fernández, and Gil Vicente) and the Portuguese rustic language (created by Gil Vicente), both of which were born of the observation of reality but were literary interpretations of it, and compares them with the Paduan dialect employed by Ruzante. She finds many stylistic similarities between the latter and Gil Vicente. "Le Diable et l'enfer dans l'oeuvre théâtrale de Gil Vicente" (pp. 137–64), first published as "Diavolo e inferno nel teatro di Gil Vicente" in *Annali dell'Instituto Universitario Orientale—Sezione Romanza*, I, 2 (1959), 31–59, and, later, in her *Ricerche*, pp. 115–55: Gil Vicente's devil is a typically medieval personage. His hell, in terms of conception, falls within the medieval Christian tradition but, in terms of staging, it betrays a culture and a mentality which belong to the Renaissance. "Le *Pater Noster* farci de Gil Vicente: interprétation" (pp. 165–75), first published as "Il *Pater Noster* farcito: interpretazione di un passo di Gil Vicente," *Annali*, III (1961), 191–98 and in her *Ricerche*, pp. 157–71: unlike other critics, Luciana Stegagno Picchio considers the *Pater Noster*, with which the *Velho da horta* opens, farcical and consonant with the tone of the entire play. In the use of sacred texts with burlesque intentions, Gil Vicente was following an extensive medieval tradition. "Un Exemple d'incohérence stylistique: le *Fidalgo aprendiz* de Francisco Manuel de Melo" (pp. 219–38); the first version in Portuguese can be found in the special issue of the literary supplement of *O Comércio do Porto* (22 November 1966) dedicated to the centenary of Francisco Manuel de Melo; an expanded version was included in her "Quatro lições sobre o teatro português," *EIP*, 28 (1967), 86–103; it also appeared in Italian in her *Ricerche*, pp. 229–53: through a comparison (pp. 221–25) of the *fidalgo aprendiz* protagonist of Melo's play, with Gil Vicente's *fidalgo pobre* (Aires Rosado and Brás da Mata of *Quem tem farelos?* and *Inês Pereira*, respectively), the author disproves the critical claim that the former is a direct descendant of the latter; rather he is similar to Pêro Marques, the half-witted *beirão* of *Inês Pereira*. See also *GVB*, no. 369.

Reviews:

a. Luiz Francisco Rebello, *CoL*, 76 (November 1983), 91–93.

b. Cosme Barreiros, *Grial*, XXII (1984), 243–45.

c. T[homas] R. H[art], *CL*, XXXVII (1985), 189–90.

282. Stegagno Picchio, Luciana. "O Purgatório de Gil Vicente: estado ou lugar?" In *TV*, pp. 159–73.

Gil Vicente's purgatory—as described in the *Auto da Barca do Purgatório*—is a temporal rather than a spatial concept. Cleansing is to take place on the riverbank, this side of the infernal river and before the crossing of no return. The riverbank is a place of concentration and assignment of the several destinations, a place where the characters are still what they had been while alive. Vicente's refusal to assign a place specifically and exclusively designed for cleansing coincides with Luther's refusal to accept the concept of a "third place." This article had appeared first in Italian ("Per una semiologia dell'aldilà: l'idea di purgatorio in Gil Vicente") in *Homenaje a Eugenio Asensio*, ed. Luisa López Grigera and Augustin Redondo (Madrid: Gredos, 1988), pp. 447–58.

283. Suárez, José I. "The Variance of the Comic Element in Vicentine Drama." In *Selected Proceedings. The Thirty–Fourth Annual (1984) Mountain Interstate Foreign Language Conference*. Ed. Eduardo Zayas–Bazán and Christa I. Hungate. Johnson City, Tennessee: East Tennessee State University, 1986, pp. 157–68.

By means of a variety of comic devices, Gil Vicente varied the degree of laughter in his plays (low–key laughter in some religious and chivalric plays, high laughter in the farces and comedies) in a manner reminiscent of the ancient Menippean satire.

284. Surtz, Ronald E. "Poetry and History in Gil Vicente's *Auto da Lusitânia*." In *Creation and Re–creation: Experiments in Literary Form in Early Modern Spain: Studies in Honor of Stephen Gilman*. Ed. Ronald E. Surtz and Nora Weinerth. Juan de la Cuesta Hispanic Monographs: *Homenajes*, II. Newark, Delaware: Juan de la Cuesta, 1983, pp. 41–48.

The play's lengthy prologue, which deals anachronistically with the Portuguese Jews, is a plea for tolerance toward the New Christians, whereas the play proper, with its pseudomythological plot, is a parody of the excesses of what often passed for Renaissance classical scholarship and a defense of Gil Vicente's artistic integrity.

Reviews (of the book):

a. Edward J. Neugaard, *Hispania*, LXVII (1984), 303.

b. Maxim. P.A.M. Kerkhof, *BHS*, LXIII (1986), 275–77.

c. Mercedes Turón, *Revista de Estudios Hispánicos* (Poughkeepsie, New York), XXI, 2 (May 1987), 113–14.

285. Tavani, Giuseppe. "Gil Vicente e a *Comédia de Rubena*." In his *Ensaios portugueses: filologia e linguística*. Temas Portugueses. Lisboa: Imprensa Nacional–Casa da Moeda, 1988, pp. 399–412.

First appeared in Italian as introduction to his critical edition of the play (Roma: Ateneo, 1965)—see *GVB*, no. 121.

Review (of the volume):

a. Helder Godinho, *CoL*, 112 (November–December 1989), 116.

286. Teyssier, Paul. "'Estrados' e 'cadeiras': estudo de alguns 'objectos culturais' em Gil Vicente e na Escola Vicentina." In *Studies in Portuguese Literature and History in Honour of Luís de Sousa Rebelo*. Ed. Helder Macedo. Colección Támesis: Série A: Monografías, CXXXXVII. London: Tamesis Books, 1992, pp. 63–71.

Gil Vicente adheres in his plays to the rigid social sitting code practiced in the Iberian Peninsula and derived from Moslem culture: men of high social standing sit on chairs with a back; those of lesser standing sit on chairs without a back; poor men, especially the peasants, use three–legged stools made of cork. Women of the aristocracy sit on daises. Poorer women sit on cork daises or mats.

Review (of the volume):

a. N. J. Lamb, *BHS*, LXXII (1995), 245–46.

287. Teyssier, Paul. *Études de littérature et de linguistique*. Civilização Portuguesa, X. Paris: Fundação Calouste Gulbenkian/Centro Cultural Português, 1990. xvii+271 pp.

Includes: "Essai d'explication du *vilancete* de Camões: *Com vossos olhos Gonçalves...*" (pp. 27–41): comments on the significance of the name of the Vicentine character Mofina Mêndez (see especially pp. 33–34); originally published in *Les Cultures ibériques en devenir: essais publiés en hommage à la mémoire de Marcel Bataillon* (Paris: Fondation Singer–Polignac, 1977), pp. 707–18. "L'Envers de l'épopée" (pp. 43–58): in the *Auto da Índia*, Gil Vicente departs from official ideology by presenting the negative side of the Portuguese voyages of discovery and expansion. His irreverent satire was part of an old tradition which the authorities had been unable to eradicate yet. The second part of the essay deals with another discordant voice, that of Fernão Mendes Pinto's *Peregrinação*. This is a revised and expanded version of the homonymous piece published in *Critique. Revue Générale des Publications Françaises et Étrangères*, XLIV, 495–496 (August–September 1988), 676–83. "Le Système des déictiques spatiaux en portugais aux XIVe, XVe et XVIe siècles" (pp. 161–98): in Part III of the study, "L'Oeuvre portugaise de Gil Vicente (XVIe siècle)," pp. 182–93, Teyssier examines the demonstratives and adverbs of place in Vicente's work. The essay appeared first in *Cahiers de Linguistique Hispanique Médiévale*, 6 (March 1981), 5–39. "L'Or et le laurier: l'étymologie du portugais *louro* ('blond')" (pp. 231–41): the author explains the semantic slip by which Portuguese *louro* came to acquire its meaning of "blond" and views it as a cultural, rather than linguistic, phenomenon. He also cites examples of the use of *louro* and related *Lourinhã* and *Laureolo* in Gil Vicente's *Romagem de agravados*, *Auto da festa*, and *Auto da sibila Cassandra*, respectively. The first version of the essay was published in *L'Or au temps de la Renaissance: du mythe à l'économie*, ed. Marie–Thérèse Jones–Davies, Centre de Recherches sur la Renaissance, III (Paris: Université de Paris–Sorbonne, Institut des Recherches sur les Civilisations de l'Occident Moderne, 1978), pp. 105–13.

Review:

a. Ernesto Rodrigues, *CoL*, 134 (October–December 1994), 161–63.

288. Teyssier, Paul. "Interpretação do *Auto da Lusitânia*." In *TV*, pp. 175–85.

The two apparently disparate parts of this play—the farcical scene of the Jewish family and the allegorical comedy on the origins of Portugal—are perfectly coherent and complementary, though antithetical. They reflect the dramatist's attitude vis–à–vis the question of the New Christians: Gil Vicente shows tolerance toward the Jews in so far as they adhere to their traditional values and religious practices. At the same time, however, he disapproves of the practices of the New Christians, symbolized by Mercúrio in the second part, and sides with the royal policy in this respect.

289. Teyssier, Paul. "Normes pour une édition critique des oeuvres de Gil Vicente." In *Actes du colloque international de critique textuelle portugaise (Paris, 20–24 octobre 1981)*. Paris: Fondation Calouste Gulbenkian/Centre Culturel Portugais, 1986, pp. 123–30.

The need to prepare a new critical edition of Gil Vicente's complete works is evident. Such an edition should be easy to read but, at the same time, it should be scientifically sound. In terms of arranging the plays, there are three possible plans: that of the *Copilaçám* of 1562, a chronological one or a partly thematic, partly chronological one. In terms of the transcription of the texts, there are certain legitimate modernizations, but there are also some traits peculiar to the language of Vicente's time which should be retained (lists of both are provided).

290. Teyssier, Paul. "Les Pauvres dans le théâtre de Gil Vicente." In *Misère et gueuserie au temps de la Renaissance*. Ed. Marie–Thérèse Jones–Davies. Centre de Recherches sur la Renaissance, I. Paris: Université de Paris–Sorbonne, Institut de Recherches sur les Civilisations de l'Occident Moderne, 1976, pp. 5–17.

Poverty appears frequently in Gil Vicente's work. In his religious plays, it is depicted as a Christian virtue. Elsewhere, the poor are rendered ridiculous and are the object of laughter, which makes the dramatist appear an ally of the ruling class which was insensitive to the poor's plight. But things are not as simple as they appear, for, on many occasions, Gil Vicente seems implacably critical of the Portuguese establishment of his time.

291. Tobar, María Luisa. "Para una edición de las comedias de Gil Vicente." In *La edición de textos. Actas del I congreso internacional de hispanistas del Siglo de Oro*. Ed. Pablo Jauralde, Dolores Noguera and Alfonso Rey. Colección Támesis, Série A: Monografías, CXXXIX. London: Tamesis Books, 1990, pp. 469–75.

A future edition of Gil Vicente's *comédias*, destined for a wider Spanish–speaking audience, should be readable (with a degree of modernization that does not alter the text); should provide a division of the text into scenes corresponding to internal division; should be accompanied by an introduction dealing with the playwright and his times, comedy in his work, previous editions, textual problems, analysis of the text (in terms of plot, structure, action, characters, theatrical technique, language, versification); when necessary, the text should be accompanied by a glossary and explicatory notes.

292. Tomlins, Jack E. "Gil Vicente's Vision of India and Its Ironic Echo in Camões's 'Velho do Restelo'." In *Empire in Transition: The Portuguese World in the Time of Camões*. Ed. Alfred Hower and Richard A. Preto–Rodas. Gainesville: University Presses of Florida, 1985, pp. 170–76.

Whereas Gil Vicente both burlesqued (*Auto da Índia*) and exalted (*Auto da Fama*) the Indian venture at the beginning of the sixteenth century, by the end of the century Camões had condemned Lusitanian pride and lust for power in the episode of the old man of Restelo (*Lusíadas*, IV, 94–104).

Reviews (of the book):

a. T. F. Earle, *Portuguese Studies*, III (1987), 216–17.

b. Marian L. Smolen, *Hispania*, LXXI (1988), 77.

293. Torrinha, Francisco. "Nótula filológica." In *Miscelânea de estudos à memória de Cláudio Basto*. Organizada por Hermínia Basto. Porto: Imprensa Portuguesa, 1948, pp. 189–91.

On the verb *dessengular* in the *Auto pastoril português* and the *Farsa dos almocreves*.

294. Tranchida, Valério. "O *Auto da feira*: uma leitura." In *TV*, pp. 187–97.

Structurally, the play can be divided into three parts, each one of which corresponds to a stage that symbolizes the ascensional movement of the soul from the darkness of the satanic world (represented by astrology and the corruption of Rome), through scenes of daily life, to the luminosity of the celestial pastures of the nine shepherdesses and the three youths. The dramatist's intention is to urge the audience to imitate the simplicity of spirit of the youth Gilberto and the religious devotion of the shepherdesses.

295. Trindade, Maria José Lagos. "Classes sociais presentes e ausentes na obra de Gil Vicente." In her *Estudos de história medieval e outros*. Perfil de Maria José Trindade por Orlando Ribeiro. Lisboa: Conselho Directivo, Faculdade de Letras de Lisboa/Cooperativa Editora, História Crítica, 1981, pp. 255–66.

Originally a "comunicação apresentada ao Simpósio Vicentino nas comemorações do V centenário do nascimento de Gil Vicente, realizado em Lisboa em 1965:" discusses the social groups which appear in Gil Vicente's works and finds that they do not reflect accurately the contemporary Portuguese society. The most common and best portrayed characters are peasants, shepherds, and friars. There is little emphasis on the merchant. In general, Vicente demonstrates a lack of interest in the social groups which arose as a result of Portuguese expansion and colonization. The characters and situations he chooses reflect his medieval makeup.

296. Velho, Selma de Vieira. "A influência indiana (hindú) nas obras de Gil Vicente." In her *A influência da mitologia hindú na literatura portuguesa dos séculos XVI e XVII*. Tese apresentada em 1983 na Universidade de Bombaím para o grau de doutoramento em literatura portuguesa (Ph.D.). Macau: Instituto Cultural de Macau, 1988. Vol. I, pp. 329–445.

Argues that Gil Vicente must have become aware of the accounts of those who returned from trips to India. Moreover, he had probably learned some of the Indian customs and philosophy from some Indian(s) who happened to be at the Portuguese court at his time. She detects echoes of Indian culture in a great many of Vicente's plays.

Review:

a. F. Pires Lopes, *Brotéria*, CXXXII (1991), 580–81.

297. Zimic, Stanislav. "Gil Vicente: *Romagem de Agravados* (ensayo de interpretación)." In *EP:HLSP*, pp. 487–505.

For certain scholars, Frei Paço's attitude in this play reflects that of the dramatist, who, like Frei Paço, disapproves of the characters' desire to change their lot. Zimic shows, however, that Gil Vicente does in no way object to the people's desire to change and better themselves socially, economically, and personally. What he criticizes is the unreasonable or immoral motives which frequently color the desire for change. In fact, he shows precisely the desperate urgency for radical changes in daily life, in society and, in particular, in its most powerful representatives, whether lay or religious.

298. Zimic, Stanislav. "Nuevas consideraciones sobre el *Auto da Lusitânia* de Gil Vicente." In *Homenaje a Alonso Zamora Vicente*. III, 1: *Literaturas medievales. Literatura española de los siglos XV–XVII*. Ed. Pedro Peira, Pablo Jauralde, Jesús Sánchez Lobato, and Jorge Urrutia. Madrid: Castalia, 1988 [1991], pp. 359–69.

The play's fundamental meaning is derived from the logical interdependence of all its parts. The happy marriage of Portugal and

Lusitânia, which symbolizes the harmonious assimilation of the foreign and the indigenous races in Portugal, represents only a fiction when contrasted with the reality of the deplorable relations between Christians and Jews (dramatized in the confrontation of the Courtier and Lediça). The satiric dialogue of Todo o Mundo e Ninguém serves to remind of the need to gauge justly the condition of the nation as a whole. In his noble desire for mutual understanding between his Christian and Jewish compatriots, Gil Vicente presents the Jewish family simply as a Portuguese family.

299. Zimic, Stanislav. "O sentido alegórico do Auto de la sibila Casandra de Gil Vicente." Trans. Manuel João Gomes. In TV, pp. 199–218.

The play enjoys a coherent and logical structure in all its details, which rests on its allegorical sense. It is a dramatization of a traditional allegory. The two central characters, Solomon and Cassandra, belong to a biblical context familiar to Vicente's audience: that of the Song of Songs. Cassandra, however, differs from the Beloved of the Song of Songs in that she personifies not the ideal Church but rather Vicente's contemporary Church, a corrupt Church that has become a sorry parody of what it should be.

C. JOURNAL ARTICLES

a. GENERAL

General

300. Côrte–Real, João Afonso. "Gil Vicente: talento poético da história luso-castelhana e do humanismo do século XVI." O Instituto, CXXXVII (1978), 1–21.

General statements about Gil Vicente as consummate playwright, satirist, patriot, recorder of historical detail, and humanist of a special kind. The article is divided into the following parts: I: A figura literária; II: "Ridendo castigat mores;" III: História luso-castelhana; IV: Humanismo do século dezasseis.

301. Gomes, António da Silva. "Das origens do teatro." Palestra, 15 (1962), 99–104.

Includes a schematic overview of Gil Vicente's early theater.

302. Nunes, V. de Carvalho. "Acerca de Gil Vicente." *Labor* (Aveiro), 3ª Série, XVIII, 133 (October 1953), 13–15.

General comments about teaching Gil Vicente in the *liceus*.

Gil Vicente, the Man

303. Guerra, Abel. "A terra natal de Gil Vicente." *Brotéria*, CXXII (1986), 278–96.

Guerra sides with those scholars who support that Gil Vicente was a native of Beira. He argues, on the basis of internal evidence from several plays (*Auto da Fama, Tragicomédia da Serra da Estrêla, Auto pastoril português, Farsa de Inês Pereira, Auto da feira, Farsa dos almocreves, Auto da festa, Auto da Cananeia, Comédia do viúvo, Comédia de Rubena*), that Vicente was born in the vicinity of Covilhã.

304. Miguel, António Dias. "Gil Vicente, mestre de retórica. . . das representações." *Humanitas* (Coimbra), XXXVII–XXXVIII (1985–86), 267–73.

In a document found in the Torre do Tombo and dated 6 April 1524, Gil Vicente is referred to as *"mestre de retórica das representações."* In this capacity, he received an income of twenty thousand *réis* per annum. This document is important in that it corrects the old belief that Vicente was King Manuel's teacher of rhetoric.

305. Silva, Valentim [Augusto] da. "Gil Vicente, beirão." *Beira Alta*, II, 1 (1943), 3–23 and III, 2 (1944), 153–79.

Argues that Gil Vicente was born in Guimarães de Tavares.

Dramatic Genres

306. Calderón Calderón, Manuel. "Una aproximación a las comedias de Gil Vicente." *Caligrama*, 4 (1991), 185–212.

Examines several aspects of the *Comédia do viúvo*, the *Comédia de Rubena*, the *Comédia sobre a divisa da cidade de Coimbra*, and *Floresta de enganos* and concludes that Vicente's *comédia* blends popular customs and manners with courtly ones, fantastic with mythic elements, since it is part of a theater closely associated with the specific circumstances and the specific place of representation (the Portuguese court). At the same time, Vicente seeks comic means in folklore and the carnival tradition; he transforms these borrowings and adapts them to the objectives of his *comédias*, bringing them into contact with the cultural atmosphere and the Neoplatonic tradition of the Renaissance.

307. Osório, Jorge A[lves]. "O testemunho de Garcia de Resende sobre o teatro vicentino. Algumas reflexões." *Humanitas* (Coimbra), XXXI–XXXII (1979–80), 71–96.

In stanza 186 of his *Miscelânea*, Garcia de Resende testifies to Gil Vicente's innovations in Portuguese theater. In an effort to determine what exactly Garcia de Resende was referring to, Osório reviews the pre–Vicentine dramatic activity in Portugal (*momos, entremezes*) and Gil Vicente's plays as parts of the larger context of Court *festas*. A discussion of the dramatist's *farsas* and *comédias* and their differences makes the author suspect that Vicente had consciously adopted a theory of comedy consistent with the medieval literary and rhetorical precepts, on the one hand, and with the norms set forth by early Renaissance Spanish writers (including Torres Naharro), on the other. It is possible then that Garcia de Resende's reference is to Vicente's *comédias* rather than his plays in general. See also no. 308.

308. R[amalho], A[mérico da] C[osta]. "Gil Vicente e a comédia." *Humanitas* (Coimbra), XXXI–XXXII (1979–80), 245–46.

Ramalho adds Dante's definition of *comoedia* (in letter X to Can Grande della Scala) to Osório's search for sources for Gil Vicente (see above, no. 307).

309. Tobar, María Luisa. "Due diversi livelli di comicità in Gil Vicente: la *Comédia do viúvo e Don Duardos.*" *QP*, 9–10 (Spring–Autumn 1981), 265–99.

Examines the structure of the two plays and its constituent elements (setting, father–daughter relationship, appearance, behavior, and mode of expression of the male protagonists) and concludes that the plays belong to different dramatic categories: the *Comédia do viúvo* adheres to the medieval notion of comedy, whereas *Dom Duardos*, in spite of its happy ending, has elements characteristic of tragedy.

310. Tobar, María Luisa. "Para una protohistoria del entremés. Gil Vicente autor de piezas entremesiles." *Nuovi Annali della Facoltà di Magistero dell'Università di Messina*, I (1983), 601–27.

The essential characteristics and structure of the *entremés* can be found in several of Gil Vicente's plays: *Auto pastoril português, Auto da*

Lusitânia, Mofina Mendes, and, above all, *Floresta de enganos* which contains two *entremeses* (that of the feigned widow and that of the "black bakerwoman").

311. Tobar, María Luisa. "'Toda comedia comienza en dolores.' Notas en torno a la comedia de Gil Vicente." *Nuovi Annali della Facoltà di Magistero dell'Università di Messina,* 4 (1985), 759–83.

Gil Vicente's conception of comedy reflects the definitions of medieval theorists (primarily Juan de Mena and the Marqués de Santillana), who point out the comedy's two salient features, namely its low and humble style and its beginning in adversity and ending in happiness. The four plays grouped as *comédias* in the Second Book of the *Copilaçám* (*Viúvo, Rubena, Divisa da cidade de Coimbra,* and *Floresta de enganos*) share these characteristics.

Poetry and Music

312. Bassagoda, Roger D. "Gil Vicente: notas y comentarios para el estudio de sus poesías líricas castellanas." *Boletín de la Academia Argentina de Letras,* X (1942), 897–940.

Bassagoda comments on a variety of irregularities (missing and irregular lines, errors in rhyme and meter) and lexical peculiarities found in Gil Vicente's Spanish poetry. He believes that most imperfections should not be attributed to the poet but rather to copyists, printers, actors, musicians. Finally, he proceeds to restore the texts to their "original" form, and offers restored versions (printed side by side with Dámaso Alonso's versions from *Poesías de Gil Vicente,* México: Séneca, 1940—see *GVB,* no. 34) of the following: "Muy graciosa es la doncella," "Del rosal vengo, mi madre," "Estánse dos hermanas," "Águila que dió tal vuelo" (pp. 938–40).

313. Becker, Danièle. "De la musique dans le théâtre religieux de Gil Vicente." *ACCP,* XXIII [*Homenagem a Paul Teyssier*] (1987), 461–86.

Gil Vicente's religious pieces are a mine of varied music. A careful examination of the numerous musical moments shows that the playwright has masterfully integrated music into the dramatic message.

313A. *López Castro, Armando. "Sobre los villancicos de Gil Vicente." *Estudios Humanísticos. Filología,* 16 (1994), 173–87.

314. Martins, Mário. "Canções marianas musicadas nos autos vicentinos." *Didaskalia*, VII (1977), 399–432.

Father Martins lists and comments on Marian songs in: *Auto pastoril castelhano, Auto dos Reis Magos, Auto da sibila Cassandra, Auto da Fé, Auto dos físicos, Auto de Mofina Mendes, Auto pastoril português, Auto da feira, Breve sumário da história de Deus, Nau de amores.* On pp. 431–32 are reproduced the musical scores of the two versions (variant lyrics) of "Norabuena vengas, Menga" from the *Cancionero musical de los siglos XV y XVI*, ed. Francisco Asenjo Barbieri (Madrid, 1890), nos 369 and 370.

315. Stegagno Picchio, Luciana (interviewer). "Stephen Reckert risponde a tre domande sulla poesia di Gil Vicente." *QP*, 9–10 (Spring–Autumn 1981), 309–20.

The general impression one gets from Gil Vicente's work is that of a series of variations on themes, sources, techniques and characters, designed to focus on a given situation from different angles or in unexpected contexts. Vicente's lyric poetry is richer in quantity than it has been assumed, amounting to more than 160 texts. In his case, it is the dramatic text that depends on the lyrical texts rather than the reverse. As a lyric poet, Vicente belongs to two traditions, the courtly and the popular, both averse to the metaphor. Therefore, he tends to be symbolic rather than metaphoric. The apparent transparency of one of his finest plays, *Dom Duardos*, is due in part to the virtual nonexistence of the metaphor, almost always replaced by the symbol.

Social and Ecclesiastical Criticism and Satire

316. Andrade Ordóñez, Marcel. "El clero en el teatro de Gil Vicente." *Universidad–Verdad*, IV (1989), 121–86.

A study of Gil Vicente's anticlerical satire, as it appears in the *Exortação da guerra, Auto de Mofina Mendes, Auto da Barca do Inferno, Auto da Barca da Glória, Auto dos físicos, Frágua de Amor, Farsa dos almocreves, Clérigo da Beira,* and *Romagem de agravados.* Vicente attacks the same clerical abuses (religious formalism, superstition, the problem of celibacy, lust, ambition, and the economic exploitation of peasantry) which served as butts of satire by Erasmus and other contemporary religious reformers.

317. Cardoso, Maria Benedita. "A dimensão da recusa em Gil Vicente." *Brotéria*, CX (1980), 167–74.

On the strength of textual evidence, Cardoso finds Gil Vicente in conflict with his times. The dramatist laments the fragmentation of society and the transformation of the social and religious man to a *homo oeconomicus*. Throughout his work, Vicente opposes usury and the materialistic tendencies of his society.

318. Carneiro, Alexandre Soares. "O rústico na corte: o auto pastoril vicentino no contexto das práticas culturais da corte portuguesa do início do século XVI." *EPA*, 19 (January–June 1992), 5–29.

Discusses the cultural context of the Portuguese royal court—within which Gil Vicente's theater originated—and Vicente's critical attitude toward the prevailing mores, making specific references to the *Monólogo do vaqueiro*, the "Sermão," and the prologue of the 1562 *Copilaçám* addressed to King João III. This study forms part of Carneiro's Master's thesis (see no. 140 above).

319. Correia de Almeida, Maria. "O auto vicentino." *Tempo Brasileiro*, 72 (January–March 1983), 48–56.

Gil Vicente's social criticism, as manifested in the *Auto da Barca do Inferno* and *O Juiz da Beira*, is formulated from the perspective of the peasantry. The *fidalgo* of the first play is damned for his oppression and exploitation of the peasants, while the *parvo* is saved not only because he is a simpleminded peasant, but also because he has been a victim of exploitation. In the second play, which contains the germ of modernity, Pêro Marques, an ingenuous peasant from Beira, inverts the values of feudal society by replacing the institutionalized justice system—of which he is ignorant—with a popular one. It is obvious that, notwithstanding his position at the court, Vicente feels free to denounce the abusive power of the nobility.

320. Dias, Aida Fernanda. "A sombra dos grandes." *RFR*, II (1984), 37–69.

Just as Gil Vicente, Sá de Miranda and others criticized in their works the lamentable state of Portuguese society in the end of the fifteenth and beginnings of the sixteenth centuries, other literati had depicted critically the same social ills. Among them Álvaro de Brito Pestana, Duarte da Gama, Nuno Pereira, João Rodrigues de Castel Branco, Diogo de Melo da Silva, Luís da Silveira, but especially Garcia de Resende, who, intellectually and artistically—though not personally—was very close to Vicente: both had common interests and points of view, they defended identical positions and can be justly considered representative of the good old Portugal. Virtually all these men of letters and their works have been undeservedly forgotten, they have been eclipsed by the great ones like Vicente and Sá de Miranda.

321. Hayashida, Masashi. "A Inquisição: Gil Vicente a propósito do conceito de conversão 'à força'." *Colóquio de Estudos Luso–Brasileiros. Anais* (Tokyo), XVIII (1984), 69–77.

On the evidence of the "Carta que Gil Vicente mandou de Santarém a El–Rei D. João III sobre o tremor da terra," the *Diálogo sobre a ressurreição de Cristo* and the *Breve sumário da história de Deus*, the author claims that Gil Vicente opposed the intolerant treatment of Jews and their forced conversion to Catholicism.

322. Malpique, Cruz. "Gil Vicente humanista." *Língua e Cultura*, II, 3 (1972), 224–40.

Gil Vicente was not a humanist in the Renaissance sense of the term, but he was a humanist in a wider sense in that he portrayed humans and things human. His anticlericalism sprang from a rock–solid orthodoxy: he attacked only the abuses of the clergy and the false, external manifestations of religiosity.

323. Malpique, Cruz. "Gil Vicente no signo de Erasmo (1465?–1537?)." *Labor* (Aveiro), 3ª Série, XXX, 241 (October 1965), 9–39.

The entire *Auto da feira* is permeated by an implacable criticism of the abuses and corruption of the clergy. Gil Vicente's anticlericalism springs not from any heterodox tendencies but from his belief that the Church ought to reform itself and return to an austere spirituality. The affinity between Vicente's anticlericalism and Erasmus's is purely coincidental: *les beaux esprits se rencontrent*.

324. Massa, Françoise. "L'Écuyer chez Gil Vicente et ses frères en misère." *Nouvelles Études Luso–Brésiliennes*, IX (1973), 11–28.

Massa studies the character of the squire in Gil Vicente (*Quem tem farelos?*, *Inês Pereira*, *Farsa dos almocreves*), *Lazarillo de Tormes*, Quevedo (*Buscón*) and Calderón (*Alcalde de Zalamea*). The differences in this character's conception and treatment in Portugal and Spain reflect each country's social situation. Whereas, in the characters of the starving squire,

Vicente criticizes a decadent, parasitic class, useless and even dangerous to the country, the Spanish authors attempt a criticism of society at its foundations, of honor as social structure and of its emptiness. This difference in attitude between Vicente and the Spanish authors is explained by the fact that in Spain the sense of caste and the cult of honor had attained a force with no parallel in Portugal.

325. Nunes, Virgínia de Carvalho. "O homem e a vida em Gil Vicente." *Revista da Universidade de Aveiro/Letras*, I (1984), 237–48.

Gil Vicente's social criticism reflects his view of contemporary Portuguese life. This view is colored by pessimism, rather than disinterest or optimism, as a result of the turmoil and corruption which characterized society in sixteenth–century Portugal. Although the purpose of Vicente's criticism is moralistic, there is no Erasmian influence.

326. Ribeiro, Maria Aparecida. "Gil Vicente e a nostalgia da ordem." *Revista Brasileira de Língua e Literatura*, V (1980), 25–29.

Ribeiro defines "farce" as a sanctioning of illegality, as a second world upside down. The farce points to what could have been but was not. Through an examination of the *Auto da Barca do Inferno* and *Inês Pereira*, she arrives at the conclusion that Gil Vicente uses parody and the grotesque to cauterize his contemporary society, which was characterized by the opposition of the productive and the parasitic classes (rustics and craftsmen, on the one hand, nobility and clergy, on the other) and by a dissolution of customs. It is this social climate of "immorality" that is at the heart of Vicente's nostalgia for the social order that was lost.

327. Ribeiro, Maria Aparecida. "Todo-o-Mundo x Ninguém: a melancolia no teatro vicentino." *QP*, 9–10 (Spring–Autumn 1981), 235–63.

Gil Vicente's work is a rejection of literary standards, since he opts for dissonance, and of social standards, since his criticism affects all social strata. Ribeiro surveys the use of parody and the grotesque (caricature, the use of vulgar expressions, the mixture of styles, disguise, jokes) in several of Vicente's plays, and she finds that, together with laughter, there are vestiges of sadness and melancholy caused by a nostalgia for a time and a social order that are lost.

328. Roig, Adrien. "Le Théâtre de Gil Vicente et le voyage aux Indes." *Quadrant*, 7 (1990), 5–23.

The voyages to India provided Gil Vicente with the subject matter of the *Auto da Índia* and of the central part of the *Triunfo do Inverno*. In both plays, the playwright criticizes and satirizes the Indian adventure in all its facets (economical, political, social, religious) by presenting us with a view of a world upside down. In other plays, however (*Exortação da guerra, Côrtes de Júpiter, Auto dos Quatro Tempos* and, especially, the *Auto da Fama*), he offers a positive view of the voyages of discovery and Portugal's preeminent role. See also Roig's "Criticism and Satire on the Indian Voyage in the Theatre of Gil Vicente," *Hispanic Horizon*, 6–7 (1989), 17–20.

329. Simões, Manuel. "A crítica e o 'tipo' do judeu em Gil Vicente." *RaI*, 3 (December 1978), 3–19.

Gil Vicente's attitude toward the Jews was a negative one, judging by most of the references to them in nineteen of his plays. Those scholars who have come to the dramatist's defense in this respect (primarily António José Saraiva and Celso Lafer) have been wrong, since they based their conclusions more on the "Sermão" and the "Carta que o poeta mandou de Santarém a El–Rei Dom João III" than on Vicente's plays.

Gil Vicente and the Menippean Tradition

330. Suárez, José I[gnacio]. "The 'Journey Through Time and Space' in Gil Vicente's Drama." *Discurso Literário*, II (1984), 31–39.

Suárez examines several of Gil Vicente's plays (*Auto pastoril castelhano, Auto da sibila Cassandra, Comédia de Rubena, Auto da Alma*, the *Barcas, Exortação da guerra*) and concludes that the playwright, in a manner reminiscent of Menippean satire, tries to exemplify abstract ideas or truths by means of a "journey through time and space" technique.

331. Suárez, José I[gnacio]. "Master Gil's 'Experimental Fantasticality'—The Traditional Supernatural." *USF Language Quarterly*, XXV, 1–2 (Fall–Winter 1986), 28–30.

Since Gil Vicente has blended the satiric with the supernatural in his work, he must be viewed as a continuator of the ancient Menippean satiric tradition.

332. Suárez, José I[gnacio]. "Moral–Psychological Abnormalities in Gil Vicente." *Journal of Evolutionary Psychology*, IX, 1–2 (March 1988), 11–16.

In several of Gil Vicente's plays (*Auto da sibila Cassandra, Comédia de Rubena, Divisa da cidade de Coimbra, Velho da horta*) we encounter unusual moral and psychic states of characters (temporary delusion, disturbed emotional state bordering on suicide, incongruous behavior, radical and unexpected psychological change, respectively), which is reminiscent of the ancient Menippean satire.

333. Suárez, José I[gnacio]. "The Vicentine Oxymoron within the Serio–Comic Mode." *Romance Notes,* XXVIII (1987–88), 101–7.

In a manner reminiscent of Menippean satire, Gil Vicente brings together in his plays sharply antithetical elements.

334. Trigo, Salvato. "Gil Vicente e a teatralização das linguagens." *Revista da Faculdade de Letras—Línguas e Literaturas* (Porto), II Série, I (1984), 209–25.

Gil Vicente's theater is essentially a theater of languages which he succeeded in integrating, despite their phonic or semantic antagonisms, thus achieving an authentically carnivalesque and Menippean polyphony.

Love and Marriage

335. Hart, Thomas R. "Two Vicentine Heroines." *QP,* 9–10 (Spring–Autumn 1981), 33–53.

In both the *Auto da sibila Cassandra* and the *Auto de Inês Pereira* character is more important than action. At the beginning of each play, each protagonist is at odds with those around her, for her refusal to accept the values of her society: Cassandra refuses to marry Solomon, since she presumptuously believes that she is destined to be the Virgin, Inês rejects her social class and the sort of marriage expected of her. At the end of the plays, both protagonists get what they want but they no longer want what they wanted in the beginning; both are reintegrated into their respective societies whose values they had initially rejected.

336. Zimic, Stanislav. "Estudios sobre el teatro de Gil Vicente (obras de tema amoroso)." *Boletín de la Biblioteca de Menéndez Pelayo,* LVII (1981), 45–103, LVIII (1982), 5–66, LIX (1983), 11–78.

In an opening statement, Zimic proposes a new classification of Gil Vicente's works: *Obras de tema amoroso, Obras de devoción, Obras de crítica social y religiosa, Obras de circunstancias.* Then he proceeds to study six plays which belong to the first category and which represent well

Gil Vicente's view of love. *LVII*: in "*Don Duardos*: espiritualización de la aventura caballeresca" (pp. 47–103), Zimic discusses the symbolism of the play and the psychology of the love relationship between Don Duardos and Flérida. This extraordinary love relationship is the fundamental theme of the play and is of a platonic, spiritual, almost mystical nature. All episodes revolving around it (including that of Camilote) form a close-knit whole on a metaphorical level. To carry out his analysis of the play, Zimic makes extensive use of the *Song of Songs* which, he believes, must have inspired Gil Vicente, and of Fray Luis de León's *Exposición del Cantar de los cantares* which appears to be more an explication of *Dom Duardos* than of the *Song of Songs*, a fact which suggests that Vicente's play may have been used as a model for Fray Luis's commentary. *LVIII*: in "*La comedia del viudo*: supervivencia del espíritu" (pp. 3–37), Zimic makes a strong case for the dramatic unity of the play, disproving some critics' claim that the opening scene bears no relation to the true dramatic action centered on Don Rosvel's love for Paula and Melícia. He argues that the widower's personal problem constitutes the central action of the play and all other episodes serve only to reveal and develop it. The widower's lament and despair at the death of his wife, at the beginning of the play, turn into a happy praise of life at the end. In "*O velho da horta*: un amor quijotesco" (pp. 38–66), Zimic finds many parallels between the *velho* and Don Quijote. As an escape from his tempestuous married life, the *velho* delves in the *cancioneros* and sentimental novels, to the extent that he comes to consider himself a true courtly lover, in the same way that Don Quijote thought of himself as a knight errant after having read so many books of chivalry. Like Don Quijote, the *velho* reaches the point where he cannot distinguish between fiction and reality. Also like Don Quijote, he goes through three stages: normal mental state, obsession, and, finally, recovery of reason. *LIX*: in "*La Comédia de Rubena*: seducida y abandonada" (pp. 11–39), Zimic argues for an extraordinary unity in the play's structure, by interpreting the action and characters beyond the first scene as the products of Rubena's hallucinations. Cismena herself and her actions are nothing but the creation of her mother's imagination at a moment of profound emotional crisis. In "*Auto da Índia*: la casada infiel" (pp. 40–51), Zimic claims that the play is an ingenious dramatization of matrimonial disaster due principally to the husband's stupidity. In "Algunas consideraciones sobre la estructura dramática y el tiempo en el *Auto da Índia*" (pp. 52–58), Zimic argues that the apparent discrepancies in the time scheme of the play are due to the critics' failure to perceive the proper scene division. His interpretation shows that there is logic in the time scheme. In *"Auto de Inês Pereira*: la imperfecta casada" (pp. 59–74), Zimic asserts that the temperamental peculiarities and conduct of Inês, before and after her two marriages, are to be attributed, at least in part, to her home environment and the unreasonable restrictions imposed on her by her mother, whom the dramatist presents as unwise in her maternal role. Because she has had no contact with the world, Inês is incapable of distinguishing between her notion of an ideal husband and reality. Her final transformation from innocence and nobility to cynicism and vulgarity points to an essentially tragic conception of the play, in spite of the many comic episodes and details one finds in it. There is a "Bibliografía selecta" on pp. 75–78.

Miscellaneous

337. Anonymous. "V Centenário de Gil Vicente: espectáculos promovidos pero S.N.I." *Panorama*, IV Série, 15 (September 1965), 91–94.

On the occasion of the fifth centenary of the dramatist's presumed birth date, the Secretariado Nacional da Informação organized and promoted the staging of some of Vicente's plays (the complete *Comédia de Rubena* and scenes from nine others), under the direction of Francisco Ribeiro, in several Portuguese and Spanish cities, between 24 July and 2 September 1965. The account includes several photographs by João Martins of the plays staged.

338. *Barreto, Luís Filipe. "Gil Vicente e os descobrimentos." *História*, 25 (November 1980), 48–60.

339. Brandão, Fiama Hasse Pais. "Discretas releituras vicentinas." *Boletim de Filologia*, XXIX [*Homenagem a Manuel Rodrigues Lapa, II*] (1984), 205–13.

Explicates the Midwife's prayer in the *Comédia de Rubena* and line 107 of the *Auto da Índia*.

340. Carneiro, Alexandre Soares. "Aspectos do auto pastoril vicentino: sua importância, seu significado político e seu lugar na literatura de corte do período." *EPA*, 22 (July–December 1993), 65–87.

Gil Vicente's pastoral plays are a political act. Placed in a social milieu—the court—in which such an act was, to a certain extent, anticipated, it is worth remembering that there are some manifest elements which define this milieu and the meaning of the rules that govern it. As a prudent moralist counselor and great courtier, Vicente does not despise them. On the contrary, through the rhetorical and theatrical device of the humble shepherd, he can ingeniously use them to his advantage. This article forms part of Carneiro's Master's thesis (see no. 140 above).

341. Castello Branco, Lúcia. "Entes sobrenaturais no teatro vicentino: a reordenação do universo medieval." *MGSL*, 859 (19 March 1983), 1–2.

The dramatic tension of certain of Gil Vicente's plays rests upon the clashing of positive and negative forces, whether supernatural (angels and devils, witches and fairies, as in the *Auto da Alma, Autos das Barcas, Comédia de Rubena*) or human (civilized persons and wild men, philosopher and simpleton, etc., as in *Dom Duardos, A divisa da cidade de Coimbra, Floresta de enganos*). The final victory of the positive forces and the return to harmony give Vicente's theater a moralizing function consistent with the tenets of medieval Christian ideology.

342. Delgado Morales, Manuel. "Alegoría y tropología en tres autos de Navidad de Gil Vicente." *BHS*, LXV (1988), 39–48.

The *Auto pastoril castellano*, the *Auto de los Reyes Magos*, and the *Auto de los cuatro tiempos* (all three related to the Nativity cycle) can be described as tropological allegories, addressed to the particular believer so that he may accept Christ's message and adapt his behavior to the demands of the faith.

343. Duarte, Lélia Maria Parreira. "A ambigüidade em Gil Vicente." *MGSL*, 566 (6 August 1977), 6–7.

Through a brief survey of Vicentine criticism, Duarte shows that some scholars tend to view Gil Vicente's theater as a reflection of contemporary ideology, while others regard it as a symbolic whole of high tension. She examines the linguistic and social ambiguities in *Inês Pereira* and concludes that the dramatist oscillates between the evasion and the reflection of the reality of his times.

344. Gambetta, Agostinho Ferreira. "Gil Vicente moedeiro." *Boletim Cultural da Junta Distrital de Lisboa*, 65–66 (1966), 75–156.

The article is divided into three parts. *Part I* (pp. 76–111) reproduces Gambetta's "Gil Vicente moedeiro"—with a few additions—originally published in *Nummus*, VII, 23 (December 1962), 3–36 (see *GVB*, no. 503), in which he outlines and sides with Braamcamp Freire's arguments in support of the identification of Vicente, the dramatist, with Vicente, the *ourives–moedeiro*. Part *II* (pp. 112–22) consists of the text of Américo da Costa Ramalho's "A 'feia acção' de Gil Vicente" (pp. 112–17), reprinted from the *Diário de Notícias* (Lisboa, 27 July 1965)—see *GVB*, nos 352–53—followed by an exchange of letters on the subject between Gambetta and Ramalho. Part *III* (pp. 123–56) is a series of letters exchanged between Reis Brasil (i.e., José Gomes Braz) and Gambetta on the occasion of the former's edition of the first volume (1966) of a projected *Obras completas de Gil Vicente* (see *GVB*, no. 5). The exchange consists primarily of textual observations on numismatic matters.

345. *Geada, Maria Emília. "Alguns aspectos da técnica teatral vicentina." *Boletim do Teatro Universitário do Porto*, 4 (1966), 16–22.

346. Gonçalves, Joaquim Cerqueira. "Gil Vicente e a temporalidade." *Euphrosyne*, Nova Série, X (1980), 141–53.

Gil Vicente's theological affiliation seems to be Augustinian which, in principle, stimulates temporality. The dramatist is concerned with the ills of the present, but he also celebrates the political present of Portugal. While the religious past is definitive, the secular past, notwithstanding its exemplarity, is surpassed by the present which the dramatist celebrates. There is no attention to the future, no plan for society, in Gil Vicente's work.

347. Lancastre, Maria José de. "Hipótese de uma cronologia vicentina." *QP*, 9–10 (Spring–Autumn 1981), 13–18.

An attempt at the chronology of Gil Vicente's life and works.

348. Lisboa, J. L. "Autos de Vicente (a partir de uma conversa com Osório Mateus)." *Vértice*, II Série, 9 (December 1988), 107–08.

Describes the Vicente project undertaken by a group of scholars under the direction of Osório Mateus. See nos 178–83.

349. *Lopes, Óscar. "Gil Vicente, nosso contemporâneo." *Boletim do Teatro Universitário do Porto*, 4 (1966), 29–36.

349A. López Castro, Armando. "Gil Vicente y *La Celestina*." *Incipit*, XIII (1993), 105–19.

Similarities with the *Celestina* can be seen primarily in several of Gil Vicente's secular plays. Vicente imitates the type of the procuress and the various linguistic modes with which she expresses herself, but he does so guided by the fact that his plays are destined for a court audience.

350. Luz, Pedro Natal da. "A sociedade quinhentista na obra de Gil Vicente." *História*, 76 (February 1985), 56–79.

Gil Vicente tried to remain faithful to his social and cultural environment when he created his characters, and, therefore, his work can be used as a documentary source to draw a portrait of sixteenth–century Portuguese society. Luz attempts to do so by studying the social types represented in the *Auto da Barca do Inferno*.

351. Mateus, Osório. "Cinco autos de Gil Vicente." *RFLUL*, 5ª Série, 11 (April 1989), 109–10.

Mateus abstracts his doctoral thesis for the University of Lisbon (1987)—see above, no. 34. The five *autos* he discusses are: *São Martinho, Índia, Côrtes de Júpiter, Divisa da cidade de Coimbra*, and the "Carta a El-Rei D. João III" (1531).

352. Mateus, Osório. "Vicente 1586." *RFLUL*, 5ª Série, 13–14 (December 1990) [*Homenagem a José V. de Pina Martins*], 413–15.

Describes in detail the *Copilaçám* of 1586 and compares it to that of 1562. The 1586 edition, subjected to a more stringent Inquisitional censorship, has fewer texts and many more errors. But it includes a different version of *Dom Duardos*, a manifesto by the dramatist on his work, and many more woodcuts which are of interest both to the art of typography and to the history of the theater.

353. Mateus, Osório. "Vicente numa exposição." *CoL*, 86 (July 1985), 60–62.

Reviews Maria Leonor Carvalhão Buescu's edition of the *Copilaçám* (see above, no. 1) and Stephen Reckert's *Espírito e letra de Gil Vicente* (see above, no. 166), both of which were included in the seventeenth European Exhibit of Art, Science and Culture (Portugal 1983).

354. Moser, Fernando de Mello. "Gil Vicente e Shakespeare: funções do drama e processo de secularização da cultura." *QP*, 9–10 (Spring–Autumn 1981), 19–32.

In spite of the fact that both Vicente and Shakespeare were writing while the process of secularization of culture and institutions, initiated in the Middle Ages, was still in progress, a comparison of their works reveals the persistence of the entertaining and the didactic functions. The edifying function, a specific variant of the didactic, is more explicit in Vicente, since he wrote plays specifically intended for religious festivals, whereas in Shakespeare it is relegated to a secondary level of importance.

354A. Palla, Maria José. "Le Discours du costume chez Gil Vicente." *Nouvelle Revue du Seizième Siècle*, XIII, 2 (1995), 165–77.
    A reelaboration of parts of no. 164.

355. Palla, Maria José. "La Symbolique des poils et des cheveux au seizième siècle au Portugal à partir du théâtre de Gil Vicente." *Medieval Folklore*, II (Fall 1992), 67–86.
    The opposition of well–groomed and disorderly hair establishes the distance between city and country, between more civilized and less civilized status, between Christian and non-Christian beings. Well-trimmed and combed hair generally typifies the man of the city. Dirty and disheveled hair typifies the shepherd, the peasant in general, and the sorceress. The presence of a beard in men is indicative of virility and honor; its absence is indicative of purity. Baldness in women can be a sign of shame and folly. Pulling out one's hair (with reference to women) can be a sign of mourning, psychological disorder, or shame.

356. Parker, J[ack] H[orace]. "A encenação das comédias de Gil Vicente." *Revista Canadiense de Estudios Hispánicos*, VI (1982), 331–39.
    The staging of Gil Vicente's plays must have been more or less elaborate, according to the circumstances and place of their performance. His staging technique was most developed in the plays that formed part of court festivals. In spite of his close ties with the Middle Ages, Vicente was a very modern director in the staging of his plays.

357. *Pestana, Sebastião. "Gil Vicente 'embarracado'." *Revista de Portugal*, Número especial (1984), 5–8.

358. Pestana, Sebastião. "Temática gil–vicentina." *Boletim de Trabalhos Históricos* (Guimarães), XXXI (1980), 53–80.
    In Part I (pp. 53–58), Pestana points out similarities and differences in the strophic and rhymic patterns of the first two editions (1518 and 1562) of the *Auto da Barca do Inferno*. Part II (pp. 58–70) is a philological commentary on a scene from the *Juiz da Beira* involving Pêro

Marques, a squire and his manservant. Part III (pp. 70–80) is a slightly shorter version of no. 437.

359. Rossi, Nelson. "A propósito de Gil Vicente (Aula aos alunos da Escola de Teatro da Universidade da Bahia, em 14 de agôsto de 1956)." *Arquivos da Faculdade de Filosofia da Universidade de Bahia*, V (1956), 101–7.

Rossi repeats I. S. Révah's conclusions about the unreliability of the text of the *Copilaçám* of 1562 (see *GVB*, no. 88) and proposes a few corrections to the text of the *Auto da Cananeia*.

360. Stegagno Picchio, Luciana. "Editoriale." *QP*, 9–10 (Spring–Autumn 1981), 9–12.

Explains the dedication of the double issue (9–10) of this journal to Gil Vicente, and introduces the articles and texts of interviews contained in it (see nos 309, 315, 327, 335, 347, 354, 361–62, 407, 432, 439, 443, 445).

361. Stegagno Picchio, Luciana (interviewer). "Alberto Pimenta risponde a tre domande sul ruolo del Diavolo nel teatro di Gil Vicente." *QP*, 9–10 (Spring–Autumn 1981), 321–26.

Alberto Pimenta comments on Gil Vicente's devil and his own experience of having interpreted him on stage. He believes that Vicente's devil is of flesh and blood, like all medieval devils. Following the Middle Ages, the devil was replaced by human figures embodying his traditional attributes. There is a plate of Pimenta as Devil on p. 327.

362. Stegagno Picchio, Luciana (interviewer). "Paul Teyssier risponde a tre domande sulla lingua di Gil Vicente." *QP*, 9–10 (Spring–Autumn 1981), 301–8.

Teyssier evaluates his own book, *La Langue de Gil Vicente* (see *GVB*, no. 293), in the light of recent linguistic trends (structuralism, semiotics, generative grammar, etc.). He comments on the major contributions to the study of Gil Vicente since 1959, and points the direction that, in his opinion, Vicentine scholarship ought to take.

363. Suárez, José I[gnacio]. "The 'Scandalous' and the 'Eccentric' in Vicentine Playlets." *USF Language Quarterly*, XXIII, 1–2 (Fall–Winter 1984), 42–44.

Gil Vicente makes use of scandalous and eccentric situations and language (as in *Quem tem farelos?*, *Mofina Mendes*, *Inês Pereira*, *Auto da Índia*, *Sibila Cassandra*) in order to make his plays more human and set them apart from the official solemnity of court life.

364. Teyssier, Paul. "*Glória* dans Gil Vicente et Camões." *Iberica*, I (1977), 295–311.

The word "glória" and its derivatives occur 139 times in the works of Gil Vicente and 152 in Camões. Vicente uses the term predominantly in a religious sense (96 times to Camões's 12). Furthermore, Vicente, unlike Camões, does not confuse *glória* with *fama*, which makes him appear "comme un homme d'avant la Renaissance humaniste et italianisante."

b. INDIVIDUAL PLAYS

O monólogo do vaqueiro (1502)

See above, nos 223, 318.

Auto de São Martinho (1504)

365. Mateus, Osório. "'Teatro ao corpo de Deos'." *CoL*, 95 (January–February 1987), 13–20.

Mateus attempts to reconstruct the staging of the *Auto de São Martinho* in the church of Caldas da Raínha in 1504. He theorizes that Gil Vicente himself played the part of the Poor and also that the text of the playlet we now have is only a fragment: the *Copilaçám* of 1562 may only include the part enacted within the church. A second part, dealing with the miracle which occurs in the known story of St. Martin, may have been played outside, during the Corpus Christi procession.

See also above, no. 351.

Auto da Índia (1509)

366. Duarte, Denis M. Canellas de Castro. "La figura femenina central del *Auto da Índia*: ¿tipo individualizado o personaje dramático?" *RFR*, II (1984), 249–60.

The male characters of the play are mere social types, since they behave and speak as one would expect them to. The Maid is a highly individualized type with psychological features which set her apart from her male counterparts. Unlike them all, Constança is a complex dramatic character whose actions and words are unpredictable. In her character, the playwright offers us a complex and almost complete study in feminine psychology.

367. Ferreira, Ana Paula. "Intersecting Historical Performances: Gil Vicente's *Auto da Índia*." *Gestos*, 17 [*Postmodernism and Cultural Criticism: Chicano, Latin American, Luso–Brazilian, Spanish, and U.S. Latino Theaters*, ed. Anne J. Cruz and Ana Paula Ferreira] (April 1994), 99–113.

"What is being revisited in the *Auto da Índia* is the figural, performative quality of the play's mode of historical interpretation." The play speaks to the present "because it gestures toward its own theatricality as part and parcel of the theatricality of history."

368. Marques, Maria Aldina de Bessa Ferreira R. "Uma abordagem linguística do *Auto da Índia* de Gil Vicente (reflexão sobre o uso de cadeias anafóricas nominais)." *Diacrítica*, 8 (1993), 235–46.

Deals with the functioning of some of the paradigmatic options the speaker makes use of in order to establish, on the textual surface, referential continuity through anaphoric chains, and attempts to integrate these linguistic instruments into the category of "pró-formas nominais."

369. McGrady, Donald. "The Italian Sources of Gil Vicente's *Auto da Índia*." *RPhi*, XXX (1976–77), 321–30.

Giovanni Boccaccio's *Decamerone* (VIII, 7) and Masuccio Salernitano's *Il novellino* (novella 29).

370. Stathatos, Constantin C. "The Date of Gil Vicente's *Auto da Índia*." *L–BR*, XXXI, 1 (Summer 1994), 91–95.

In relatively recent times, there have been three attempts to challenge the date that the *editio princeps* of Gil Vicente's complete works assigns to the play (1509). Álvaro Júlio da Costa Pimpão claims that the play was first staged in 1508; Selma de Vieira Velho believes that it was composed between 1510 and 1511; finally, Mário Fiúza argues that it was performed in 1510. All three try to make the play conform to historical time and events, denying the dramatist the right to use history in accordance with his own aesthetic needs. The text itself does not support the conclusions proposed.

See also above, nos 150, 172, 191, 256, 279–80, 287, 292, 328, 336, 339, 351, 363, and below, nos 430, 619.

Auto pastoril castelhano (1509)

371. Lemos, Nuno Tovar de. "O *Auto pastoril castelhano* de Gil Vicente." *Brotéria*, CXXV (1987), 164–70.

    The theme of the play is the opposition of the two Vicentine worlds (*segres*) or of "Todo o mundo" and "Ninguém." Gil Terrón, the central character, is "Ninguém" while the other shepherds are "Todo o mundo." The scene of the games the shepherds play, which forms the transition between the two parts of the *auto*, illustrates the struggle between these two worlds. In the end, all shepherds hasten to appear before the newborn Jesus, the true, divine "Ninguém." Although it is again Gil who stands out, all shepherds unite in praising Mother and Son. There is peace and harmony finally.

372. Pestana, [Eduardo] Antonino. "O Natal madeirense num auto de Gil Vicente." *Das Artes e da História da Madeira*, V, 27 (1957), 1–9.

    There are strong similarities between the celebration of Christmas mass in the rural churches of the island of Madeira (the visit of the shepherds at midnight mass, the "pensação do Menino," etc.) and the second part of Gil Vicente's *Auto pastoril castelhano*.

See also above, nos 196, 223, 238, 245, 252, 267, 314, 330, 342.

Auto dos Reis Magos (1510)

See above, nos 267, 314, 342.

Auto da Fé (1510)

See above, nos 179.7, 196, 223, 267, 278.

O velho da horta (1512)

See above, nos 191, 193, 246, 249, 265, 281, 332, 336, and below, no. 476.

Auto dos Quatro Tempos (1513)

See above, nos 181.1, 223, 239, 267, 328, 342.

Auto da sibila Cassandra (1513)

373. Delgado Morales, Manuel. "La tropología navideña del *Auto de la Sibila Casandra.*" *Bulletin Hispanique*, LXXXVIII (1986), 190–201.
      The *auto* is a true moral sermon, in which Gil Vicente attempts to explain the theological and spiritual content of Christ's birth. He uses Cassandra as a symbol of a Christian whose presumption and egotism incapacitate him to receive the Messiah. Cassandra's vices distance her from God and make her an antithesis of Virgin Mary; her reintegration into the world of the redeemed occurs only after she has renounced her presumption. Vicente's moral sermon extends also to the Church itself, which is urged to imitate the Virgin and to combat injustice, greed, and presumptuousness. Delgado Morales goes on to defend the relevance of the final *villancico* to the rest of the play, arguing that the combat preached in both is of the same spiritual nature.

374. Ferré, Pere. "El romance *Él reguñir, yo regañar* en el *Auto de la Sibila Casandra* de Gil Vicente." *RevL*, Nova Série, 3 (1982–83), 55–67.
      Seeks parallels between some lines of Gil Vicente's *Cassandra* and the ballad "Él reguñir, yo regañar." If these parallels are valid, Vicente's glossed text antedates by more than a century the first documented version of the ballad theme.

375. McGinniss, Cheryl Folkins. "The Dance, a Metamorphic Symbol in Gil Vicente's *Auto de la sibila Casandra.*" *HR*, LII (1984), 163–68.
      The *Auto da sibila Cassandra* is structurally unified by four dances: *chacota, folía, chacota, danza baja*. These dances serve as symbols of change in scene and characterization, providing the visual means by which this change may be perceived. The concept of change is fundamental to the didactic purpose of the play which is summarized in the final *villancico*. This article is a reworking of pp. 84–97 of no. 238 above.

See also above, nos 158, 197, 223, 238, 262, 267, 287, 299, 314, 330, 332, 335, 363, and below, nos 524, 618.

Exortação da guerra (1514)

376. Bechara Filho, Gabriel. "Gil Vicente e a *Exortação da guerra.*" *Encontro*, 4 (July–December 1984), 61–69.

This play, more than any other, reflects the ideology of the Portuguese court, with which the dramatist identified and which he served. Since it is a work of political propaganda, everything is subordinated to the exaltation of the Portuguese Crown's foreign policy. The play also reveals the true dimension of Gil Vicente's vision of Portuguese expansion, which he conceives as an evangelical mission to propagate the faith rather than an attempt to conquer new ports of commerce.

See also above, nos 316, 328, 330.

Quem tem farelos? (1515)

377. Zimic, Stanislav. "Estudios sobre el teatro de Gil Vicente: obras de crítica social y religiosa. III: *Quem tem farelos?.*" *ActaN*, XVIII (1985), 11–29.

In the first part of the article (pp. 11–18), Zimic argues against the critics' tendency to view this play as lacking in unity and as inconclusive. In his view, all episodes are logically interrelated and the final scene of the altercation between Isabel and her mother is relevant to the development of the dramatic action. Although the satire of Aires Rosado occupies a central place in the farce, it is subordinated to a satire of a despotic mother who, determined to control and manipulate her daughter's life, imposes on her unreasonable modes of behavior which center on appearance only—as in Aires Rosado's case—with total disregard for Isabel's inclinations and personal dignity. This causes Isabel's vehement reaction and their final altercation points to hostile future relations between them. In the second part of the article (pp. 18–29), Zimic undertakes a detailed comparison of Aires Rosado and Apariço of Vicente's farce with their counterparts in chapter III of *Lazarillo de Tormes*, which reveals such extraordinary similarities in the general situations as well as in particular details (attitudes, psychology, verbal expression, narrative technique, etc.) that make it virtually impossible that chapter III of *Lazarillo* could have been written without access to *Quem tem farelos?*.

See also above, nos 172, 184, 281, 324, 363.

Auto de Mofina Mendes (1515)

378. Dias, Graça Silva. "De Gil Vicente a Camões: culturas e mentalidades." *Revista de História das Ideias*, II (1978–79), 355–400.
     An expanded version of no. 205 above.

379. Maleval, Maria do Amparo Tavares. "A propósito de um título
vicentino." *Boletim Informativo do Centro de Estudos Portugueses da
Universidade de São Paulo*, 2ª Série, 12 (July–December 1983), 31–39.
     The substitution of the secular title (*Auto de Mofina Mendes*) for the
sacred one (*Os mistérios da Virgem*) by the people reflects not so much
a modification as a variation of the original title, since Mofina Mendes,
at first sight an inversion of Virgin Mary, becomes like her in the end. The
two principal characters are portrayed as opposites: Mary as the *pastora*,
in the Biblical sense, who is concerned with her flock (mankind); Mofina
as the *anti–pastora*, who is completely unconcerned with the flock in her
charge; until they come to be alike in the condemnation of human material
values.

380. Melo, Gladstone Chaves de. "O prólogo do *Auto da Mofina Mendes*
de Gil Vicente: uma nova leitura." *Lusorama*, 8 (November 1988), 51–61.
     Melo disagrees with those scholars who find no sense in the first
eighty-five lines of the friar's speech, which opens the play. He argues that
the friar was Gil Vicente himself who simulated madness in order to say
sensible things. The friar's speech (a logical paraphrase of which is
provided) was meant to excoriate the Franciscan friars of Santarém, the
very same friars whom Gil Vicente had taken to task in his sermon.

381. Reyre, Dominique. "La Mystérieuse identité d'un personnage de Gil
Vicente: Mofina Mendes." *BEPB*, Nouvelle Série, XXXIX–XL (1978–79),
13–18.
     The episode of Mofina Mendes is more than a pastoral interlude
designed to entertain. The character of Mofina Mendes confers to it a
symbolic dimension. She brought about the loss of the flock (a symbol for
God's children who went astray before Redemption) and betrayed Paio
Vaz (as the Jews betrayed Christ, refusing to recognize him as the Savior).
Mofina Mendes also symbolizes the Jewish minority whose support the
kings sought to maintain, because they considered its skills necessary.

See also above, nos 195, 205, 215, 223, 244, 267, 287, 310, 314, 316, 363.

Autos das Barcas (*Inferno*: 1517, **Purgatório**: 1518, **Glória**: 1519)

382. Costa, Dalila Pereira da. "A trilogia de Gil Vicente." *Revista Letras* (Curitiba), 24 (December 1975), 121–38.

Gil Vicente's world view is both national and universal. In his three *Barcas*, he deals with the eternal and universal questions of human freedom, Good and Evil, and man's salvation. Of central importance is the question of whether salvation depends more on faith than works. This, in turn, brings forth the problem of predestination. Rather than reflect Lutheran preoccupations, the view expressed is based on divine grace which, though implying justification by faith, does not exclude man's collaboration.

383. Costa Fontes, Manuel da. "*Barca Bela* in the Portuguese Oral Tradition." *RPhi*, XXXVII (1983–84), 282–92.

Costa Fontes discusses the forms in which the ballad "Barca bela" has been preserved by the Portuguese oral tradition and establishes a connection between it and "Conde Arnaldos" and Gil Vicente's "Remando van remadores" (*Purgatório*), concluding that Vicente's ballad is not an original composition but, rather, was inspired by "Barca bela."

384. Mazzara, Richard A. "Two Modern *autos* by Ariano Suassuna." *Estudos Ibero–Americanos*, IV (1978), 109–12.

Makes some general comparative statements about Gil Vicente's *Barcas* and Ariano Suassuna's *Compadecida* and *A pena e a lei*, and tries to show the latter's indebtedness to the former.

385. *Moraes, Bernarda Bastos. "A percepção carnavalesca do mundo no *Auto da Barca do Inferno*, de Gil Vicente." *Arquivos*, III, 3 (1979), 57–66.

386. Palla e Carmo, Maria José. "Os objectos de civilização no *Auto da Barca* de Gil Vicente." *Boletim Cultural da Assembleia Distrital de Lisboa*, III Série, 88 (1982), 111–43.

The author examines the objects present in the *Auto da Barca do Inferno* (the boat, the boarding plank, the oars, the objects associated with the characters, etc.) and concludes that, although relatively small in number, their importance is fundamental, for, in addition to their technical function, they have a symbolic one. The author also finds that the play can be read on several levels of meaning: literal, moral, symbolic, and allegoric.

386A. Quiroz, Roderick S. "La gran teatralidad en el *Auto da barca da Gloria*, de Gil Vicente." *Entorno*, 36–37 (Summer–Fall 1995), 84–88.

This play is informed by multiple theatrical elements and by a structure of great esthetic appeal. For these reasons, a modern *mise-en-scène* of it could have almost the same impact as the audience felt in 1519.

387. Suárez, José I[gnacio]. "The Tri–levelled Structure of Gil Vicente's *Trilogia das Barcas*." *Michigan Academician*, XVI, 2 (Winter 1984), 179–85.

The trilogy of the *Barcas* resembles closely the trilevelled structure of the ancient Menippean satire, with Lucian's *Dialogues of the Dead* possibly serving as a genetic link between Menippus's satire and Vicente's drama.

See also above, nos 145, 156, 165, 172, 183.2, 191, 193, 196, 199–200, 204, 207, 209, 220, 222–23, 232, 236, 243, 247A, 249, 255–56, 260, 267–68, 272, 277, 282, 316, 319, 326, 330, 341, 350, 358, and below, nos 517, 568, 574, 579, 603, 609, 611.

Auto da Alma (1518)

388. Carter, Janet E. "From Sign to Symbol: The Structure of a Portuguese Allegory." *Portuguese Studies*, IV (1988), 1–15.

A structural analysis of the *Auto da Alma* reveals a surprising richness and perfection of form and meaning. There is a progression from signs to a structure of signs and symbols, and then, to pure symbols. The allegorical level is transmitted through signs, the tropological through the fusion of signs and symbols, and the anagogical through pure symbols.

389. Carvalho, Júlio. "Descrição da forma do gênero dramático: uma proposição à leitura do *Auto da Alma*." *Vozes*, LXV (1971), 149–52.

Carvalho summarizes the theory of dramatic form expounded by Steen Jansen in "Esquisse d'une théorie de la forme dramatique," *Langages*, 12 (December 1968), 71–93 (having to do with the distinction, in a dramatic work, between form and substance, which, in turn, is subordinated to that between expression and content), and attempts to apply it to an interpretation of the *Auto da Alma*.

390. Darbord, Bernard. "*Auto da Alma* de Gil Vicente: sur les deux composantes de l'allégorie." *ACCP*, XXIII [*Homenagem a Paul Teyssier*] (1987), 417–25.

In the play's allegory, metaphor is a convenient tool to refer to life here on earth. Metonymy, as used in the Devil's speech, serves to characterize temporal riches and pleasure, whereas in the speech of the Doctors of the Church, it describes the nearly ineffable, the mystery of the Redemption.

391. Fonseca, Pedro L. "O *Auto da Alma* de Gil Vicente e a semiose da moralidade II." *MGSL*, 1170 (28 September 1991), 2–6, and 1173 (25 January 1992), 2–5.

A semiotic approach to the play in the light of the theories of Genette, Greimas, Lekomtsev and others.

392. Matias, Elze M. H. Vonk. "'Modernidade' do *Auto da Alma* de Gil Vicente." *Brotéria*, CXIX (1984), 521–29.

The play offers a moral lesson and falls within the medieval traditions of the morality play and the didactic liturgical representation. Besides continuing previous traditions, it treats the Renaissance issue of free will, the defense of which shows Gil Vicente's "modernity."

See also above, nos 136, 142, 148, 195, 221, 330, 341, and below, nos 492, 517, 574, 611.

Auto da Fama (1520)

See above, nos 292, 303, 328.

Côrtes de Júpiter (1521)

See above, nos 328, 351, and below, nos 591, 598.

Comédia de Rubena (1521)

393. Albuquerque, Irene Truninger de. "A propósito da cena do eco na *Comédia de Rubena* de Gil Vicente." *RFLUL*, 5ª Série, 5 (April 1986), 33–42.

Albuquerque traces the development of repetitive forms from ancient Semitic poetry to the Peninsular literature of the early Renaissance. Then she analyzes the echo scene in the *Comédia de Rubena* and compares it to the episode of Narcissus and Echo in Ovid's *Metamorphoses* and to the echo scene in Juan del Encina's *Égloga de Plácida y Vitoriano*. She concludes that Vicente has put the dramatic and lyrical possibilities of the Ovidian legend to better use.

394. *Porto, Carlos. "Modernidad de un renacentista." *El Público*, 85 (1991), 94–95.
    Review of a staging of the *Comédia de Rubena*.

395. Salema, Maria Emília Freire. "Da realidade linguística de Mestre Gil Vicente, na *Comédia de Rubena*." *Panorama*, IV Série, 41 (March 1972), 19–27.
    Following Ferdinand de Saussure's tenets of linguistic structuralism, Salema examines the speech patterns in the play and finds that the dramatist has masterfully used speech as a tool for characterization.

See also above, nos 152, 155, 177, 181.10, 242, 249, 275, 285, 303, 306, 311, 330, 332, 336–37, 339, 341, and below, nos 533, 618.

Auto das ciganas (1521)

396. Zimic, Stanislav. "Estudios sobre el teatro de Gil Vicente: obras de crítica social. I: El sentido satírico del *Auto de las gitanas*." *ActaN*, XVI (1983), 3–12.
    This play may lack the structural complexity and wealth of satiric implications characteristic of the best Vicentine farces, but it still has a genuine theatrical atmosphere and considerable dramatic possibilities. Rather than being a mere audience, the court ladies, whose fortune the gypsies tell, are revealed in the end as the protagonists. In the written text of the play, they are not assigned speaking parts nor are their precise acts described, since they were not to play predetermined fictional roles but to react spontaneously; fired by their excitement over the gypsies' flattery and prophecies, they shed their inhibitions and, unconsciously, reveal their true selves and several uncomplimentary facets of their personalities. The playwright has anticipated their reactions correctly and, in addition to satirizing their superstitious beliefs in the prophecies of the gypsies, he compels the reader to view them as persons of very questionable inclinations.

See also above, no. 206, and below, nos 537, 618.

Tragicomédia de Dom Duardos (1522)

397. Brandão, Fiama Hasse Pais. "Em torno do Infante Dom Luís e de Luís de Camões." *Arquipélago*, 3 (January 1981), 157–66.

Brandão sides with the first bibliographers who attributed *Dom Duardos* to the Infante Dom Luís. The play contains elements typical of the philosophy of the Illuminati which are absent from other Vicentine plays. Dom Luís and Camões were close philosophically, which accounts for the affinities between *Dom Duardos* and the *Auto de Filodemo*.

398. Calderón Calderón, Manuel. "La transmisión del Romance de Flérida y Don Duardos." *Incipit*, XI (1991), 107–23 plus 2 pages of tables.

A study of the modifications (verbal, prosodic, discursive, formal, and of content) which have occurred in the process of transmission—both oral and written—of the concluding *romance* of *Dom Duardos*. The two decisive factors in these modifications are the language employed and the remembrance of the play.

399. Carvalho, Mário Vieira de. "Do teatro de Gil Vicente ao teatro de Wagner (uma leitura do libreto de *D. Duardos e Flérida*, de F. Lopes–Graça)." *Vértice*, XLIII, 454 (May–June 1983), 29–39.

Carvalho discusses the social aspects of the love relationship between Dom Duardos and Flérida (Flérida does not fall in love with the rustic as such, but with the rustic of the speech and manners of a prince). He then lists parallel motifs between the libretto of *Dom Duardos*—elaborated by F. Lopes–Graça for his cantata–melodrama—and Wagner's *Tristan und Isolde*, *Lohengrin*, and *Götterdämmerung*.

400. Costa Fontes, Manuel da. "*D. Duardos* in the Portuguese Oral Tradition." *RPhi*, XXX (1976–77), 589–608.

The ballad "en el mes era de abril," with which *Dom Duardos* concludes, has survived in the Portuguese oral tradition. Costa Fontes studies several versions of it collected in continental Portugal as well as the Azores and Madeira, and finds that the latter differ significantly from the former.

401. Costa Fontes, Manuel da. "*Lizarda*: A Rare Vicentine Ballad in California." *RPhi*, XXXII (1978–79), 308–14.

Discusses two versions of "Lizarda"—collected from Portuguese immigrants in California—in which portions of *Dom Duardos* have survived in oral tradition.

402. Costa Fontes, Manuel da. "Novas versões de *Flérida* na tradição oral transmontana." *RevL*, Nova Série, 2 (1981), 17–29.

Costa Fontes compares seven oral versions of the ballad of "Flérida," which he collected in the district of Bragança in 1980, with the original Vicentine text and other versions from the oral tradition already published. He concludes that through four and a half centuries of oral transmission this ballad has suffered certain changes in form as well as content.

403. Daniels, Marie Cort. "*Falsos paños*: Lineage and Dress in Gil Vicente's *Don Duardos*." *Revista de Estudios Hispánicos* (Río Piedras, P.R.), IX (1982), 47–54.

Gil Vicente has transformed his chivalric source for this play (*Primaleón*) into an allegory of identity. At the thematic focus of the play is the philosophical and social dilemma of the correspondence between *linaje* and *ser* in the Lisbon of Vicente's time. Don Duardos, disguised as a peasant in *viles paños*, becomes a spokesman for the *converso* minority. His insistence that he be accepted for himself expresses a generalized plea for men to be accepted for what they are, regardless of the social roles assigned to them. Flérida's reluctance to accept him, dressed in his *falsos paños*, is indicative of the pressures which obstructed social integration.

404. Madrigal, José A. "Una revalorización del caballero salvaje en *La Tragicomedia de Don Duardos* (Gil Vicente)." *Romance Notes*, XXVI (1985–86), 125–28.

Gil Vicente was the first to employ the wild man as a dramatic character. Camilote, the ugly and grotesque wild knight who sees beauty and perfection in ugliness and whose love for ugly Maimonda remains unrequited, serves as a mirror to Don Duardos and Flérida. By introducing such a character, the playwright was perhaps suggesting to Flérida that she ought to love Don Duardos even though he might be a humble gardener, and to Don Duardos that a test of true love was the willingness to love a lady without expecting this love to be returned. In their ultimate acceptance of true love, Don Duardos and Flérida imitate Camilote's philosophy and conduct.

405. Martín Gaite, Carmen. "Una reelaboración de *Don Duardos.*" *Primer Acto*, 2ª época, 182 (December 1979), 107–10.

The author explains how she went about adapting Gil Vicente's play for C.E.N.I.N.A.T. Her adaptation was staged twice in the Fall of 1979 at San Carlos del Valle and at the Church of San Agustín (Almagro) under the direction of José María Morera. A shorter version of this article, titled "*Don Duardos* de Gil Vicente," appeared in *Pipirijaina*, XI (1979), 16–17.

See also above, nos 157–58, 171, 181.4, 217, 219, 225, 262–64, 272, 309, 315, 336, 341, 352, and below, nos 456, 524, 531, 541, 566, 603.

Auto de Inês Pereira (1523)

406. Bismut, R[oger]. "Note vicentine: sur l'épisode final de l'*Auto de Inês Pereira.*" *BEPB*, Nouvelle Série, XXXV–XXXVI (1974–75), 247–51.

Discusses similarities between Gil Vicente's play and *Tristan et Yseult.*

407. Carvalho, Ilka V. de. "A linguagem sólida de *Inês Pereira.*" *QP*, 9–10 (Spring–Autumn 1981), 109–43.

An examination of the play as theatrical spectacle by focusing on its physical language (stage settings, costumes and accessories, gestures and movement on stage, music). The article is a slightly revised version of a chapter from the author's doctoral thesis (see no. 143 above).

408. Frèches, Claude–Henri. "Le Dénouement de la *Farce d'Inês Pereira.*" *Cahiers d'Études Romanes*, 7 (1982), 103–06.

Examines the concluding passage of the play both in terms of staging and of meaning, and concludes that Gil Vicente reveals once again his ties with medieval popular literature by dramatizing the proverb "mais quero asno que me leve que cavalo que me derrube" in two moments: Inês's matrimonial failure with the squire (the horse that throws one down) and her success with a born cuckold (the ass that carries one).

409. Guerreiro, M. Viegas. "Gil Vicente e os motivos populares: um conto na *Farsa de Inês Pereira.*" *RevL*, Nova Série, 2 (1981), 31–60.

By comparing eleven versions of the popular tale of Domingos Ovelha, from various areas of Portugal and Galicia, with the last episode of *Inês Pereira*, Guerreiro shows how masterfully Gil Vicente has exploited popular tradition to serve his own dramatic purpose. Two versions of the tale are quoted in the body of the article, whereas the remaining nine are found in an appendix (pp. 51–60). A plate is also included on p. 61.

410. Massa, Françoise. "Types et personnages dans la farce de *Inês Pereira*." *Études Portugaises et Brésiliennes*, Nouvelle Série, V (1983), 7–22.

Thanks to the truth with which the playwright has endowed the characters of this play, the modern spectator sees in them a reflection of his own problems and aspirations. It is not necessary to be familiar with the customs and problems of Gil Vicente's times to appreciate the play.

411. Pestana, Sebastião. "Do núcleo da *Farsa de Inês Pereira* de Gil Vicente." *Revista dos Cursos de Letras* (Sá da Bandeira, Angola), I (1974), 5–15.

Deals with the proverb "mais quero asno que me leve, que cavalo que me derrube" which served as point of departure for the play. The article was reprinted in vol. II of Pestana's *Estudos gil–vicentinos* (Sá da Bandeira: Tip. Imprex, 1975), pp. 47–54 (see *GVB*, no. 277).

412. Roig, Adrien. "La Duplicité, fondement de la farce d'*Inês Pereira* de Gil Vicente." *Revista da Universidade de Coimbra*, XXX (1983), 347–67.

Gil Vicente has succeeded admirably in blending a variety of comic elements in *Inês Pereira*. He has structured the play on duplicity of characters and their words. Duplicity runs throughout the play and involves all characters with the exception of Inês's mother, who represents sincerity and good sense in her desire to see her daughter happy in a good marriage, and Pêro Marques, who becomes the victim of Inês and her hermit lover. Except for the squire, all characters who use duplicity derive some profit. The playwright has presented us with a world upside–down, in which no one keeps one's place: all characters, with the two exceptions mentioned, have objectives which are contrary to their thoughts and sentiments. The play's humor rests upon this opposition between internal real nature and external deceptive appearance.

See also above, nos 143, 147, 151, 172, 198, 222, 227, 281, 303, 324, 326, 335–36, 343, 363, and below, nos 524, 543, 579, 603, 618.

Auto pastoril português (1523)

See above, nos 223, 267, 293, 303, 310, 314.

Tragicomédia de Amadis de Gaula (1523)

413. Zimic, Stanislav. "*Amadis de Gaula* de Gil Vicente: de la novela al drama." *Boletín de la Biblioteca de Menéndez Pelayo*, LXIII (1987), 35–56.

Gil Vicente has chosen as the central theme of his dramatization of the story of Amadis the heroic aspect of the latter's love for Oriana. There is no textual evidence, as some scholars believe, that the playwright intended either to portray Amadis as childishly ostentatious and gossipy regarding his love, or that he treated Amadis's knightly exploits in a burlesque fashion.

See also above, nos 182.6, 272, and below, nos 492, 517, 525, 566.

Comédia do viúvo (1524)

See above, nos 152, 177, 191, 206, 238, 303, 306, 309, 311, 336.

Frágua de Amor (1524)

See above, nos 258–59, 316.

Farsa dos físicos (1524)

414. Bismut, Roger. "Notes camoniennes." *BEPB*, Nouvelle Série, XXXV–XXXVI (1974–75), 253–58.

In Note II (pp. 255–57), Bismut shows that Camões borrowed from Gil Vicente the three–line *mote* "Quem ora soubesse..." to begin a *cantiga*. The lines derive from the final scene of the *Farsa dos físicos*. Bismut also argues that Camões's *cantiga* helps to establish 1512 (end of winter) as the year in which the *Farsa dos físicos* was staged.

415. Frèches, Claude–Henri. "Satire et morale dans l'*Auto dos físicos*." *BEPB*, Nouvelle Série, XLI (1980), 89–98.

In this play, Gil Vicente aims his satiric barbs at the enamoured priest and the four doctors who are powerless to cure his malady. In doing so, the playwright seeks to produce laughter rather than avenge the morality offended by the priest or support the marriage of clergymen.

See also above, nos 259, 314, 316, and below, no. 585.

O Juiz da Beira (1525 or 1526)

416. Dantas, Francisco José Costa. "Comicidade e humanismo na *Farsa do Juiz da Beira*." *EPA*, 4 (1984), 98–131.
    A reading of the play in the light of Henri Bergson's theories on laughter. Gil Vicente avails himself of the most legitimate comic devices in the production of laughter: the parodic inversion of the ceremonial aspect of the court hearings; the transformation of what is solemn and formal into familiar; of what is essential into formal; the automatic repetition of witty responses; the process of inversion by which plaintiffs turn into defendants, etc.

417. Sousa, Carlos Mendes de. "*O Juiz da Beira*—unidade na pluralidade." *Cadernos de Literatura*, 17 (April 1984), 47–57.
    The play is not a mere succession of unconnected scenes. Justice is the dominant thematic force and Pêro Marques, the peasant judge, its key character. Besides serving as judge, Pêro Marques is the object of judgment. Hence the implicit need of a moral and juridical defense on his part, having to do with his professional integrity. His defense rests on the good sense of the sentences he pronounces. It is on these apparently paradoxical sentences that the internal unity of the play is based.

418. Zimic, Stanislav. "[Estudios sobre el teatro de Gil Vicente: obras de crítica social y religiosa.] IV: *O Juiz da Beira*." *ActaN*, XVIII (1985), 31–47.
    In spite of Pêro Marques's limited mental capacity, all his judgments, in his audience before the King, are correct and wise because they are based on a pinch of common sense and an elementary understanding of reality. Vicente's satire is not aimed at country judges but, implicitly, at the court judges, who were given to an unthinking and mechanical application of the letter of the *Ordenações* with no concern for common sense and reality.

See also above, nos 172, 190–91, 202, 222, 319, 358, and below, no. 543.

Templo de Apolo (1526)

See above, no. 240, and below, no. 462.

Auto da feira (1526)

419. Alçada, João Nuno. "O Saque de Roma, *caput/coda mundi* e o *Auto da Feira.*" *ACCP*, XXIV (1988), 149–305 (includes plates, too).

By inserting the study of the *Auto da feira* in the political, religious and cultural context in which the sack of Rome took place, Alçada shows that there is internal thematic coherence in the play, based on several subtle elements by which Gil Vicente alludes to this historical event. Interpreting its causes next, with the aid of several contemporary sources, the author draws the evident conclusions in order to reinforce the moral allegory presented to the spectators.

Review (of the article):

a. G. M., *Moreana*, XXIX, 109 (March 1992), 112.

See also above, nos 149, 179.9, 223, 229, 256, 267, 294, 303, 314, 323.

Nau de amores (1527)

420. Martins, Mário. "*Tristán de Leonis* e a *Nau d'amores* de Gil Vicente.*" *Brotéria*, CXX (1985), 167–72.

The *Nau de amores* may have been inspired in the legend of Tristan and Yseult as set forth in the Spanish version of the *Libro del esforçado cavallero don Tristán de Leonís y de sus grandes hechos en armas* (Valladolid, 1501). The last part of this romance was probably the source of the melancholy which envelops love in Vicente's play. The *Nau de amores* is not a frivolous play; its characters symbolize mankind in search of the Isle of Fortune.

421. Rodrigues, Maria Idalina Resina. "Lisboa, um Rei que regressa e uma *Nao d'Amores.*" *ACCP*, XXIII [*Homenagem a Paul Teyssier*] (1987), 427–59.

Gil Vicente had the *Nao de amores* staged as part of the ceremonies welcoming D. João III and D. Catarina to Lisbon in 1527 following a long absence caused by the plague in the capital. The play is pure entertainment but it is also important for its interest to the historian of royal receptions, the information it provides about the dramatist's position vis–à–vis the Crown's expansionist policy, and the fact that it helps to show the aesthetic direction the playwright followed after 1521. Rodrigues then engages in an analysis of the play, comparing it frequently with the *Autos das Barcas* which belong to an earlier period of Vicente's art.

See also above, nos 178.3, 258, 269, 314.

Comédia sobre a divisa da cidade de Coimbra (1527)

422. Mateus, Osório. "Ou como do vivo a ũa imagem." *Cadernos de Literatura*, 16 (December 1983), 28–36.

Mateus examines the structure of the *Comédia sobre a divisa da cidade de Coimbra* and tries to recreate the details surrounding its staging in a palace of Coimbra in 1527.

See also above, nos 177, 225, 306, 311, 332, 341, 351.

Farsa dos almocreves (1527)

423. Pestana, Sebastião. "Uma parte do diálogo Pêro Vaz—Vasco Afonso da *Farsa dos Almocreves* de Gil Vicente." *Revista da Biblioteca Nacional de Lisboa*, I (1981), 223–52.

Pestana quotes the last part of the dialogue between Pêro Vaz and Vasco Afonso and comments briefly on the temperamental differences of the two characters. He analyzes the passage metrically and discusses the terms *ta, gasalhado, molher, magoar, yeramaa, apre, arre, dix, uxtix, vendeyro, mu, chão, pesar, desingular, perder, Jam Diz, noo, soo, meyjoada, pequice, Cornaga, Cucanha.*

424. Zimic, Stanislav. "[Estudios sobre el teatro de Gil Vicente: obras de crítica social.] II: La *Farsa dos almocreves* de Gil Vicente: relevancia dramática y moral del título." *ActaN*, XVI (1983), 13–23.

Unlike most critics, Zimic feels that the title of the play is fitting both in terms of its dramatic structure and its satirical intention. Just as Pêro, the professional carrier, treats his mule, the Nobleman treats his servitors and they—except for the Goldsmith—their own victims. The playwright, then, has used the term *almocreves* to refer symbolically to several characters. The Nobleman is obviously the "carrier" par excellence and is the principal target of the play's satire, for his ridiculous vanity and his cynical and brutal exploitation of the others. The play presents an altogether pessimistic view of the entire Portuguese society.

See also above, nos 293, 303, 316, 324, and below, nos 517, 547.

Tragicomédia pastoril da Serra da Estrêla (1527)

See above, no. 303.

Breve sumário da história de Deus (1527)

425. Moser, Fernando de Melo. "O *Breve sumário da história de Deus*: sua unidade e equilíbrio tectónico." *Ocidente*, Número Especial (1981), 5–11.

The *auto* condenses theological history from Creation to Resurrection admirably. Though the content is immutable in its essentials, as part of the Christian tradition, the dramatist has excelled in his treatment of it thanks to his masterful selection, dramatic structure, and lyrical expression.

426. Ribeiro, José António Pinto. "*Breve sumário da história de Deus*: uma visão augustiniana da História?" *Revista da Universidade de Aveiro/Letras*, I (1984), 249–85.

In the play, which falls within the tradition of medieval *summae*, humanity has access to salvation. The exercise of free will, which will determine the separation of the just from the bad, is safeguarded. There is a conscious periodization and a meticulous selection of figures. There is a linear conception of irreversible time; all events lead to the resurrection of Christ. Thus it can be argued that the play constitutes a theological vision of history. Furthermore, one can perceive an affinity between Vicente's interpretation of history and the Augustinian conception as expressed in *De civitate Dei*, with which the dramatist was certainly familiar.

See also above, nos 211, 230, 244, 256, 268, 314, 321, and below, nos 517, 558.

Diálogo sobre a ressurreição de Cristo (1527)

427. Zacherl, Elisabeth. "Der Jude in Gil Vicentes *Diálogo sobre a ressurreição*." *Aufsätze zur Portugiesischen Kulturgeschichte*, XV (1978), 83–89.

In his works, Gil Vicente is both a critic and a defender of Jews. While he directs his criticism against errors and weaknesses, he calls for greater religious tolerance. In the *Diálogo sobre a ressurreição*, the Jew is portrayed not as the man who cannot believe but rather as the man who will not, since he prefers earthly goods to God. Zacherl also examines the linguistic peculiarities of the Jews in the play.

See also above, nos 222, 321.

Auto das fadas (1527)

428. Alçada, João Nuno. "Charivari, Rébus e heresia na fala do Diabo picardo do *Auto das fadas.*" *QP*, 15–24 (1984–88), 51–147.
   Alçada rereads the dialogue between the sorceress Genebra Pereira and the Devil she has conjured up, in the light of several manifestations of medieval cultural tradition (*charivari*, carnival, *sotties*, morality plays). Deciphering the *rebus* of the Devil's speech in the dialect of Picardy, he finds that Genebra Pereira is a personification of the Church and that, in addressing her, the Devil delivers a violent verbal attack, denouncing the abuses committed.

See also above, nos 155, 212, 249, and below, nos 547, 618.

Auto da festa (1527 or 1528)

See above, nos 225, 287, 303, and below, nos 462, 537.

O triunfo do Inverno (1529)

429. Palla, Maria José. "O *Triunfo do Inverno* de Gil Vicente." *Vértice*, 2ª Série, 44 (November 1991), 67–76.
   This play, which celebrates time and the seasons of the year, is one of contrasts: cold and hot, old age and youth. It was designed to commemorate the birth of a princess, a moment of fertility. Vicente tries to bring into relief cyclical and cosmic time. Man is conditioned on cosmic time, that of the seasons of the year, and linear time, that of human life. The dramatist was inspired by a variety of traditions and other sources in giving form to this original work.

430. Simões, Manuel. "Disforia e euforia em *Triunfo do Inverno* de Gil Vicente." *RaI*, 26 (September 1986), 3–15.
   In the *Auto da Índia* and the *Triunfo do Inverno*, Gil Vicente is at odds with the prevalent ideology of Portuguese expansion in the East. The scene of the tempest, which occupies the central position in the *Triunfo*

do Inverno, has a caricaturesque and satiric function. In it, the dramatist questions—through the incompetence of the pilots—the ships and the organization of the expeditions to India. Even the second part of the play (the "triunfo do Verão") ends in abeyance, in spite of Vicente's explicit intention to create a festive atmosphere.

See also above, nos 145, 163, 181.6, 190, 210, 225, 271, 328.

O clérigo da Beira (1529 or 1530)

431. Frèches, Claude-Henri. "*O clérigo da Beira*, source d'informations." *ACCP*, XIX (1983), 501–20.
　　Under the pretext of entertainment, the *Clérigo da Beira* casts a caustic glance at the clergy, the peasantry, and the slaves. Gil Vicente brings to light the role of money in Portugal around the second quarter of the sixteenth century. The lower clergy cry famine. The *fidalgos aprendizes* are hard up and live by their own wits. Former slaves become vagabonds and thieves. The nobles are lured by profit and the rich want to become richer.

432. Peloso, Silvano. "Gil Vicente, Sá de Miranda e il *Clérigo da Beira*: una farsa per molte occasioni." *QP*, 9–10 (Spring–Autumn 1981), 199–234.
　　Disproves Anselmo Braamcamp Freire's contention (see *GVB*, no. 234) that Vicente composed the *Clérigo da Beira* to retaliate against Sá de Miranda who, in his turn, had criticized Vicente's *Comédia sobre a divisa da cidade de Coimbra* and had composed his *Fábula de Mondego* as a response to Vicente's play. Peloso proposes 1526 as the date of performance of the *Clérigo da Beira*. He also favors the hypothesis that the *Auto de Pedreanes*, mentioned in the Index of 1551, was not, as is generally believed, the same play as the *Clérigo da Beira* but a sequel of it.

See also above, nos 249, 258, 316.

Jubileu de Amor (1531)

See above, nos 171, 183.8.

Auto da Lusitânia (1532)

433. Alçada, João Nuno. "Para um novo significado da presença de *Todo o Mundo* e *Ninguém* no *Auto da Lusitânia*." *ACCP*, XXI (1985), 199–271.

Taking as a point of departure Carolina Michaëlis's assertion that *Todo o Mundo* and *Ninguém* are "duas figuras internacionais pré–existentes" (see *GVB*, no. 267), Alçada offers a new reading of the play's meaning, relying on the cultural tradition of Northern Europe, to which both *Niemand* and *Elck* belong. This tradition could have been transmitted via Antwerp. There are literary and iconographic references to it, in the context of the Reformation and in Bosch and Breughel respectively. *Ninguém=Niemand* (identified with the Jews of the Diaspora) and *Todo o Mundo=Elck* (identified with the ambition for power and wealth) are the central figures of the *auto* (considered a triptych). They explain the two worlds of Lediça (Introduction) and Lusitânia (Farce) which are parallel but, at the same time, antagonistic in terms of Christian moral values according to Erasmus's vision: *Ninguém* is the wise and virtuous fool that stands in opposition to *Todo o Mundo* (collective for every man), who considers virtue a useless folly. See also no. 187.

434. Lemaire, Ria. "Hombres y mujeres en el umbral de los tiempos modernos." *Foro Hispánico*, V [*La mujer en la literatura hispánica de la Edad Media y el Siglo de Oro*, ed. Rina Walthaus (Amsterdam: Rodopi, 1993)], 57–69.

The case of the Jewish family of the first part of the *Auto da Lusitânia* demonstrates the profound economic and social changes which accompanied the transition from the Middle Ages to the modern age in Portugal. Whereas the parents, Juda and Hecer, still live on the threshold of modern times, their children, Lediça and Samuel, have already crossed it.

See also above, nos 145–46, 178.1, 222, 284, 288, 298, 310.

Romagem de agravados (1533)

435. Castelo–Branco, Fernando. "O 'Ilheo de Peniche' na *Romagem de agravados* de Gil Vicente." *ACCP*, XI (1977), 283–90.

Castelo–Branco corrects Paul Teyssier's belief (see *GVB*, no. 166) that the reference to the *Ilhéu de Peniche* was a slip on Vicente's part.

Although Peniche ceased to be an island long before Vicente's time, it continued to be referred to as such in documents well into the seventeenth century. Castelo–Branco also adds that the dramatist's intention here is to ridicule the ambitions of Frei Narciso, who aspires to becoming bishop of the islet.

436. Girodon, Jean. "A propos d'un *auto* de Gil Vicente, *Romagem dos agravados.*" *ACCP*, XV (1980), 541–50.

Girodon discusses the play's title and its symbolic meaning (*romagem* stands for life on earth, *romaria* for the beyond). He proceeds to study the play's structure, and he discovers a surprising symmetry in its bipartite division, the number of lines per part, the conclusion of each part in song and dance, and in the distribution of characters by class (nobility, clergy, peasantry) and sex (seven men and seven women).

437. Pestana, Sebastião. "Um troço do diálogo 'Cerro Ventoso—Frei Narciso' da *Romagem de Agravados* de Gil Vicente." *ACCP*, XVII (1982), 829–43.

Quotes a twenty–line passage from the dialogue between Cerro Ventoso and Frei Narciso, analyzes it metrically, provides a commentary on its vocabulary, and comments briefly on the two characters. See also no. 358 above.

438. *Pestana, Sebastião. "Um verso da *Romagem de Agravados* de Gil Vicente." *Revista de Portugal*, Número especial (1983), 5–11.

See also above, nos 171, 190, 196, 287, 297, 316, and below, no. 590.

Auto da Cananeia (1534)

See above, nos 196, 230, 303, 359, and below, no. 476.

Floresta de enganos (1536)

See above, nos 177, 182.9, 248, 306, 310–11, 341.

c. MISCELLANEOUS WORKS AND THE CUSTÓDIA DE BELÉM

439. Alçada, João Nuno. "Sobre o Epitáfio e Sepultura de Gil Vicente." *QP*, 9–10 (Spring–Autumn 1981), 145–98.

Alçada examines Gil Vicente's epitaph and the drawing of the tombstone, as they appear in the *Copilaçám*. His detailed analysis of the intrinsic meanings of the words and the symbolism of the decorative motifs which surround them leads him to the conclusion that the epitaph is a *speculum morale* of Vicente's entire work.

440. Couto, João. "A Custódia de Belém." *Palestra*, 13 (1962), 132–35.

A detailed description of the masterpiece and its restoration in the first half of this century.

441. David–Peyre, Yvonne. "Maria Parda, témoin de son temps." *ACCP*, XXVIII (1990), 437–46.

1522, the year in which the *Pranto de Maria Parda* was written, was a calamitous one for Lisbon because of the plague, drought, famine, and the death of Manuel I. It is in this context, familiar to all Portuguese, that Gil Vicente has placed Maria Parda, a poor, starving, dipsomaniac, and syphilitic mulatto prostitute. He has chosen to focus on Maria Parda's marginal life in order to render everyone's daily life more tolerable through cathartic laughter. Irreverence and cynicism, however, serve only as a disguise to an underlying meditation in the manner of *ubi sunt?* and *sic transit gloria mundi.*

442. Gonçalves, António Manuel. "A custódia de Belém." *Panorama*, III Série, 11 (September 1958), 9 pp. with 15 plates (this issue lacks pagination).

Detailed description of the work and its history.

443. Mateus, Osório. "Vicente, Abrantes, 1506." *QP*, 9–10 (Spring–Autumn 1981), 89–108.

The "Sermão" of Abrantes is different from ordinary sermons. Whereas sermons are normally in prose and are delivered in church by religious preachers, Vicente's is in verse and is given by a layman (Vicente himself in a preacher's habit) in the Queen's chamber. Vicente's "Sermão" is metaphor, it is theater.

444. Mateus, Osório. "Vicente, Santarém, 1531." *CoL*, 71 (January 1983), 16–23.

In a letter to D. João III, on the occasion of the earthquake which shook Portugal on 26 January 1531 and which, according to the friars of Santarém, was caused by the sins of the *conversos*, Gil Vicente includes the statement: "E porém saberá V. A. que este auto foi de tanto seu serviço. . . ." Mateus takes the term *auto* as point of departure to argue that this letter is a summary version of a theatrical action which Vicente presented before the friars in the Church of São Francisco in Santarém.

445. Periñán, Blanca. "Una lectura del 'Sermam pregado em Abrantes'." *QP*, 9–10 (Spring–Autumn 1981), 55–88.

Periñán analyzes in detail the form and content of the "Sermão" on the basis of the *artes praedicandi*. She finds that its unity lies in the oxymoron of wise madness. On the surface, the sermon is an entertaining parody of preachers, but it also reveals a hostile attitude toward hollow lucubrations and arbitrary interpretations and toward the Church's excessive vigor and irrationality in dealing with practical moral problems. There are echoes of Erasmus in this work, though this is not to say that Vicente was necessarily influenced by him.

446. Silva, Carlos H. do C. "Sobre o 'Sermão de Abrantes:' dos aspectos da parenética formal a uma sageza implícita em Gil Vicente." *Itinerarium*, 142 (January–April 1992), 101–24.

The overall structure of the "Sermão" is informed by dialectic and sapiential coherence.

447. *Silva, José da. "Uma prédica de Gil Vicente a certos frades alarmistas." *Diário Popular* (Lisboa), 25 January 1983.

448. Silva, Nuno Vassallo e. "O ouro de Quíloa." *Oceanos*, 10 (April 1992), 54–61 (including plates).

Surveys the historical background of the creation of the monstrance of Belém, which Gil Vicente—Dona Leonor's goldsmith—completed in 1506, describes the work and explains its symbolism, and reviews the controversy surrounding the identity of Gil Vicente, the goldsmith.

See also above, nos 163, 178.2, 178.7, 181.5, 183.10, 188, 222, 239, 266, 318, 321, 329, 351, and below, nos 480–81, 552, 586–87, 595.

D. *HISTORIES AND DICTIONARIES OF LITERATURE, CULTURE, MUSIC, ART, AND BRIEFER MENTIONS*

449. Abdala Júnior, Benjamin and Maria Aparecida Paschoalin. *História social da literatura portuguesa*. São Paulo: Ática, 1982, pp. 25–30.

450. Alonso, Dámaso. "La caza de amor es de altanería (sobre los precedentes de una poesía de San Juan de la Cruz)." In his *Obras completas*. II: *Estudios y ensayos sobre literatura. Primera Parte: Desde los orígenes románicos hasta finales del siglo XVI*. Madrid: Gredos, 1973, pp. 1057–75.

Originally published in the *Boletín de la Real Academia Española*, XXVI (1947), 63–79. It reappeared in his *De los siglos oscuros al de oro (Notas y artículos a través de 700 años de letras españolas)*. Biblioteca Románica Hispánica, VII: Campo Abierto, 14. 2d ed. Madrid: Gredos, 1964, pp. 271–93 (First ed., 1958). An earlier, shorter version can be found in his *La poesía de San Juan de la Cruz (Desde esta ladera)*. Madrid: CSIC, 1942, pp. 119–22 (later editions too), and in his *Obras completas*, II, pp. 956–61.

451. Alonso, Dámaso. "Escila y Caribdis de la literatura española." In his *Obras completas*. V: *Góngora y el gongorismo*. Madrid: Gredos, 1978, pp. 243–58.

Originally published in *Cruz y Raya*, 7 (October 1933), 77–102. It reappeared in his *Ensayos sobre poesía española*. Madrid: Revista Occidente, 1944, pp. 9–27 (2d ed.: Buenos Aires, 1946), and as Prologue to his *Estudios y ensayos gongorinos*. Biblioteca Románica Hispánica, II: Estudios y Ensayos, 18. 3d ed. Madrid: Gredos, 1970, pp. 11–28 (First ed., 1955; second, 1960). It can also be found in *En busca de España*. Ed. Frank Paul Casa. New York: Harcourt, Brace & World, 1968, pp. 182–92. Gil Vicente, among others, exemplifies the duality which characterizes Spanish literature.

452. Alonso, Dámaso. "Poesía de Navidad: De Fray Ambrosio Montesino a Lope de Vega." In his *Obras completas*. II: *Estudios y ensayos sobre literatura. Primera Parte: Desde los orígenes románicos hasta finales del siglo XVI*. Madrid: Gredos, 1973, pp. 455–60.

Originally appeared in *ABC* (Madrid, 23 December 1945) and later in his *De los siglos oscuros al de oro (Notas y artículos a través de 700 años de letras españolas)*. Biblioteca Románica Hispánica, VII: Campo

Abierto, 14. 2d ed. Madrid: Gredos 1964, pp. 137–43 (First ed., 1958). It includes Gil Vicente's "Ro, ro, ro" (*Cassandra*), "la más emocionante canción de cuna de la literatura universal."

453. Alonso, Martín. *Historia de la literatura mundial. I: Mundo antiguo, medieval y renacentista.* Madrid: E.D.A.F., 1969, pp. 612–13, 737–38, 1145–47 (texts of three lyrics) *et passim.*

454. Armiño, Mauro. *Historia de la literatura española e hispanoamericana.* Biblioteca Hispania. Barcelona: Sopena, 1980, pp. 170–72.

455. Armiño, Mauro. *Qué es verdaderamente el Siglo de Oro.* Qué es Verdaderamente, XXII. Madrid: Doncel, 1973, pp. 52–55.

456. Armistead, Samuel G., and Joseph H. Silverman. "El falso hortelano." In their *The Judeo–Spanish Ballad Chapbooks of Yacob Abraham Yoná.* Folk Literature of the Sephardic Jews, I. Berkeley: University of California Press, 1971, pp. 274–93.
    The authors discuss the ballad of the "False Gardener" and compare it to its source, Gil Vicente's *Dom Duardos.*

457. Aub, Max. *Manual de historia de la literatura española.* Madrid: AKAL, 1974, pp. 182–83 *et passim.*
    First appeared in 2 vols (México: Pormaca, 1966).
    Review:
    a. Rafael Ferreres, *Revista Valenciana de Filología,* VII (1975), 308–09.

458. Aullón de Haro, Pedro, and Javier Huerta Calvo, Juan Palette, Pío E. Serrano, Carlos Tirado. *Historia breve de la literatura española en su contexto.* Madrid: Playor, 1981, pp. 199–200.

459. Avalle–Arce, Juan Bautista, Antonio Prieto, Antonio Gallego Morell, Cristóbal Cuevas, José María Díez Borque, Emilio Orozco, Luciano García Lorenzo, Pilar Palomo, Joaquín de Entrambasaguas, and Manuel Fernández Nieto. *Historia de la literatura española.* Dir. José María Díez Borque. II: *Renacimiento y Barroco.* Persiles, CXVII. Madrid: Taurus, 1980, pp. 334–41.
    Part of ch. XI ("el teatro en el siglo XVI"—pp. 321–89) by José María Díez Borque.

Review:
a. Margaret Wilson, *BHS*, LIX (1982), 337–38.

460. Azevedo Filho, Leodegário A. de. *Literatura portuguesa: história e emergência do novo.* Coleção Diagrama, XVII. Rio de Janeiro: Tempo Brasileiro/Universidade Federal Fluminense, 1987. 157 pp.
Ch. 2: "O teatro de Gil Vicente entre dois mundos" (pp. 37–44).

461. Baubeta, Patricia Anne Odber de. *Anticlerical Satire in Medieval Portuguese Literature.* Lewiston, New York: Edwin Mellen Press, 1992. 346 pp.
Numerous references to Gil Vicente.
Review:
a. Stephen Parkinson, *BHS*, LXXII (1995), 422–23.

462. Belchior, Maria de Lourdes. "Poesia e realidade." In *Miscelânea de estudos em honra do Prof. Vitorino Nemésio.* Lisboa: Publicações da Faculdade de Letras da Universidade de Lisboa, 1971, pp. 47–59.
On pp. 54–57, Belchior discusses Gil Vicente's geographical allusions and finds that they are to known places. She also points out the flagrant coincidences between Janeafonso's speech in the *Auto da festa* and that of the peasant in the *Templo de Apolo*.

463. Bell, Aubrey F. G., C. Bowra, and William J. Entwistle. *Da poesia medieval portuguesa.* Trans. António Álvaro Dória. 2d expanded ed. Lisboa: Edição da Revista Ocidente, 1947. 102 pp.
Many references to Gil Vicente throughout. It contains: Aubrey F. G. Bell, "Algumas observações sobre as *cantigas de amigo*," pp. 7–24: originally published in *Revue Hispanique*, LXXVII (1929), 270–83. Bell, "A origem das cantigas encadeadas *(cossantes)*," pp. 25–43: appeared first in *MLR*, XXVII (1932), 175–85. C. Bowra, "Paralelo entre cantares gregos e portugueses," pp. 45–71. William J. Entwistle, "Dos *cossantes* às *cantigas de amor*," pp. 73–99.

464. Braga, Teófilo. *História da literatura portuguesa. II: Renascença.* Temas Portugueses. Lisboa: Imprensa Nacional–Casa da Moeda, 1984, pp. 34–79, *et passim.*
First published in 1914 (Porto: Livraria Chardron).
Review:
a. A. R., *Brotéria*, CXXIII (1986), 115.

465. Bragança, António. *Lições de literatura portuguesa*. I: *Século XII a XVI* (6° ano dos liceus). 6ª ed. Porto: Livraria Escolar Infante, [1971], pp. 297–351.

466. Briesemeister, Dietrich. "Hof und Theater in Portugal in der ersten Hälfte des 16. Jahrhunderts." In *Europäische Hofkultur im 16. und 17. Jahrhundert: Vorträge und Referate gehalten anlässlich des Kongresses des Wolfenbütteler Arbeitskreises für Renaissanceforschung und des Internationalen Arbeitskreises für Barockliteratur in der Herzog August Bibliothek Wolfenbüttel vom 4. bis 8. September 1979. II: Referate der Sektionen 1 bis 5.* Ed. August Buck, Georg Kauffmann, Blake Lee Spahr, Conrad Wiedemann. Wolfenbütteler Arbeiten zur Barockforschung, IX. Hamburg: Ernst Hauswedell & Co., 1981, pp. 269–76.

One of the central motifs in Gil Vicente's plays is the praise of Portugal and the glorification of its historic mission. Thus theater becomes the means for political self–portrayal. In order to legitimize Portuguese claims, the dramatist mixes indiscriminately popular and learned, Christian and pagan elements. Along with the glorification of the king and the Portuguese empire, there is social criticism and satire, which may betray a split between personal conviction and the poet's office.

467. Brinches, Victor. *Dicionário biobibliográfico luso–brasileiro*. Rio de Janeiro: Fundo de Cultura, 1965, pp. 147–50.

468. Buescu, Maria Leonor Carvalhão. *História da literatura*. Sínteses da Cultura Portuguesa, Europália, LXXXXI. Lisboa: Imprensa Nacional–Casa da Moeda, 1991. 100 pp.
    Pp. 32–36: "Gil Vicente: contradições em cena."
    Review:
    a. Ernesto Rodrigues, *CoL*, 131 (January–March 1994), 244.

469. *The Cambridge Guide to World Theatre*. Ed. Martin Banham. Cambridge: Cambridge University Press, 1988. 1104 pp.
    Entry on "Vicente, Gil" (pp. 1043–44) by L[aurence] K[eates]. See also entry "Portugal" (pp. 785–88) by the same author for other references to Gil Vicente.

469A. Caro Baroja, Julio. *Vidas mágicas e Inquisición*. Vol. I. Barcelona: Círculo de Lectores, 1990, pp. 126–28.

Brief discussion of sorcery and sorceresses in the *Velho da horta* (Branca Gil), *Auto da Barca do Inferno* (Brízida Vaz), *Auto das fadas* (Genebra Pereira) and *Comédia de Rubena* (feiticeira).

470. Carpeaux, Otto Maria. *História da literatura ocidental.* Vol. I. Rio de Janeiro: O Cruzeiro, 1959, pp. 585–89 *et passim.*

471. *Cassell's Encyclopaedia of World Literature.* Ed. S. H. Steinberg. 2 vols. New York: Funk & Wagnalls, 1954.
    Entry on "Vicente, Gil" by T. P. Waldron (II, 1599–1600). See also under "Portuguese Literature" by the same contributor (I, 438).

472. Castro Calvo, José María. *Historia de la literatura española.* Vol. I. Barcelona: CREDSA, 1965, pp. 181–84.

473. Chabás, Juan. *Nueva y manual historia de la literatura española.* 2d ed. La Habana: Cultural, 1953, pp. 132–33 *et passim.* (First ed., 1944).

474. Chase, Gilbert. *The Music of Spain.* 2d rev. ed. New York: Dover Publications, 1959. 383 pp. (First ed. : New York: W.W. Norton, 1941).
    Pp. 92–94: "Music in the Plays of Gil Vicente."

475. Chicharro [Chamorro], Dámaso. *Orígenes del teatro. "La Celestina."* *El teatro prelopista.* Cuadernos de Estudio, Serie Literatura, IV. Madrid: Editorial Cincel, 1980 (reprinted in 1983), pp. 69–74.

476. Cintra, Luís Filipe Lindley. *"Tu e vós,* como formas de tratamento de Deus, em orações e na poesia em língua portuguesa." In *Miscelânea de estudos em honra do Prof. Vitorino Nemésio.* Lisboa: Publicações da Faculdade de Letras da Universidade de Lisboa, 1971, pp. 145–76.
    On pp. 159–61, Cintra examines the dominical prayer of the *Auto da Cananeia* and the *Pater Noster* of the *Velho da horta* and concludes that in the work of Gil Vicente man addresses God in the second person singular and only Virgin Mary in the second person plural.

477. Cohen, J. M. *A History of Western Literature.* Rev. ed. Chicago: Aldine Publishing Co., 1963, pp. 91–94.
    Later reprints (1965, 1968). First ed. by Penguin Books (Harmondsworth, 1956).

478. *A Companion to the Medieval Theatre.* Ed. Ronald W. Vince. New York: Greenwood Press, 1989. xxxiii+420 pp.

Entry on "Vicente, Gil" (pp. 369–71) by Charlotte Stern. Other passing references also.

479. Costa Pimpão, Álvaro Júlio. *História da literatura portuguesa.* Vol. II. Coimbra: Edições Quadrante, [1947], pp. 123–212.

Reviews:

a. João Maia, *Brotéria,* LII (1951), 583–89.

b. João Mendes, *Brotéria,* LVII (1953), 201–5 (see also no. 239 above).

480. Couto, João. "A arte da ourivesaria em Portugal—elementos decorativos." In *Arte portuguesa.* III: *As artes decorativas.* Dir. João Barreira. [Lisboa]: Excelsior, n.d., pp. 15–74.

Pp. 33 (B&W plate of the *custódia de Belém*), 34–35 (three B&W detailed views of same), 37.

481. Couto, João and António M. Gonçalves. *A ourivesaria em Portugal.* [Lisboa]: Livros Horizonte, 1960, pp. 103–06.

Description of the *custódia de Belém* (1 B&W and 1 color plates included). Relevant notes on pp. 129–31. Two B&W detailed views of the work on p. 61 of the appendix ("Documentação fotográfica"). The description is virtually the same as that in Gonçalves's "A custódia de Belém," *Panorama,* 11 (September 1958). Cf. Couto's *Ourivesaria portuguesa. Exposição portuguesa em Sevilla.* Lisboa: Imprensa Nacional, 1929, pp. 20–21 (full–page B&W plate of the *custódia* on p. 19).

482. Cruz, Duarte Ivo. *Introdução à história do teatro português.* Lisboa: Guimarães, 1983, pp. 35–41.

Review:

a. O[sório] M[ateus], *CoL,* 89 (January 1986), 78.

483. Cunha, Celso. "Valor das grafias *–eu* e *–eo* do século XIII ao século XVI." In *EP:HLSP,* pp. 913–27.

See especially pp. 921–23, 926. It was Gil Vicente who, influenced probably by the Spanish phonological system, introduced the freedom of rhyme among open and closed tonic vowels to Portuguese versification.

484. Dalmasso, Osvaldo B. *El teatro prelopesco*. Buenos Aires: Centro Editor de América Latina, 1968, pp. 19–23.

485. Dias, Aida Fernanda. *O "Cancioneiro geral" e a poesia peninsular de Quatrocentos (contactos e sobrevivência)*. Coimbra: Almedina, 1978. xvi +418 pp.
Her doctoral thesis for the Universidade de Coimbra. Many references to Gil Vicente.

486. Díaz–Plaja, Guillermo. *Historia de la literatura española encuadrada en la universal a través de la crítica y de los textos*. Ilustrada con gráficos y mapas. Lecturas seleccionadas de escritores clásicos españoles. De acuerdo con los nuevos planes de estudio. 10ª edición argentina de acuerdo con la 30ª edición española al cuidado de Ángel Mazzei. Buenos Aires: Ciordia, 1967, pp. 155, 177–78.

487. Díaz–Plaja, Guillermo. *A History of Spanish Literature*. Trans. and ed. Hugh A. Harter. New York: New York University Press, 1971, pp. 101–3.
Review:
a. A. V. Ebersole, *Hispanófila*, 47 (January 1973), 90–91.

488. *Diccionario de autores de todos los tiempos y de todos los países*. Vol. III. Barcelona: Montaner y Simón, 1973, p. 906.
Reprint of first ed., 1963. Entry on "Vicente, Gil" by J. do Prado Coelho.

489. *Diccionario de literatura española e hispanoamericana*. Dir. Ricardo Gullón. Vol. II. Madrid: Alianza Editorial, 1993, pp. 1725–28.
Entry on "Vicente, Gil" by M.A.P.P.

490. *Dicionário cronológico de autores portugueses*. Organizado pelo Instituto Português do Livro. Coordenação de Eugénio Lisboa. Vol. I. Mem Martins: Europa–América, 1985, pp. 132–36.
Entry on "Vicente, Gil" by Luís de Sousa Rebelo.
Review:
a. Manuel Simões, *RaI*, 27 (December 1986), 65–66.

491. *Dicionário de história de Portugal.* Dir. Joel Serrão. Vol. IV. Lisboa: Iniciativas Editoriais, 1971, pp. 292–94.
Entry on "Vicente, Gil" by A[ntónio] J[osé] S[araiva].

492. *Dicionário do teatro português.* Dir. Luiz Francisco Rebello. Lisboa: Prelo, [1968]– .
First fascicle (48 pp.) includes the following two entries by Luciana Stegagno Picchio: "Alma, Auto da" (pp. 33–34) and "Amadis de Gaula" (pp. 43–44).

493. *Dicionário ilustrado da história de Portugal.* Coordenação de José Costa Pereira. Vol. II. [Lisboa]: Publicações Alfa, 1986, pp. 325–26.
Entry on "Vicente, Gil" by António Dias Miguel.

494. *Dictionary of the Literature of the Iberian Peninsula.* Ed. Germán Bleiberg, Maureen Ihrie, and Janet Pérez. 2 vols. Westport, Connecticut: Greenwood Press, 1993. Vol. I: xxi+906 pp., Vol. II: xxi+1806 pp. (continuous pagination).
Entry on "Vicente, Gil" (II, pp. 1690–93) by Deborah Compte.

495. Díez Borque, José María. *Los géneros dramáticos en el siglo XVI: el teatro hasta Lope de Vega.* Historia Crítica de la Literatura Hispánica, VIII. Madrid: Taurus, 1987, pp. 24–25, 28–29, 33, 84–89.

496. Díez de Revenga, Francisco Javier. "Teatro clásico y canción tradicional." *Cuadernos de Teatro Clásico,* 3 (1989), 29–44.
On pp. 33–34, he discusses briefly Gil Vicente's use of traditional songs and claims that "de todos los autores del XVI, el que mejor manejó la fórmula de introducir intermedios líricos en sus obras dramáticas fue Gil Vicente."

497. *Dizionario letterario Bompiani degli autori di tutti i tempi e di tutte le letterature.* Vol. III. Milano: Bompiani, 1957, p. 808.
Entry on "Vicente, Gil" by Jacinto do Prado Coelho.

498. Dos Passos, John. *The Portugal Story: Three Centuries of Exploration and Discovery.* Garden City, New York: Doubleday, 1969, pp. 263-64.

499. Elizalde, Ignacio. "La interpretación teológica de los autos sacramentales." In *Varia hispanica: Homenaje a Alberto Porqueras Mayo.* Ed. Joseph L. Laurenti and Vern Williamsen. Kassel: Reichenberger, 1989, pp. 147–61.

500. Eminescu, Roxana. *Preliminarii la o istorie a literaturii portugheze.* Colecţia Eseuri. Bucureşti: Editura Univers, 1979, pp. 98–112 *et passim.*

501. *Enciclopédia brasileira Mérito.* Vol. XX. São Paulo: Mérito, 1967, pp. 329–30.
    Anonymous entry on "Vicente, Gil."

502. *Enciclopedia cattolica.* Vol. IX. Città del Vaticano: Ente per l'Enciclopedia Cattolica e per il Libro Cattolico, 1952, p. 1800.
    Entry on "Vicente, Gil" by Giuseppe Carlo Rossi.

503. *Enciclopedia de la cultura española.* Dir. Florentino Pérez–Embid. Vol. V. Madrid: Editorial Nacional, 1963, pp. 639–41.
    Entry on "Vicente, Gil" by Rafael Morales.

504. *Enciclopédia luso–brasileira de cultura.* Vol. XVIII. Lisboa: Verbo, 1976, cols 1023–26.
    Entry on "Vicente, Gil" by João Mendes and L. da Silva Pereira.

505. *Enciclopedia universal ilustrada europeo–americana.* Vol. LXVIII. Madrid: Espasa–Calpe, 1966, pp. 542–43.
    Anonymous entry on "Vicente, (Gil)."

506. *Encyclopaedia universalis.* Vol. XVI. Paris: Encyclopaedia Universalis France, 1973, pp. 749–50.
    Entry on "Vicente, Gil" by B. S.

507. *The Encyclopedia Americana: International Edition.* Vol. XXVIII. Danbury, Connecticut: Grolier, 1990, pp. 77–78.
    Entry on "Vicente, Gil" by Jack Horace Parker.

508. Enríquez Calleja, Isidoro. *Tercer curso de lengua y literatura.* De acuerdo con los programas oficiales. 6th ed. México: Esfinge, 1964, pp. 132–35. (First ed., 1954).

509. *European Authors (1000–1900): A Biographical Dictionary of European Literature.* Ed. Stanley J. Kunitz and Vineta Colby. New York: H.W. Wilson Co., 1967, pp. 962–63.

Entry on "Vicente, Gil" by Robert E. Osborne.

510. Ferrario de Orduna, Lilia E. "Texto dramático y espectador en el teatro castellano primitivo." In *Studia hispanica medievalia: Actas de las II jornadas de literatura española medieval (Agosto 20–23, 1987, Buenos Aires).* Ed. L. Teresa Valdivieso and Jorge H. Valdivieso. Buenos Aires: Universidad Católica Argentina, 1987 [1988], pp. 31–44.

On pp. 38–41, the author surveys the secondary dramatic texts (explicit and implicit stage directions) of several of Gil Vicente's plays.

511. Ferreira de Vasconcellos, Jorge. *Comedia Eufrosina.* Texto de la edición príncipe de 1555 con las variantes de 1561 y 1566. Edición, prólogo y notas de Eugenio Asensio. Biblioteca Hispano–Lusitana, I. Madrid: CSIC, 1951, pp. lxxvii–lxxxiii.

On Erasmus's influence on Gil Vicente and Jorge Ferreira de Vasconcellos.

512. Finello, Dominick. *Pastoral Themes and Forms in Cervantes's Fiction.* Lewisburg, Pennsylvania: Bucknell University Press, 1994, pp. 152–53.

513. Frenk Alatorre, Margit. *Entre folklore y literatura (lírica hispánica antigua).* Centro de Estudios Lingüísticos y Literarios. Jornadas, LXVIII. México: El Colegio de México, 1971. 104 pp.

Frequent references to Gil Vicente.

514. Gerstinger, Heinz. *Lope de Vega and Spanish Drama.* Trans. Samuel R. Rosenbaum. New York: Ungar, 1974, pp. 82–91.

Pp. 83–90 are occupied by plates.

515. González Mas, Ezequiel. *Historia de la literatura española: Renacimiento (siglo XVI).* San Juan: Universidad de Puerto Rico, 1973, pp. 163–69, 178–79 *et passim.*

516. Granda [Gutiérrez], Germán de. "Sobre el origen del 'habla de negro' en la literatura peninsular del Siglo de Oro." In his *Estudios lingüísticos*

hispánicos, afrohispánicos y criollos. Biblioteca Románica Hispánica, II: Estudios y Ensayos, 282. Madrid: Gredos, 1978, pp. 216–33.

517. *Grande dicionário de literatura portuguesa e de teoria literária.* Dir. João José Cochofel. Lisboa: Iniciativas Editoriais, 1970–.
It is being issued in fascicles. The completed first volume includes the following entries: "Alma, Auto da" (pp. 141–42) by Luís Francisco Rebelo; "Almocreves, Farsa dos" (p. 170) by Stephen Reckert; "Amadis de Gaula (Auto de)" (pp. 201–02) by Luís Francisco Rebelo; "Auto" (pp. 519–21) by Luciana Stegagno Picchio; "Barcas (Autos das)" (pp. 607–24) by Stephen Reckert (revised version of this entry in *GVB*, no. 285A). The first fascicles of vol. II include an entry on "Breve sumário da história de Deus" (p. 156) by Jean Colomès.

518. *Grande dizionario enciclopedico.* Fondato da Pietro Fedele. 3rd rev. ed. Vol. XIX. Torino: Unione Tipografico–Editrice Torinense, 1973, pp. 432–33.
Entry on "Vicente, Gil" by Paolo Pignata.

519. *Grande enciclopédia Delta Larousse.* Vol. XV. Rio de Janeiro: Delta, 1971, p. 7006.
Anonymous entry on "Vicente, Gil."

520. *Grande enciclopédia portuguesa e brasileira.* Ilustrada com cêrca de 15.000 gravuras e 400 hors–textes a côres. 40 vols. Lisboa/Rio de Janeiro: Editorial Enciclopédia, 1936–60. Vol. XXXV (n.d.), pp. 86–95.
Anonymous entry on "Vicente, Gil."

521. *Grande enciclopedia Vallardi.* Vol. XVI. Milano: Francesco Vallardi, 1971, pp. 509–10.
Anonymous entry on "Vicente, Gil."

522. *Gran enciclopedia Larousse en diez volúmenes.* Vol. X. Barcelona: Planeta, 1974, pp. 753–54.
Anonymous entry on "Vicente, Gil."

523. *Great Foreign Language Writers.* Ed. James Vinson and Daniel Kirkpatrick. New York: St. Martin's Press, 1984, pp. 598–600.
Entry on "Vicente, Gil" by C. C. Stathatos (see also below, no. 579).

524. Hart, Thomas R. "Camões's *Auto do Filodemo.*" In *Iberia: Literary and Historical Issues. Studies in Honour of Harold V. Livermore.* Ed. R. O. W. Goertz. Calgary: University of Calgary Press, 1985, pp. 41–48.

Hart discusses Camões's play and finds certain affinities with Gil Vicente's romantic comedies, especially *Dom Duardos.* Central to both *Filodemo* and *Dom Duardos* is the motif of the disguised prince. Dionisa's complaints about her situation as a woman echo Vicente's *autos* of the *Sibila Cassandra* and *Inês Pereira.*

Review (of the book):

a. N. J. Lamb, *BHS*, LXV (1988), 403.

525. Hathaway, Robert L. "Frustrated Lovers' Farewells in the Early Iberian Theatre." In *From Dante to García Márquez: Studies in Romance Literatures and Linguistics Presented to Anson Conant Piper by Former Students, Colleagues and Friends.* Ed. Gene H. Bell–Villada, Antonio Giménez, and George Pistorius. Williamstown, Massachusetts: Williams College, 1987, pp. 12–23.

On pp. 20–21, he deals with Amadis's farewell to the world, in Vicente's *Tragicomédia de Amadis de Gaula* and contends that the dramatist's purpose in his dramatization of portions of the chivalric novel was not a serious one.

526. Hermenegildo, Alfredo. *Historia de la literatura española.* XV: *El teatro del siglo XVI.* Ed. Ricardo de la Fuente. Madrid: Ediciones Júcar, 1994, pp. 43–54 *et passim.*

527. Hermenegildo, Alfredo. "La neutralización del signo carnavalesco: el pastor del teatro primitivo castellano." In *Texte, Kontexte, Strukturen: Beiträge zur französischen, spanischen und hispanoamerikanischen Literatur. Festschrift zum 60. Geburtstag von Karl Alfred Blüher.* Herausgegeben von Alfonso de Toro. Tübingen: Gunter Narr Verlag, 1987, pp. 283–95.

528. Hermenegildo, Alfredo. "Sobre la dimensión social del teatro primitivo español." *Prohemio*, II (1971), 25–50.

529. Herrán, Laurentino María. *Santa María en las literaturas hispánicas.* Biblioteca NT Religión, V. Pamplona: EUNSA, 1979, pp. 81–82, 127–29, 157–58, 232.

530. *Histoire de la littérature espagnole*. I: *Moyen Âge–XVIe siècle–XVIIe siècle*. Dir. Jean Canavaggio. Paris: Fayard, 1993, pp. 364–68, 373–76 (by Pierre Heugas) *et passim*.

531. *Historia y crítica de la literatura española*. Ed. Francisco Rico. II: *Siglos de Oro: Renacimiento*. Ed. Francisco López Estrada. Barcelona: Editorial Crítica, 1980. xx+748 pp.

Includes Luciana Stegagno Picchio's "Trayectoria de Gil Vicente," pp. 558–63 (taken from her *Profilo storico della letteratura portoghese*, Milano: Vallardi, 1967, pp. 8–16) and Stephen Reckert's "*Don Duardos*: las innovaciones de Gil Vicente," pp. 564–69 (taken from his *Gil Vicente: Espíritu y letra*, I: *Estudios*, Biblioteca Románica Hispánica, IV: Textos, 10, Madrid: Gredos, 1977, pp. 31–32, 38–45, 46–49, 54–55, 56–58—see *GVB*, no. 285A). See also pp. 543–45 *et passim* of Mercedes de los Reyes Peña's "El teatro prelopesco" (pp. 540–48).

532. *International Dictionary of Theatre*. II: *Playwrights*. Ed. Mark Hawkins–Dady. Detroit: St. James Press, 1994, pp. 1005–8.

Entry on "Vicente, Gil" by Juliet Perkins.

533. Jarvis, Bárbara M. "El halcón y la presa: Identidades ambiguas en *Crónica de una muerte anunciada*." Trans. Daniel Iglesias. In *En el punto de mira: Gabriel García Márquez*. Ed. Ana María Hernández de López. Colección Pliegos de Ensayo. Madrid: Editorial Pliegos, 1985, pp. 219–29.

Gabriel García Márquez borrowed two lines ("La caza de amor / es de altanería") from Gil Vicente's *villancico* "Halcón que se atreve" (*Comédia de Rubena*) for his epigraph in *Crónica de una muerte anunciada*, and another three lines ("Halcón que se atreve / con garza guerrera / peligros espera") to which he gave crucial importance in the story.

534. Johnson, Harvey L. "Longfellow and Portuguese Language and Literature." *CL*, XVII (1965), 225–33.

Some references to Gil Vicente. Also includes Longfellow's verse translations of "Si dormís, doncella" (*Farelos*) and "Muy graciosa es la doncella" (*Cassandra*) on p. 230.

535. Kayser, Wolfgang [Johannes]. *Interpretación y análisis de la obra literaria*. Trans. María D. Mouton and V. García Yebra. 4th rev. ed.

Biblioteca Románica Hispánica, I: Tratados y Monografías, 3. Madrid: Gredos, 1970, pp. 78–80, 229–30 *et passim*. (First ed., 1954).

Translation of *Das sprachlicke Kunstwerk; eine Einführung in die Literaturwissenschaft* (Bern: A. Francke, 1948). There is also a Portuguese translation: *Fundamentos da interpretação e da análise literária*, Colecção Studium: Temas Filosóficos, Jurídicos e Sociais, LXI–II (São Paulo: Livraria Acadêmica, 1948).

536. Kayserling, Meyer. *História dos judeus em Portugal*. Trans. Gabriele Borchardt Corrêa da Silva and Anita Novinsky. Ed. Anita Novinsky. São Paulo: Pioneira, 1971, pp. 155–58.

Translation of *Geschichte der Juden in Portugal* (Leipzig: O. Leiner, 1867). Gil Vicente raised his voice against the friars of Santarém's claim that the *conversos* were responsible to a large degree for incurring God's wrath and thus prompting the 1531 earthquake. Included in these pages is also the almost complete text of the "Carta que Gil Vicente mandou de Santarém a El–Rei D. João III."

537. Leblon, Bernard. *Les Gitans dans la littérature espagnole*. Collection Thèses et Recherches, XI. Toulouse: Institut d'Études Hispaniques et Hispano–Américaines, Université de Toulouse–Le Mirail, 1982. 251 pp.

Constant references to Gil Vicente's *Auto da festa* and *Auto das ciganas*. With these two plays, Vicente initiated the gypsy genre in the theater. See pp. 12, 52, 54, 55, 99–100, 101, 103, 104, 105, 106, 107, 108, 115, 117, 123–24, 126–27, 129, 131, 132, 136, 139, 152–53, 177, 178, 179, 180, 181, 207.

538. Lihani, John. "A Literary Jargon of Early Spanish Drama: The Sayagués Dialect." In *Linguistic Approaches to the Romance Lexicon*. Ed. Frank H. Nuessel, Jr. Washington, D.C.: Georgetown University Press, 1978, pp. 39–44.

539. Luft, Celso Pedro. *Dicionário de literatura portuguêsa e brasileira*. Pôrto Alegre: Globo, 1967, pp. 306–9.

540. Macrì, Oreste. "Saggio sulla poesia di Rafael Alberti (*Marinero en tierra e Retornos*)." *Quaderni Ibero–Americani*, 71 (1992), 372–418.

Numerous references to Gil Vicente (see pp. 379–82 especially) who influenced Rafael Alberti so profoundly.

541. Madrigal, José A. "Las diferentes caras del hombre salvaje en el teatro del siglo XVI: un ensayo sobre la génesis de su temática." *Revista de Literatura*, XLVII (1985), 65–79.

On pp. 67–68, Madrigal discusses Camilote in Gil Vicente's *Dom Duardos*, the first dramatic work to employ the character of the wild man. See also above, no. 404.

542. Márquez, Antonio. *Literatura e Inquisición en España (1478–1834)*. Persiles, CXXIV. Madrid: Taurus, 1980. 274 pp.

Several references to Gil Vicente and his work as objects of inquisitional censorship. See especially ch. IX ("La censura inquisitorial del teatro renacentista [1514–1551]"), pp. 189–200.

Reviews:

a. Francisco Márquez Villanueva, *Ínsula*, 428–29 (July–August 1982), 22.

b. Terence O'Reilly, *BHS*, LIX (1982), 336–37.

c. Emilietta Panizza, *RaI*, 13 (April 1982), 49–51.

d. Victoriano Ugalde, *Revista Canadiense de Estudios Hispánicos*, VIII (1984), 296–300.

543. Márquez Villanueva, Francisco. "*La Celestina* as Hispano–Semitic Anthropology." *Revue de Littérature Comparée*, LXI (1987), 425–53.

On pp. 425–26, 427, 442–43, especially, the author deals with proxenetism in Gil Vicente's *Inês Pereira* and *O Juiz da Beira*.

544. Márquez Villanueva, Francisco. *Espiritualidad y literatura en el siglo XVI*. Hombres, Hechos e Ideas, XVI. Madrid/Barcelona: Alfaguara, 1968, pp. 76–77, 80, 86, 114, 134–35.

544A. Márquez Villanueva, Francisco. *Orígenes y sociología del tema celestinesco*. Colección Hispanistas: Creación, Pensamiento, Sociedad, II. Barcelona: Anthropos, 1993, pp. 19–20, 22–23, 142–44, 148, 150, 151, 152, 158.

See above, no. 543.

Review:

a. Tatiana Bubnova, *NRFH*, XLIII (1995), 205–12.

b. Michael T. Ward, *Hispania*, LXXVIII (1995), 794–95.

545. Martins, José V. de Pina. *Cultura portuguesa*. Colecção Presenças, XX. Lisboa: Verbo, 1974, pp. 28, 167, 201, 213, 238–39, 244, 258, 262, 286–87, 292–93, 296–97.

546. Martins, José V. de Pina. "L'Humanisme chrétien au Portugal (XVIe siècle)." In *L'Humanisme portugais et l'Europe. Actes du XXIe colloque international d'études humanistes (Tours, 3–13 juillet 1978)*. Ed. Jean–Claude Margolin and José V. de Pina Martins. Centre d'Études Superieures de la Renaissance, Université de Tours. Paris: Fondation Calouste Gulbenkian/Centre Culturel Portugais, 1984, pp. 15–29.

Discusses Gil Vicente on p. 18, and opposes the view that the dramatist was an Erasmian.

547. Mateus, Osório. "O título roubado." *Românica*, 1–2 (1992–93) [*Homenagem a Maria de Lourdes Belchior*], 317–21.

Two plays which appeared anonymously on the 1551 Index (*Aderência do Paço* and *Vida do Paço*) could possibly be the same as Gil Vicente's *Farsa dos almocreves* and *Auto das fadas*, respectively. But *Vida do Paço* or *Aderência do Paço* could also be a different title for António Ribeiro Chiado's *Prática d'oito feguras*. Chiado may have changed the title to *Prática d'oito feguras* after 1551 in order to deceive censorship.

548. *The McGraw–Hill Encyclopedia of World Biography*. An International Reference Work in Twelve Volumes Including an Index. Vol. XI. New York: McGraw–Hill, 1973, pp. 139–41.

Entry on "Vicente, Gil" by Juan Bautista Avalle–Arce.

549. McKendrick, Melveena. *Theatre in Spain 1490–1700*. Cambridge: Cambridge University Press, 1989, pp. 19–26, *et passim*.

Reviews:
a. Peter N. Dunn, *MLN*, CVI (1991), 443–47.
b. A. Robert Lauer, *Symposium*, XLV (1991), 157–59.
c. James A. Parr, *Hispania*, LXXIV (1991), 308.

550. McPheeters, Dean W. "*La Celestina* en Portugal en el siglo XVI." In "*La Celestina*" *y su contorno social. Actas del I congreso internacional sobre "La Celestina."* Ed. Manuel Criado de Val. Barcelona: Hispam, 1977, pp. 367–76.

On pp. 367–69, the influence of the *Celestina* in several of Gil Vicente's plays is traced.

551. Mendes, João. *Literatura portuguesa I*. Ed. Alves Pires, S. J. Colecção Presenças, XXI. Lisboa: Verbo, 1974, pp. 137–82.

552. Mendonça, Maria José de. "As artes ornamentais no século XVI." In Mário Chicó, Maria José de Mendonça, Fernando de Pamplona, Damião Peres, *História da arte em Portugal*. Vol. II. Porto: Portucalense, 1948 [1953], pp. 405–43.
   Short entry on the *custódia de Belém* (pp. 418–19); B&W plate of it (no. 385) occupies p. 413.

553. Michaëlis de Vasconcelos, Carolina. *Estudos sobre o romanceiro peninsular: Romances velhos em Portugal*. Biblioteca Iniciação Literária, VI. Porto: Lello & Irmão, 1980. 416 pp.
   Originally published in *Cultura Española*, 7–15 (1907–9). Numerous references to Gil Vicente.

554. Miguel, Jorge. *Curso de literatura*. São Paulo: Harper & Row do Brasil, 1986, pp. 41–42, 44–46.

555. *Moderne Encyclopedie der Wereldliteratuur*. Dir. J. Aerts, A. G. H. Bachrach, Achilles Mussche, G. Stuiveling, M. H. Würzner. Vol. IX. Bussum: Paul Brand/C. de Boer Jr., 1977, pp. 118–19.
   Entry on "Vicente, Gil" by J. van den Besselaar.

556. Moisés, Massaud. *A literatura portuguesa*. São Paulo: Cultrix, 1989, pp. 50–57.

557. Mongelli, Lênia Márcia de Medeiros, Maria do Amparo Tavares Maleval, and Yara Frateschi Vieira. *A literatura portuguesa em perspectiva*. I: *Trovadorismo, Humanismo*. Dir. Massaud Moisés. São Paulo: Atlas, 1992. 214 pp.
   "Gil Vicente," by Maria do Amparo Tavares Maleval, on pp. 170–90.

558. Moser, F[ernando] de Mello. "Misericórdia na tradição dramática medieval e renascentista." *Biblos*, LVII [*Homenagem a M. Paiva Boléo*] (1981), 437–65.
   In section 7 ("Gil Vicente e a História de Deus"), pp. 453–58, Moser traces the theme of God's mercy in *Breve sumário da história de Deus* and other works of Gil Vicente.

559. *Die Musik in Geschichte und Gegenwart*. Allgemeine Enzyklopädie der Musik. Unter Mitarbeit zahlreicher Musikforscher des In- und Auslandes herausgegeben von Friedrich Blume. XIII. Basel: Bärenreiter Kassel, 1966, col. 1582.

Entry on "Vicente, Gil" by José Subirá, trans. Ingeborg Robert.

560. *New Catholic Encyclopedia*. Vol. XIV. New York: McGraw–Hill, 1967, pp. 643–44.

Entry on "Vicente, Gil" by T. R. Hart.

561. *The New Encyclopaedia Britannica*. 15th ed. Vol. XII. Chicago: Encyclopaedia Britannica, 1989, p. 344.

Anonymous entry on "Vicente, Gil."

562. Newmark, Maxim. *Dictionary of Spanish Literature*. Totowa, New Jersey: Littlefield, Adams & Co., 1965, pp. 343–44. (First ed., New York: Philosophical Library, 1956).

563. Oliveira, Cândido de. *Súmulas de literatura portuguêsa*. 13th ed. São Paulo: Biblos, 1969, pp. 56–60.

564. *The Oxford Companion to Spanish Literature*. Ed. Philip Ward. Oxford: Clarendon Press, 1978, pp. 606–8.

Anonymous entry on "Vicente, Gil." See also *Diccionario Oxford de literatura española e hispanoamericana*, ed. Philip Ward (Barcelona: Editorial Crítica, 1984).

Reviews:

a. M. E. Venier, *NRFH*, XXVIII (1979), 401–02.

b. J. L. Brooks, *Quinquereme*, III (1980), 132–33.

c. Kathleen McCullough, *American Reference Books Annual*, XI (1980), 597– 98.

d. D. W. Foster, *Rocky Mountain Review of Language and Literature*, XXXV (1981), 84–85.

e. Geoffrey Ribbans, *BHS*, LVIII (1981), 252–54.

565. Pandolfi, Vito. *Historia universale del teatro drammatico*. Vol. I. Torino: Unione Tipografico–Editrice Torinense, 1964, pp. 469–71.

566. Parker, Alexander A. *The Philosophy of Love in Spanish Literature. 1480–1680*. Ed. Terence O'Reilly. Edinburgh: Edinburgh University Press, 1985, pp. 29–31.

Discusses Gil Vicente's *Amadis de Gaula* and *Dom Duardos* in terms of courtly love. There is also a Spanish translation: *La filosofía del amor en la literatura española (1480–1680)*. Madrid: Cátedra, 1986.

Reviews:
a. Roger Boase, *JHP*, IX (1984–85), 67–73.
b. Alastair Fowler, *TLS*, 4310 (8 November 1985), 1260.
c. Elide Pittarello, *RaI*, 24 (December 1985), 24–27.
d. T[homas] R. H[art], *CL*, XXXVIII (1986), 101–02.
e. Heinrich Merkl and Kathryn Hawken, *Archiv für das Studium der Neueren Sprachen und Literaturen*, CCXXIII (1986), 222–23.
f. Luis Miguel Serrano, *RFR*, IV (1986), 382–85 [review of the Spanish edition].
g. Mary E. Giles, *Studia Mystica*, X (1987), 64–69.
h. Arthur Terry, "Lectures in Love's Philosophy: A.A. Parker on Human and Divine Love in Golden–Age Literature," *BHS*, LXV (1988), 169–74.

567. Pedraza Jiménez, Felipe–B. and Milagros Rodríguez Cáceres. *Manual de literatura española*. II: *Renacimiento*. Tafalla: Cénlit Ediciones, 1980, pp. 280–87 *et passim*.

568. *Pequeno dicionário de literatura portuguesa*. Dir. Massaud Moisés. São Paulo: Cultrix, 1981, pp. 375–76, 393–95.

Entries on "Trilogia das Barcas (A)" and "Vicente, Gil" (respectively) by M.H.R.C.

569. Perdigão, Henrique. *Dicionário universal de literatura (bio–bibliográfico e cronológico)*. 2d ed., illustrated. Porto: Livraria Latina, 1940, pp. 56–57.

570. Pereira, Maria Helena da Rocha. "O mito de Medeia na poesia portuguesa." *Humanitas* (Coimbra), XV (1963), 348–66.

Surveys the use of the myth of Medea in several Portuguese authors including Gil Vicente (see pp. 352–53).

571. Pinheiro, Célio. *Introdução à literatura portuguesa*. São Paulo: Livraria Pioneira Editora, 1991. xiv+330 pp.

On Gil Vicente pp. 29–44, *et passim* (includes an excerpt from the *Auto da Alma* on pp. 32–39).

572. Pinheiro, Fernandes (Cônego). *Curso de literatura nacional.* 3d ed. Apresentação de Mário Portugal Fernandes Pinheiro. Rio de Janeiro: Livraria Editôra Cátedra / Brasília: Instituto Nacional do Livro, Ministério da Educação e Cultura, 1978, pp. 77–83. (First ed., 1862, 2d 1883).

573. *Portugal: breviário da pátria para os portugueses ausentes.* Lisboa: Edições SNI, 1946, pp. 313–16 *et passim.*
Part of "Visão da literatura portuguesa" by José Osório de Oliveira, pp. 303–62.

574. Potter, Robert. *The English Morality Play: Origins, History and Influence of a Dramatic Tradition.* London: Routledge & Kegan Paul, 1975, pp. 182–84.
On the three *Barcas* and the *Auto da Alma.* Includes the text and Aubrey F. G. Bell's verse translation into English of "Remando vam remadores" (*Purgatório*) on p. 183.

574A. Profeti, Maria Grazia. *Introduzione allo studio del teatro spagnolo.* Teatri Nazionali, II. Firenze: Casa Usher, 1994. 334 pp.
Several references to Gil Vicente.

575. Rebello, Luiz Francisco. *O primitivo teatro português.* Biblioteca Breve, Série Literatura, V. Amadora: Instituto de Cultura Portuguesa, M.E.I.C., Secretaria de Estado da Investigação Científica, 1977. 119 pp.
Constant references to Gil Vicente.
Review:
a. Mário Martins, *CoL,* 51 (September 1979), 89–92.

576. Rebello, Luiz Francisco. *Variações sobre o teatro de Camões.* Lisboa: Caminho, 1980. 128 pp.
Numerous references to Gil Vicente.

577. Rebelo, Luís de Sousa. *A tradição clássica na literatura portuguesa.* Colecção Horizonte Universitário, XXX. Lisboa: Livros Horizonte, 1982, pp. 147–48, 173–75 *et passim.*

577A. Reckert, Stephen. *Beyond Chrysanthemums: Perspectives on Poetry East and West.* Oxford: Clarendon Press, 1993, pp. 44–45, 86–87, 93–94, 96–98, 115–16, 144–47 *et passim.*

Includes also renderings in English of "Vanse mis amores, madre" and "Donde vindes, filha" (both from the *Auto da Lusitânia*), on pp. 45 and 94 respectively; "Canas do amor, canas" (*Inês Pereira*), on p. 91; "En la huerta nasce la rosa" (*Auto dos Quatro Tempos*), on p. 97; and "Llevántate, amiga mía" (*Auto pastoril castelhano*), on p. 144.

> *Review:*
> a. Alan Deyermond, "The Language Problem and Comparative Literature: Stephen Reckert's *Beyond Chrysanthemums*," *Portuguese Studies*, XI (1995), 200–15.

578. Reckert, Stephen. "The Shoemaker's Wife and the Joker." In *Lorca, Poet and Playwright: Essays in Honour of J. M. Aguirre.* Ed. Robert Havard. Cardiff: University of Wales Press/New York: St. Martins, 1992, pp. 93–106.

Several echoes of Gil Vicente in Lorca's *La zapatera prodigiosa* (see pp. 99–100).

579. *Reference Guide to World Literature.* 2d ed. Ed. Lesley Henderson. 2 vols. New York: St. James Press, 1995. 1520 pp.

Vol. II includes: C. C. Stathatos, "Vicente, Gil" (pp. 1281–83); P. A. Odber de Baubeta, "*Auto da Barca do Inferno, Auto da Barca do Purgatório, Auto da Barca da Glória.* Plays by Gil Vicente, 1517, 1518, 1519" (pp. 1283–84), and "*Farsa de Inês Pereira.* Play by Gil Vicente, 1523" (p. 1285).

580. Riquer, Martín de. *Historia de la literatura universal.* I: *De la antigüedad al Renacimiento.* Barcelona: Noguer, 1957, pp. 501–03 *et passim.*

581. Romera–Navarro, M[iguel]. *Historia de la literatura española.* 2d ed., corrected and expanded. Boston: D.C. Heath, 1949, pp. 112–14. (First ed., 1928).

582. Romeu Figueras, José. "La colección *Cantares de diversas sonadas* y la serie 'Pus que no'm voleu amar'—'Pues (que) no me queréys amar,' o 'hablar.'" *Anuario Musical*, XXII (1967), 97–143.

Several references to Gil Vicente.

583. Salazar, Adolfo. *La música de España: desde el siglo XVI a Manuel de Falla*. Colección Austral. Madrid: Espasa–Calpe, 1972, vol. I, pp. 68–71, 72, 73, 74–75.

The same as *La música de España: la música en la cultura española*. Buenos Aires: Espasa–Calpe Argentina, 1953, pp. 213–18 *et passim*.

584. Salomon, Noël. *Recherches sur le thème paysan dans la "comedia" au temps de Lope de Vega*. Bibliothèque des Hautes Études Hispaniques, XXXI. Bordeaux: Féret & Fils, 1965. xxiv+946 pp.

Many references to Gil Vicente. See pp. 7–8, 10, 12, 27, 43, 44, 47, 54, 55–56, 57, 58, 63, 65, 67–68, 70–71, 72, 76, 78, 100–01, 128, 138, 141, 145–46, 148, 150, 152, 161, 406, 428, 438–39, 441, 442, 462, 464, 465, 476, 538–39, 575, 576, 579, 611, 732–33, 750, 844. See also the Spanish translation by Beatriz Chenot, *Lo villano en el teatro del Siglo de Oro*, Literatura y Sociedad, XXXVI (Madrid: Castalia, 1985), 772 pp.

585. Sánchez Romeralo, Antonio. "Razón y sinrazón en la creación tradicional." In *El Romancero hoy: poética (Segundo coloquio internacional sobre el Romancero)*. Ed. Diego Catalán, Samuel G. Armistead, and Antonio Sánchez Romeralo. Romancero y Poesía Oral, III. Madrid: Cátedra Seminario Menéndez Pidal & Gredos, 1979, pp. 13–28.

Pp. 13–15: brief commentary on the ballad "En el mes era de mayo" (*Auto dos físicos*). The text appears on p. 14.

586. Santos, Reynaldo dos. *Historia del arte portugués*. Prólogo de José Camón Aznar. Barcelona: Labor, 1960. x+383 pp.

Pp. 289–91 on the *custódia de Belém* (p. 291 is a B&W plate of it).

587. Santos, Reynaldo dos. *Oito séculos de arte portuguesa: história e espírito*. Vol. III. Lisboa: Empresa Nacional de Publicidade, 1970. 480 pp.

Pp. 369–70 on the *custódia de Belém*; full–page color plate of it facing p. 370.

588. Saraiva, António José. *A cultura em Portugal. Teoria e história.* I: *Introdução geral à cultura portuguesa*. Amadora: Livraria Bertrand, 1981 [1982], pp. 176–79 *et passim*.

589. Saraiva, António José. *Iniciação na literatura portuguesa*. Colecção Saber, VII. Mem Martins: Europa–América, 1984. 172 pp.

Pp. 40–47: "Gil Vicente e o teatro medieval."

590. Saraiva, José Hermano. *História concisa de Portugal*. Colecção Saber. [Lisboa]: Europa–América, 1978, pp. 172–78.

Gil Vicente was a courageous social thinker. In his *Romagem de agravados* (1533), he analyzed the social consequences of Portuguese expansion, especially the proliferation of the parasitic classes at the expense of the productive ones. This argument can be found also in no. 171 above.

591. Sasportes, José. "Gil Vicente, mestre coreógrafo." In his *História da dança em Portugal*. Lisboa: Fundação Calouste Gulbenkian, 1970, pp. 79–109.

Sasportes makes a strong case for the representational aspect of Gil Vicente's theater. *Côrtes de Júpiter* illustrates best the inherent importance of spectacle and choreography in Vicente's entire production. A selection from the same play is included (pp. 99–106).

592. Sasportes, José. *Trajectória da dança teatral em Portugal*. Biblioteca Breve, XXVII. Série Artes Visuais. Lisboa: Instituto de Cultura Portuguesa, Secretaria de Estado de Cultura, Presidência do Concelho de Ministros, 1979. 98 pp.

Ch. II (pp. 23–27) on Gil Vicente as choreographer.

593. Scholberg, Kenneth R. *Algunos aspectos de la sátira en el siglo XVI*. Utah Studies in Literature and Linguistics, XII. Berne/Frankfurt am Main/ Las Vegas: Peter Lang, 1979. 202 pp.

Numerous references to Gil Vicente: pp. 21, 24–25, 28, 30, 33–35, 38, 40, 46, 49–50, 64, 68, 75–76, 82, 89–91, 93–94, 98–100, 106–07, 117–18, 124, 126, 131, 157–58, 162–64, 174, 176, 179–81. *Contents*: Nota preliminar. La misoginia en el siglo XVI. Sátira de profesionales y de tipos sociales. Sátira de costumbres y vicios. Sátira anticlerical y de prácticas religiosas. Rivalidades regionales y mofas de otras gentes. Los ataques de carácter político. Dos cuestiones relacionadas con la sátira del siglo XVI. Observaciones finales. Bibliografía. Índice.

Review:

a. John Lihani, *Hispania*, LXIV (1981), 154.

594. Selvagem, Carlos, and Hernâni Cidade. "Gil Vicente." In their *Cultura portuguesa*. Vol. IV. [Lisboa]: Empresa Nacional de Publicidade, 1970, pp. 129–38.

595. Smith, Robert C. *The Art of Portugal (1500–1800)*. New York: Meredith Press, 1968. 320 pp.

P. 265 on the *custódia de Belém*. Color plate of it (XV) also.

596. Souto, José Correia do. *Dicionário da literatura portuguesa*. Vol. IV. [Porto]: n. pub., [1983?], pp. 206–09.

597. *Spain: A Companion to Spanish Studies*. Ed. P. E. Russell. London: Methuen, 1973, pp. 347–48.

Part of "Spanish Literature (1474–1681)" by the editor.

598. Stegagno Picchio, Luciana. "O *thíasos* marinho na literatura portuguesa de Gil Vicente a Gonzaga." In *Studies in Portuguese Literature and History in Honour of Luís de Sousa Rebelo*. Ed. Helder Macedo. Colección Támesis: Série A: Monografías, CXXXXVII. London: Tamesis Books, 1992, pp. 73–81.

On pp. 74–77, Stegagno Picchio discusses the sea–*thíasos* and its iconographic sources in Gil Vicente's *Côrtes de Júpiter*, the most inventive, active, and poetic treatment of the motif that Portuguese literature has transmitted to us.

Review (of the volume):

a. N. J. Lamb, *BHS*, LXXII (1995), 245–46.

599. Stern, Charlotte. "The Genesis of the Spanish Pastoral: From Lyric to Drama." *Kentucky Romance Quarterly*, XXV (1978), 413–34.

600. Subirá, José. *Historia de la música teatral en España*. Colección Labor. Biblioteca de Iniciación Cultural. Sección V: Música, 429. Barcelona: Labor, 1945, pp. 35–37.

601. Surtz, Ronald E. *The Birth of a Theater: Dramatic Convention in the Spanish Theater from Juan del Encina to Lope de Vega*. Princeton and Madrid: Princeton University and Editorial Castalia, 1979. 205 pp.

Numerous references to Gil Vicente: pp. 9–10, 30–31, 32–33, 46–47, 49, 53, 54, 58–59, 60–61, 62, 63, 65, 66, 85–86, 87–88, 89, 91–92, 93–95, 115, 126–27, 133–34, 139–41, 142, 151, 152–54, 157–58, 170. *Contents*: Introduction. The Origins of the Castilian Drama. Liturgy and Theater. The Court Entertainment in the Fifteenth Century. Pageantry and Drama. The Function of the Dramatic Prologue. Representation and

Reading. The Castilian Drama in the Late Sixteenth and Early Seventeenth Centuries.
Review:
a. D. W. McPheeters, *BCom*, XXXV (1983), 113–15.

601A. Surtz, Ronald E., Manuel Sito Alba, Marc Vitse, Frédéric Serralta, Javier Huerta Calvo, and José María Díez Borque. *Historia del teatro en España*. I: *Edad Media, siglo XVI, siglo XVII*. Dir. José María Díez Borque. Persiles, CLII. Madrid: Taurus, 1983, pp. 198–215, 440–44, *et passim*.
Part of ch. III ("El teatro en el siglo XVI [desde finales de la Edad Media a comienzos del siglo XVII]"—pp. 155–471) by Manuel Sito Alba.

602. *El teatro de Sebastián de Horozco*. Estudio y edición crítica por Oleh Mazur. Con una breve historia del teatro español anterior a Lope de Vega: tipos, modos y temas. Madrid: Rocana, 1977. 222 pp.
Many references to Gil Vicente in the appendix ("Breve historia del teatro español anterior a Lope de Vega: tipos, modos y temas"), pp. 147–90.
Reviews:
a. Anthony J. Farrell, *BCom*, XXX (1978), 135–36.
b. Juan María Marín Martínez, *Segismundo*, 27–32 (1980), 289–90.

603. *Teatro mundial: 1700 argumentos de obras de teatro antiguo y moderno, nacional y extranjero, con descripciones, listas de personajes, críticas y bibliografía*. Comp. Arturo del Hoyo. Madrid: Aguilar, 1955, pp. 1075–77.
Entries by José Ares Montes on the *Barca da Glória, Barca do Inferno, Barca do Purgatório, Inês Pereira, Dom Duardos*.

604. Teyssier, Paul. "Le Théâtre populaire portugais après Gil Vicente: quelques travaux imprimés et inédits." *BEPB*, XLIV–XLV (1983–85), 475–98.
Many references to Gil Vicente.

605. Tocco, Valeria. "Osservazioni sul bilinguismo in Portogallo (sec. XV–XVII)." *Il Confronto Letterario*, 20 (November 1993), 319–34.

606. Trapero, Maximiano. "Tradicionalismo en el primitivo teatro castellano: los autos del ciclo del *Officium Pastorum*." In *Calderón: Actas*

del congreso internacional sobre Calderón y el teatro español del Siglo de Oro (Madrid, 8–13 de junio de 1981). Dir. Luciano García Lorenzo. Anejos de la Revista "Segismundo," VI. Madrid: CSIC, 1983, vol. III, pp. 1715–30.

Gil Vicente and his contemporary Spanish dramatists were following a popular religious dramatic tradition.

Review (of the *Actas*):

a. Franco Meregalli, *RaI*, 19 (February 1984), 35–38.

607. Trend, J. B. *Medieval Lyrics in Spain and Portugal.* Cambridge: Printed by R. I. Severs Ltd, 1952. 25 pp.

On Gil Vicente, pp. 9–10 *et passim.* Pp. 9–10 include the text of "Muy graciosa es la doncella" (*Cassandra*) and the author's verse translation of it. On p. 17, the text of "Del rosal vengo, mi madre" (*Inverno*) is reproduced and a version of its missing fourth stanza is proposed.

608. Trilse, Christoph, Klaus Hammer, and Rolf Kabel. *Theater Lexicon.* Berlin: Henschelverlag, 1977, p. 582.

609. Trisler, Barbara Jean. "A Comparative Study of the Character Portrayal of 'Celestina' and Other Golden Age Celestinesque Protagonists." Doctoral thesis, University of Oklahoma, 1977, pp. 51–53 *et passim.* (See *DAI*, XXXVIII [1977–78], 2165–A).

Deals with Brízida Vaz of the *Auto da Barca do Inferno.*

610. Valbuena Prat, Ángel. *Historia de la literatura española.* II: *Renacimiento.* 9ª ed. ampliada y puesta al día por Antonio Prieto. Barcelona: Gustavo Gil, 1981, pp. 47–61, 67–69 *et passim.*

611. Valle–Killeen, Suzanne Dolores. *The Satiric Perspective: A Structural Analysis of Late Medieval, Early Renaissance Satiric Treatises.* Senda de Estudios y Ensayos. New York: Senda Nueva de Ediciones, 1980, pp. 174–86.

The framework of the journey in the *Barcas* and the *Auto da Alma* affords Gil Vicente the opportunity to expose social, political, and ecclesiastical ills.

612. Valverde, José María. *Breve historia de la literatura española.* 2d ed. Colección Punto Omega, LXXXVI. Madrid: Guadarrama, 1980, pp. 60–62. (First ed., 1969).

613. Vázquez Cuesta, Pilar. "O bilinguismo castelhano–português na época de Camões." *ACCP,* XVI (1981), 807–27.

614. Ventura, Augusta Faria Gersão. *A máquina do mundo: resumo das idéias cosmológicas desde os tempos primitivos até ao fim do século XIX.* Porto: Portucalense Editora, 1944. 143 pp.
   Pp. 58–63 on Gil Vicente. Other passing references also. Examines several passages from Gil Vicente's plays and concludes that the dramatist is trying consistently to destroy the belief in astral influence by ridiculing both belief and believers.

615. Vian, Cesco. *Storia delle letterature portoghese e brasiliana.* Letteratura Universale (a cura di Luigi Santucci), XIX. Milano: Fratelli Fabbri, 1969, pp. 26–29.

616. Weber de Kurlat, Frida. "Acerca del portuguesismo de Diego Sánchez de Badajoz (portugueses en farsas españolas del siglo XVI)." In *Homenaje a William L. Fichter: Estudios sobre el teatro antiguo hispánico y otros ensayos.* Ed. A. David Kossoff and José Amor y Vázquez. Madrid: Castalia, 1971, pp. 785–800.

617. Weber de Kurlat, Frida. "El teatro prelopesco: líneas de investigación en los años setenta." *NRFH,* XXIX (1980), 172–85.
   Reviews in detail Robert L. Hathaway's *Love in the Early Spanish Theatre* (Madrid: Plaza Mayor, 1975) and John Brotherton's *The "Pastor–Bobo" in the Spanish Theatre Before the Time of Lope de Vega* (London: Tamesis, 1975) on pp. 173–77 and 177–82 respectively. Both works deal extensively with Gil Vicente (see *GVB,* nos 324 and 388).

618. Ynduráin, Francisco. "Variaciones en torno a una imagen poética, 'La garza'." In his *Relección de clásicos.* Madrid: Prensa Española, 1969, pp. 257–79.
   Discusses the use of the image in Gil Vicente's *Auto das fadas, Sibila Cassandra, Auto das ciganas, Inês Pereira* and *Comédia de Rubena* on pp. 267–71.

619. Zimic, Stanislav. *"La cueva de Salamanca*: parábola de la tontería."
Anales Cervantinos, XXI (1983), 135–52.

In note 29 (p. 146), Zimic suggests that among the possible sources
of Cervantes's *entremés* is Gil Vicente's *Auto da Índia*. There are several
episodic coincidences in the two plays, including the wife's cynicism in
deceiving her husband and the latter's stupidity.

620. Ziomek, Henryk. *A History of Spanish Golden Age Drama*. Studies
in Romance Languages, XXIX. Lexington: The University Press of
Kentucky, 1984, pp. 16–17.

Reviews:

a. C. Alan Soons, *JHP*, IX (1984–85), 257–61.
b. Frank A. Domínguez, *South Atlantic Review*, L (1985), 111–12.
c. Edward H. Friedman, *BCom*, XXXVII (1985), 149–51.
d. J. Vinci, *Choice*, XXII (1985), 823.
e. Alfredo Hermenegildo, *HR*, LIV (1986), 94–95.
f. Harvey L. Johnson, *Hispanófila*, 87 (May 1986), 69–73.
g. Nigel Griffin, *MLR*, LXXXII (1987), 996–98.
h. Margaret Wilson, *BHS*, LXIV (1987), 365–66.

INDEX OF SCHOLARS AND TRANSLATORS

Unless otherwise indicated, numbers refer to entries. Those preceded by *B* correspond to entries in the section on Bibliographies. Names incidentally mentioned (e.g., editors of *Festschriften* in which articles on Gil Vicente are published) are excluded from this index.

SUBJECT INDEX

Numbers indicate entries.